ASTON VILLA
REVIEW 1995

Published by Sports Projects Ltd

ACKNOWLEDGEMENTS

Aston Villa Review 1995
First published in Great Britain in July 1995
by Sports Projects Limited

© 1995 Sports Projects Limited
188 Lightwoods Hill, Smethwick, Warley,
West Midlands B67 5EH.

ISBN 0 946866 23 6

Printed and bound in Great Britain
by The Bath Press

Editor: Dennis Shaw

Photographs: Bernard Gallagher and Terry Weir

Design, layout and graphics: Bernard Gallagher,
Nadine Goldingay, Phil Lees and Vic Millward

Special thanks to: Trevor Hartley, Steve Stride,
Neil Gallagher, Mike Beddow, Dave and Pam
Bridgewater, David Hodges, Rod Evans.

KEY

❏	Player booked
■	Player sent off
32	Figure in goals column indicates time of goal
†56	First substitute and time of substitution
†	First player substituted
‡56	Second substitute and time of substitution
‡	Second player substituted

Notes:

● *Players are listed in order of position, goalkeeper, defenders, midfield and then forwards, except in European games when teams are listed by number.*

● *The first named substitute is always the substitute goalkeeper.*

● *In friendly games, where several substitutes may have appeared, additional symbols are used in the following order: #, §, ††, ‡‡, ##, §§, ≠.*

Aston Villa's successful struggle against adversity

This third volume of the *Aston Villa Review* fits comfortably into the unique collection which quickly found popular appeal when introduced in 1993.

However, while the 1994 issue happily recorded the winning of the Coca-Cola Cup the latest instalment's story-line proves to be of a successful struggle against adversity.

Football is a world of peaks and troughs and season 1994-1995 was, for Villa, memorable for the tormentingly gradual u-turn away from the threat of relegation.

Thus the value of the publication is in its faithful continuing documentation of Aston Villa's history as it happens, warts and all.

Virtually every fact and statistic of season 1994-95 is recorded in these pages along with match description and comment.

As in its two previous volumes the *Aston Villa Review 1995* takes the reader along the match-by-match journey from August to May while also filling in with close season tours, friendly matches and matters of interest.

Like the majority of the other 21 top clubs who set out on the 42 fixture league programme Villa found the pruning of the FA Carling Premiership from 22 clubs to 20 a punishing, fear-ridden process.

By November 9 the danger of being among the four clubs to go down into the Endsleigh First Division had become worryingly real.

Only one point had been taken from the previous nine games with 20 goals conceded against eight scored. Significantly, the one point won during that confidence-sapping spell was in a home draw against Norwich, one of the four relegated clubs.

As a result of such a sterile sequence of results, which saw the club in 19th position with only two wins from 14 Premiership games all season, home and away, Ron Atkinson was dismissed and subsequently replaced by Brian Little.

In making the managerial change the club pointed out that the inadequate Premiership results actually stretched back over a full 42-match period during which time the club had been relegation material.

A further disappointment was removal from the UEFA Cup after two rounds by the Turkish side, Trabzonspor, on away goals.

All this frustration on the playing side was set against the backcloth of massive upgrading of Villa Park to one of the finest stadiums in Great Britain. Following the successful completion of the double-decker Doug Ellis Stand a similar construction was completed by the turn of the year to replace the famous old Holte End terracing.

Plunged into a difficult situation, Little was in charge for 30 matches and fortunately, on the Premiership front, there was a steady improvement. By mid-February an inviting seventh place briefly beckoned until a further slump created new and serious difficulties.

With such high rewards at stake for Premiership status and several clubs of approximately equal strength competing point-for-point, it became one of the most fraught relegation-fighting finishes ever.

Safety for Villa arrived only in the very last game when Crystal Palace, who needed to win, lost at Newcastle while Villa achieved the draw they, at worst, required to stay up.

The detailed story of all these rises and falls is contained in the ensuing pages. Along with its two earlier versions Aston Villa Review 1995 is essential for, not only the avid collector, but every Villa supporter who wants the full picture at his or her finger tips.

Dennis Shaw
May 1995

CONTENTS

CONTENTS

FRIENDLY MATCHES

APPENDIX

Saturday 20th August 1994 • Goodison Park • 3.00pm

EVERTON 2 ASTON VILLA 2

Half-time 1-0 • *Attendance* 35,544

Referee Kelvin MORTON (Bury St Edmunds)

Linesmen M. FLETCHER and B. LOWE

Blue Shirts, White Shorts	Goals	Green, Black and Red Striped Shirts, Black Shorts	Goals
1 Neville SOUTHALL		13 Mark BOSNICH	
2 Matthew JACKSON		6 Kevin RICHARDSON ❏	
5 Dave WATSON		5 Paul McGRATH	
26 David UNSWORTH		16 Ugo EHIOGU	
6 Gary ABLETT		3 Steve STAUNTON †	
8 Graham STUART	22	7 Ray HOUGHTON	
14 John EBBRELL		14 Garry PARKER	
7 Vinny SAMWAYS		11 Andy TOWNSEND ❏	
17 Anders LIMPAR		18 Dwight YORKE ❏	
9 Tony COTTEE		8 John FASHANU	66
15 Paul RIDEOUT	70	9 Dean SAUNDERS	74
Substitutes		*Substitutes*	
13 Jason KEARTON		30 Michael OAKES	
18 Joe PARKINSON †29		15 Phil KING †65	
22 Brett ANGELL		10 Dalian ATKINSON	

BEFORE	P	W	D	L	F	A	pts	AFTER	P	W	D	L	F	A	pts
Villa	0	0	0	0	0	0	0	Villa	1	0	1	0	2	1	1
Everton	0	0	0	0	0	0	0	Everton	1	0	1	0	2	1	1

FACTFILE

John Fashanu marks his Villa Premiership debut with a goal... Phil King is another debutant, substituting for Steve Staunton... It's Everton's first Premiership match under new manager Mike Walker... Kevin Richardson fills the right-back role in place of suspended Earl Barrett... Garry Parker's 100th Villa game.

New signings show the way

Season number three of the FA Premiership arrives with talk of red and yellow cards cascading like confetti as tighter, World Cup-style refereeing is introduced.

A degree of conflict between supporters and the professionals emerges in the pre-season media build-up.

Most managers reckon that too many players will get sent off and that the game will suffer. Many fans and pundits believe that, if negative aspects are removed from the game, it will actually benefit as a spectacle in the long-term. Ron Atkinson fears the worst, forecasts a record 20 sendings-off on Day One, but reserves judgement on the amount of good sense referees will bring to bear.

As for Villa, the squad has been reshaped and updated rather than transformed.

Major focus of attention in the opening game at Goodison Park is on £1.35m John Fashanu, signed from Wimbledon two weeks earlier to provide a new physical presence at the sharp end of the attack. Of the other two close season imports, Ghanaian international Nii Lamptey is excluded while Phil King, from Sheffield Wednesday, is on the bench.

Two notable absentees are Dalian Atkinson and Shaun Teale, the latter having lost his place alongside Paul McGrath to the ever-improving Ugo Ehiogu. One problem position is at right back, where Earl Barrett is recovering from surgery and skipper Kevin Richardson is moved back from midfield as emergency cover.

Everton, at the start of Mike Walker's first full-season as boss, unveils a big new signing, too, in Vinny Samways from Spurs for £2.2m.

Goodison, now smartly all-seater, is virtually full and humming with anticipation of the start of a new era.

The football flows freely, scoring chances are there in abundance and Walker observes afterwards that the final score could have been 7-6 either way, though it was Mark Bosnich who was required to make the most saves.

Everton draw first blood through Graham Stuart's 22nd minute cross which to Bosnich's alarm, deflects past him into the net.

Early in the second half, still at 1-0 down, Villa lose Steve Staunton who limps off with a calf strain, thus enabling King to make his first appearance as sub at left back.

It proves an inspired introduction. After 16 minutes on the park it is the versatile former Hillsborough man who is the provider for the equaliser.

King's well-flighted right wing corner to the near post is headed in by Fash for the first of what, hopefully, could be a useful Villa career goals haul.

Soon, however, Villa are a goal down again as ex-Villa Park striker Paul Rideout drives in Everton's 70th minute second from a Tony Cottee assist.

The action is unrelenting now with Villa showing an encouraging degree of determination, led by Fashanu's purposeful example.

This time Everton's lead survives for only four minutes before King directs a superb cross-field pass to Ray Houghton whose centre is headed in by Dean Saunders.

"It was great to see both our front men get off the mark with a goal," said Atkinson. "And also that King did so well for us when he came on. A satisfactory start..."

**Phil King – a
promising start**

Wednesday 24th August 1994 • Villa Park • 7.45pm

ASTON VILLA 1 SOUTHAMPTON 1

Half-time 1-0 • Attendance 24,179

Referee Philip DON (Middlesex)

Linesmen R.J. HARRIS and D.C. MADGWICK

Claret Shirts with Blue Stripes, White Shorts		Goals	Red and White Striped Shirts, Black Shorts		Goals
13	Mark BOSNICH		1	Bruce GROBBELAAR	
6	Kevin RICHARDSON		5	Richard HALL	
5	Paul McGRATH		21	Tommy WIDDRINGTON †	
16	Ugo EHIOGU ❑		3	Francis BENALI ❑	
15	Phil KING		2	Jeff KENNA	
7	Ray HOUGHTON		11	Paul ALLEN	
14	Garry PARKER ‡		4	Jim MAGILTON	
11	Andy TOWNSEND		10	Neil MADDISON	
18	Dwight YORKE		14	Simon CHARLTON	
8	Dean SAUNDERS	33	7	Matthew LE TISSIER	89
9	John FASHANU †		16	Nicky BANGER	
	Substitutes			*Substitutes*	
1	Nigel SPINK		13	Dave BEASANT	
10	Dalian ATKINSON †70		12	Neil HEANEY †60	
2	Earl BARRETT ‡75		20	Peter WHISTON	

BEFORE	P	W	D	L	F	A	pts	AFTER		P	W	D	L	F	A	pts
Villa	1	0	1	0	2	2	1	12	Villa	2	0	2	0	3	3	2
Saints	1	0	1	0	1	1	1	13	Saints	2	0	2	0	2	2	2

FACTFILE

Earl Barrett back from suspension, but on the bench... Kevin Richardson keeps right-back spot... Home debuts for new signings Phil King and John Fashanu... Southampton's seventh point off Villa in three starts... Deano's second goal in two games...

Villa denied by Le Tissier magic

The first home fixture of the season revives unpleasant memories of 1993-94 and home and away defeats by the Saints who went on to narrowly avoid relegation.

One name in the opposition ranks, looms large. Matthew Le Tissier scored both goals in Southampton's 2-0 win at Villa Park last November. He then conjured another two at The Dell at the end of April when Saints, battling fiercely for survival, won by an emphatic 4-1 scoreline.

And, not satisfied with that four-goal scourge of the claret-and-blue, it seems, the supremely-talented Channel Islander is poised to weave another spell of scoring magic to Villa's acute discomfort.

Villa start confidently enough, though Steve Staunton has not recovered from the calf strain which caused him to limp off at Goodison on Saturday. Phil King is the natural deputy at left back while Kevin Richardson again deputises for Earl Barrett, who is to make his return in the second half as substitute.

Supporters see Villa Park from the inside for the first time with no Holte End terraces and the huge framework of the new double-decker stand taking shape.

Southampton cause something of a surprise with the style and quality of their game. There is no negative defensive attitude, though when they defend they do so in numbers. Going forward they pass the ball crisply, to feet, in similar fashion to Villa and the outcome is a closely-contested game which swings this way and that as they virtually cancel each other out.

Half-way through the first half there is a flurry of scoring attempts, Ehiogu heading Parker's assist just wide and Bosnich saving from Banger. John Fashanu has a great chance to mark his Villa Park debut with a goal but, after taking Dean Saunders' right wing low cross he turns and shoots straight at Grobbelaar.

Villa's breakthrough, for what seems the winner until Southampton's last throw of the dice, comes two minutes later with Deano's second goal in two games. King's long upfield ball is headed down by Fash for the Welsh cap to fire a terrific low shot from 20 yards out of the former Liverpool keeper's grasp.

Southampton immediately signal their intention of fighting back at the start of the second half when Charlton gets a good cross in from the left which Bosnich fumbles and McGrath has to clear in haste as Banger moves in.

On the hour Villa are close to making it 2-0 when Richardson, clearly missed in midfield, threads an immaculate long, angled pass forward for Saunders to escape the visiting back line. In possession, unmarked on the 18-yard line, a golden chance would be beckoning but for the experienced Grobbelaar's expertise in nipping straight out to the Villa man to deprive him of a shooting chance.

At this point Fashanu is withdrawn to allow Dalian Atkinson, wounded pride showing in the hunger of his running, to dash on and stir things up.

In the most entertaining period of the game both sides are close to scoring but Villa's always-precarious lead survives somewhat breathlessly to the 88th minute and still looks under no threat when Le Tissier, ready and waiting for his England call, gets possession 30 plus yards out of Bosnich's North Stand goal.

The goalkeeper has advanced, a shade too far it emerges, and the star Saint's looping missile goes over his head and under the bar for a goal-of-the-season contender.

"It's the norm for him," shrugs his boss, Alan Ball. "A special goal from a special player," agrees Big Ron. Four points gone out of the first six. Life in the Premiership doesn't get any easier...

Saturday 27th August 1994 • Villa Park • 3.00pm

ASTON VILLA 1 CRYSTAL PALACE 1

Half-time 0-0 • Attendance 23,305

Referee Joe WORRALL (Warrington)

Linesmen R. GOULD and D.C. RICHARDS

Claret Shirts with Blue Stripes, White Shorts		Goals	Yellow Shirts, Light Blue Shorts		Goals
13	Mark BOSNICH		1	Nigel MARTYN	
2	Earl BARRETT		22	Darren PATTERSON ❑	87
5	Paul McGRATH		14	Richard SHAW	
16	Ugo EHIOGU		6	Chris COLEMAN	
3	Steve STAUNTON	46	3	Dean GORDON ❑	
10	Dalian ATKINSON		23	Ricky NEWMAN	
6	Kevin RICHARDSON		7	Simon RODGER †	
11	Andy TOWNSEND		4	Gareth SOUTHGATE	
7	Ray HOUGHTON †		11	John SALAKO	
9	Dean SAUNDERS		10	Bruce DYER ‡	
8	John FASHANU		9	Chris ARMSTRONG	
	Substitutes			*Substitutes*	
1	Nigel SPINK		13	Rhys WILMOT	
18	Dwight YORKE †88		21	Ian COX †78	
15	Phil KING		16	Darren PITCHER ‡78	

BEFORE	P	W	D	L	F	A	pts	AFTER	P	W	D	L	F	A	pts
12 Villa	2	0	2	0	3	3	2	13 Villa	3	0	3	0	4	4	3
20 Palace	2	0	1	1	1	6	1	18 Palace	3	0	2	1	2	7	2

Barrett back in the full back spot... Dwight Yorke makes way for Dalian Atkinson... Steve Staunton scores direct from a corner kick – his first goal of the season... Third consecutive draw...Villa let it slip again to late equaliser... Six points dwindle from first nine...

Villa miss out on points again

Build-up to Palace's visit has tended to be over-shadowed by the excitement of the UEFA Cup first-round draw pairing Villa with Italian legends Inter Milan.

A week earlier the Selhurst Park club was greeted back to the Premiership with a six-goal blast by Liverpool and though they held Norwich 0-0 in mid-week they appear to be only a limited threat.

All the pre-match signs are good.

Steve Staunton is fit again, as is Earl Barrett, enabling Kevin Richardson to return to midfield with Garry Parker dropping out. The only 'unenforced' change is Dalian Atkinson's return to the exclusion of Dwight Yorke.

A similar pattern to the Southampton game quickly emerges with the visitors proving a shade more troublesome than fans, at least, anticipated. Although Villa have more of the possession they fail to create meaningful problems while Palace are threatening a couple of times early on.

Staunton's return brings some air balls for John Fashanu who provides a couple of knock-downs and, in earnestly searching for posses-sion, gets a hefty kick on the head by Patterson for his pains.

One neatly-executed passing move ends with a Fash header, saved by Nigel Martyn while the ex-Don feeds Ray Houghton for a curving shot which flashes a whisker wide of the post.

The interval mood is one of vague dissatis-faction with Villa having failed to take as firm a grip as anticipated, though the gloom changes within seconds.

Staunton drives over one of his perfectly-struck corners from the right-hand side at the Holte End and Martyn is taken by surprise.

As the ball travels in too close to his line for comfort Fashanu is menacingly bearing down on him and the keeper has his eye on the Villa striker rather than the ball as it flies through his hands into the far top corner.

By now Palace, apart from the odd break-out, seem ready to settle for a damage limitation exercise and a narrow defeat, but Villa fail to capitalise on their superiority.

"We didn't punish them when we had the chance," said the Villa boss afterwards. One cross by Staunton is fed to Dean Saunders whose volley is saved superbly by Martyn to partially atone for his goal lapse.

"At only 1-0 up you're never safe until it is all over," added Atkinson. "And we committed suicide out there.

"It was Wednesday all over again..."

Indeed it was as Villa seem to get a touch of the last-ditch jitters for the second time in four days. Paul McGrath and Mark Bosnich tie them-selves up into a rare old tangle with barely three minutes to go and Chris Armstrong misses a gift chance.

"We never really cleared the ball away after that," added the disappointed Villa boss.

A long ball back into the Villa goal area pro-duces another spell of panic. In the disorganised scramble which follows Gareth Southgate gets a shot in, the ball brushes Bosnich's arm, Ehiogu vainly attempts to hook it away... and two points slip away.

In the era of three points for a win three suc-cessive draws is not the satisfactory return it used to be, though Ron Atkinson, positive to the last, finds solace in a two-year flash-back.

"The year we were run-ners-up we drew our first three games," he points out.

Steve Staunton – on target at Selhurst Park

Monday 29th August 1994 • Highfield Road • 8.00pm

COVENTRY CITY 0 ASTON VILLA 1

Half-time 0-1 • Attendance 12,218

Referee Paul DURKIN (Dorset)

Linesmen R.J. HARRIS and W.M. JORDAN

Sky Blue Shirts, Sky Blue Shorts	Goals	Green, Black and Red Striped Shirts, Black Shorts	Goals
1 Steve OGRIZOVIC		13 Mark BOSNICH	
2 Brian BORROWS		2 Earl BARRETT	
6 Phil BABB		16 Ugo EHIOGU	
20 David BUSST		5 Paul McGRATH	
3 Steve MORGAN		15 Phil KING	
4 Julian DARBY		18 Dwight YORKE	3
5 David RENNIE †		6 Kevin RICHARDSON ❑	
11 Willie BOLAND		11 Andy TOWNSEND	
15 Paul COOK		3 Steve STAUNTON	
7 Sean FLYNN		8 John FASHANU	
8 Roy WEGERLE		9 Dean SAUNDERS	
Substitutes		*Substitutes*	
13 Jonathan GOULD		1 Nigel SPINK	
12 John WILLIAMS †66		12 Nii LAMPTEY	
17 Ally PICKERING		14 Garry PARKER	

BEFORE	P	W	D	L	F	A	pts	AFTER	P	W	D	L	F	A	pts
12 Villa	3	0	3	0	4	4	3	9 Villa	4	1	3	0	5	4	6
21 Coventry	3	0	1	2	1	9	1	21 Coventry	4	0	1	3	1	10	1

FACTFILE

Dean Saunders' 100th appearance for Villa... Andy Townsend's 300th League game... Staunton pushes forward in format change... Yorke's first goal of the season... Six points from 12 – Big Ron's best start... Villa move up three places... Just one goal for Coventry in their opening four games – and 10 against!

Lara watches Villa's 'Yorker'

Bank Holiday Monday evening at Highfield Road, live on Sky, and a small, lukewarm gate providing a low-key atmosphere for Villa to seek their first win of the season.

The West Midlands derby has the Premiership stage to itself. And, with Coventry having been held to a draw by Wimbledon at home and severely trounced away by Newcastle and Blackburn, Villa have caught Sky Blues at a very low ebb.

The sale of the young Republic of Ireland centre back Phil Babb has dragged on for a considerable time, but it does seem now that this will be his final game before he departs to Liverpool for a staggering £3.6m.

Ron Atkinson makes a couple of changes after the disappointing draw at home to Palace. Dwight Yorke is re-introduced to the exclusion of Dalian Atkinson on the right of the strikers, while Phil King is at left back allowing Steve Staunton to take Ray Houghton's left-side midfield role. And what significant changes they prove to be!

The manager was on record as being vaguely disappointed with Yorke's form after the Southampton draw and the West Indian, watched by his cricketing mega-star mate Brian Lara, is visibly determined to make his indelible mark on this occasion.

In the event it takes him just two minutes to inscribe his name on proceedings as goalscorer and, it is to ultimately prove, matchwinner, too.

The early and crucial strike is Sky Blue-assisted but none the less welcome for that.

Former Birmingham City man David Rennie appears to have ample time to clear Staunton's delivery but he delays long enough for Dean Saunders to pounce into the tackle.

The ball spins away to Andy Townsend whose centre into the goalmouth is nodded easily into Steve Ogrizovic's net.

For the third successive game Villa are holding a 1-0 lead and this time, with Coventry offering little and their supporters lulled into a depressed silence, they have ample time and opportunity to build up an unassailable lead.

What in fact happened afterwards was described like this by Andy Colquhoun in the Birmingham Post: "... if either side had more than one effort on target I have forgotten it.

"...this was a limp, error-strewn affair, lacking action on the field and atmosphere on the terraces.

"By the final 10 minutes the crowd had been bored into an indifferent silence. With seats costing from £14 to £19 and the visitors charged £17 it was poor value for money."

Poor value for Sky subscriptions, too! Villa were, however, good value for their three points since Coventry never looked remotely like conjuring a Palace-Southampton-style kick in the tail.

It is much more likely that Villa will double their lead especially in one of the game's better moves when Staunton crosses again and Yorke is only narrowly wide of adding his second.

Bosnich's only moment of temporary concern comes from a shot by Coventry's best player, right back Morgan, a rasping drive which necessitates a diving save.

By the final whistle the dominating emotion is that of joint-relief with Coventry glad to see it all over and Villa happy to store away their three points.

"It completes my best start for Villa," points out Atkinson, referring to an undefeated six points from four games rather than the effectiveness of the attacking play.

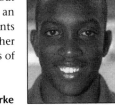

Dwight Yorke

Saturday 10th September 1994 • Villa Park • 3.00pm

ASTON VILLA 2 IPSWICH TOWN 0

Half-time 1-0 • *Attendance* 22,241

Referee Gary WILLARD (West Sussex)

Linesmen S.R. BRAND and P.V. NORMAN

Claret Shirts with Blue Stripes, White Shorts	Goals	Blue Shirts, White Shorts	Goals
1 Nigel SPINK		1 Craig FORREST	
2 Earl BARRETT		2 Mick STOCKWELL	
5 Paul McGRATH		5 John WARK	
16 Ugo EHIOGU		6 David LINIGHAN †	
15 Phil KING		19 Frank YALLOP ❑	
18 Dwight YORKE		4 Paul MASON ❑	
6 Kevin RICHARDSON		7 Geraint WILLIAMS	
11 Andy TOWNSEND ❑		17 Simon MILTON	
3 Steve STAUNTON ❑	15	21 Stuart SLATER	
8 John FASHANU †		11 Chris KIWOMYA	
9 Dean SAUNDERS ❑	85	9 Bontcho GUENTCHEV	
Substitutes		*Substitutes*	
30 Michael OAKES		13 Clive BAKER	
10 Dalian ATKINSON †75		10 Ian MARSHALL †69	
14 Garry PARKER		18 Steve PALMER	

BEFORE	P	W	D	L	F	A	pts	AFTER	P	W	D	L	F	A	pts
10 Villa	4	1	3	0	5	4	6	7 Villa	5	2	3	0	7	4	9
15 Ipswich	4	1	1	2	4	6	4	15 Ipswich	5	1	1	3	4	8	4

FACTFILE *First home win of the season... five games unbeaten... Villa hit woodwork three times... Saunders celebrates new three-year contract with late goal... Spink's first appearance of the season... Match watched by Inter 'spies'... Big Ron absent in Milan...Jim Barron takes charge... Villa jump three places to seventh spot.*

Inter spies see first home win

The visit of Ipswich Town, the fifth team from the lower reaches to face up to Villa this season, does not, on the surface, appear too much of a frightener.

There is a slight feeling of 'calm before the storm' in the air, however, with the visit to Milan for the UEFA Cup-tie first leg coming next midweek.

"It is never easy to completely dispel such thoughts from players' minds," concedes Ron Atkinson, though he makes a jolly good stab at so doing with his next verbal nudge.

This is to the effect that, with three 'non-nationals' only allowed in European competition, there is a jostle for places ahead and performances against Ipswich could be crucial to selection. The pairing with Inter has fired everyone's imagination and none of the players want to miss out on such a feature tie.

One of the selection queries could solve itself in unfortunate circumstances, namely that goalkeeper Mark Bosnich has damaged medial knee ligaments in training and is out for an unspecified period.

Nigel Spink, who sprang to fame a dozen or so years earlier in the European Cup Final, is suddenly back in the Euro-frame. If the young Aussie is still out next Thursday that will be one 'non-national' accounted for...

Spink, along with Paul McGrath the only remaining player from the 1990 trip to San Siro, sniffs the chance of a possible return to the famous Milan stadium.

Twice when needed he pulls off crucial saves to do his claims no harm at all. Manager Atkinson is in Italy to watch Inter's home game against Roma while the rival coach, Ottavia Bianchi, is at Villa Park on the reverse spying duty.

Assistant manager Jim Barron, in charge in the boss's absence, quickly gets any initial fears removed as Steve Staunton, fed by Dean Saunders, rifles a 15th minute lead from the edge of the box.

From then on Villa totally dominate the proceedings – those two Spink stops apart – but those further goals they need to add gloss to an increasingly encouraging display seem not to be forthcoming.

Dwight Yorke, urgently seeking a Milan place, is in fine and forceful form and only a brilliant piece of goalkeeping from Craig Forrest denies him the goal he deserves.

Although not a goalscorer John Fashanu adds weight and power up front, working hard to constantly put the Ipswich back line under physical and mental pressure.

Forrest's woodwork is rattled three times as the lurking danger remains of a third successive home match ending with a late opposition strike snatching away two precious Premiership points.

Mercifully it is Villa and Saunders who produce the scoring finale on this occasion, soon after the industrious Welshman has hit the post from only four yards out.

No such mishap this time, though, as he evades John Wark, draws the keeper and secures the points with the second goal Villa so badly need.

By the final whistle there is no doubt that Villa have put together their most complete display so far to create exactly the right mood of quiet confidence for San Siro.

Barron's report to his gaffer on Monday morning will get Euro-week off to a satisfactory start...

Nigel Spink – a return to goal and Europe

Thursday 15th September 1994 • San Siro, Milan • 8.30pm

INTERNAZIONALE 1 ASTON VILLA 0

Half-time 0-0 • Attendance 22,639

Referee P. MIKKELSEN

Linesmen J.P. STAERK and J. LARSEN

Officials from Denmark

White Shirts with Blue and Black Sash, White Shorts	Goals		Claret Shirts with Blue Stripes, White Shorts	Goals
1 Gianluca PAGLIUCA			1 Nigel SPINK	
2 Giuseppe BERGOMI			2 EARL BARRETT	
3 Mirko CONTE			3 Steve STAUNTON	
4 Andrea SENTO			4 Ugo EHIOGU ❑	
5 Gianluca FESTA			5 Paul McGRATH	
6 Giovanni BIA †			6 Kevin RICHARDSON	
7 Alessandro BIANCHI			7 Phil KING	
8 Wim JONK			8 John FASHANU †	
9 Nicola BERTI			9 Dean SAUNDERS	
10 Dennis BERGKAMP pen 75			10 Dalian ATKINSON	
11 Ruben SOSA ‡			11 Andy TOWNSEND	
Substitutes			*Substitutes*	
gk Luca MONDINI			gk Michael OAKES	
13 Massimo PAGANIN †70			12 Ray HOUGHTON †75	
14 Antonio MANICONE			14 Shaun TEALE	
15 Marco BAROLLO			15 Garry PARKER	
16 Marco DEL VECCHIO ‡81			16 Guy WHITTINGHAM	

Tough draw against UEFA Cup Champions... Villa's flight to Milan delayed for 90 minutes...Torrential rain storms put match in doubt... European debuts for Ehiogu, Fashanu and King... Injury keeps Bosnich out... Only Spink and McGrath remain from Villa team beaten 3-0 in the Giuseppe Meazza Stadium four years ago... Disputed late penalty gives Italians first leg lead... Villa remain in Milan overnight to fly direct to London for their game with West Ham on Saturday...

I never touched him – says Spink

By any pre-match yardstick this visit to the North Italian football nerve centre of Milan is fraught with the danger of a daunting first-leg deficit.

Four years earlier Jo Venglos's team had gone down here by an emphatic 3-0 after setting up a 2-0 lead in the memorable first leg.

Since then both sides have undergone substantial changes with only Nigel Spink and Paul McGrath remaining in the Villa ranks from that time.

Inter, the UEFA Cup holders who had a poor 1993-94 season in Serie A, have changed, too. Not, perhaps totally for the better though with the darting Uruguayan striker Ruben Sosa and the Dutchman Wim Jonk in their ranks, plus Dutch striker Dennis Bergkamp, they have not been devalued either.

It is the general aura of the tie which appears to have been downgraded. Inter's disciplinarian coach Ottavia Bianchi is said to be at odds within the club who were beaten 1-0 at home by Roma last Sunday.

Support has waned just a touch, while the high cost of admission, match coverage on TV, the presence of local electric storms and a public transport strike restricts the attendance to 22,000.

By half-time Villa are fancying their chances of returning to Villa Park for the second leg with an appetising 0-0 scoreline.

Showing great discipline, especially in defence, Villa restrict Inter mainly to shots from outside the penalty area.

There's a worrying moment when Ugo Ehiogu is booked for an ill-timed tackle on Bergkamp but Earl Barrett calms any unease with two superbly-timed tackles.

Barrett deals capably with the Ruben Sosa threat though the nimble Uruguayan is liable to crop up anywhere across the line.

Marking Bergkamp is also a problem since he operates from a very deep position, suddenly moving forward.

However the most dangerous moment of the first half is a shot by the powerful Steve Staunton which forces the Italian national goalkeeper Gianluca Pagliuca into a one-handed save.

Inter start the second-half in a higher gear, forcing Villa into lengthy spells of 10-man defence though Dean Saunders is always willing and able to motor restlessly towards the Inter goal.

By now the Italians are desperate for a home-leg goal and this is reflected vividly by Nicola Berti's two theatrical dives to demonstratively but vainly claim unwarranted penalties.

With 20 minutes left Nigel Spink has made only one save and Inter are disrupted by losing their sweeper, Bia. To cover for his crucial loss Wim Jonk is pulled back into defence from midfield.

Villa's traumatic moments arrive with 15 minutes remaining. A centre-field tussle some 20-yards or so out sees the ball played out left by Berti as Paul McGrath tackles him.

Sosa chases the speeding ball, Spink advances, hesitates, dives late to attempt a touch on the ball and the Uruguayan goes down. To the majority it looks a penalty but how can you tell?

"There was no physical contact when the gentleman fell over," insists a stoney-faced Spink who finger-jabbed his disapproval the Uruguayan's way on the final whistle.

It's not to be Villa's night. Deano makes a brilliant attempt at an 83rd minute equaliser but the keeper twists in spectacular fashion to keep it out.

"We battled and scrapped," said Big Ron. "Macca and Ugo were tremendous. It would have been nice to go back all-square."

Saturday 17th September 1994 • Upton Park • 3.00pm

WEST HAM UNITED 1 ASTON VILLA 0

Half-time 0-0 • Attendance 18,326

Referee Stephen LODGE (Barnsley)
Linesmen E.W. GREEN and M. TINGEY

Claret and Blue Shirts, White Shorts		Goals
1	Ludek MIKLOSKO	
2	Tim BREAKER ❑	
5	Alvin MARTIN	
4	Steve POTTS ❑	
12	Keith ROWLAND	
14	Matthew RUSH	
6	Martin ALLEN	
10	John MONCUR ❑	
19	Mike MARSH	
27	Tony COTTEE	86
8	Peter BUTLER †	

Substitutes

21	Tony FEUER	
16	Lee CHAPMAN †ht	
22	Adrian WHITBREAD	

Green, Black and Red Striped Shirts, Black Shorts		Goals
13	Mark BOSNICH	
2	Earl BARRETT	
16	Ugo EHIOGU	
4	Shaun TEALE ❑	
3	Steve STAUNTON	
18	Dwight YORKE †	
6	Kevin RICHARDSON	
11	Andy TOWNSEND	
7	Ray HOUGHTON	
8	John FASHANU ❑	
9	Dean SAUNDERS	

Substitutes

1	Nigel SPINK	
10	Dalian ATKINSON †57	
14	Garry PARKER	

BEFORE		P	W	D	L	F	A	pts	AFTER		P	W	D	L	F	A	pts
8	Villa	5	2	3	0	7	4	9	8	Villa	6	2	3	1	7	5	9
21	West Ham	5	0	2	3	1	7	2	17	West Ham	6	1	2	3	2	7	5

FACTFILE

Villa's first Premiership defeat... West Ham's first win and only their second goal in six games... Shaun Teale makes first appearance of the season in place of the injured Paul McGrath... Earl Barrett's 100th league appearance for Villa... Fashanu miss proves costly.

Another costly late lapse

The demands of Euro-TV coverage have left little time to prepare for Upton Park with only a 38-hour gap between the final whistle in Milan and the kick-off in East London.

The two hour flight was made yesterday from Milan to Stanstead in the disappointment of the late penalty goal conceded in San Siro stadium.

A feeling of anti-climax is hard to avoid. However, Upton Park at least seems a far friendlier place than the famous Italian stadium though, ultimately, it proves not to be the case. Ron Atkinson shuffles his pack slightly with Mark Bosnich fit to replace Nigel Spink in goal while Shaun Teale takes over from Paul McGrath, who injured his shoulder late on against Inter.

In order to spread the playing load throughout the squad, and with no 'three foreigners' rule to queer the pitch, Ray Houghton and Dwight Yorke are back.

Hammers have 'prodigal son' Tony Cottee just returned from Everton and this is to prove the most decisive factor in a most disappointing afternoon.

Perhaps the return journey to Italy has had some effect on Villa who are a touch lethargic and lacking snap and sparkle from midfield, though the manager will stand for no such alibi.

Whatever the cause few truly outstanding opportunities are created in a fairly even game which, while they are never dominating, Villa seem unlikely to lose as Hammers attack is effectively contained.

By early in the second half Dwight Yorke, slightly out-of-sorts, is suffering a breathing problem and is replaced by Dalian Atkinson. The change brings a little more promise to Villa's attack as he runs at defenders to create more space.

With seven minutes remaining the chance to lock away three welcome Premiership points arrives as Atkinson weaves his way forward from the near the half-way line and West Ham are caught square.

Atkinson's pass puts John Fashanu in a first-class scoring position with goalkeeper Ludo Miklosko stranded without cover.

Sadly, the £1.35m ex-Don misses the chance of the game and what an expensive error that proves to be. "Am I imagining things or was that a glaring miss or what," manager Atkinson is to ask afterwards with a heavy helping of irony.

"He could have gone down and headed it in. The trouble was it fell to his wrong feet."

It's no laughing matter, though, four minutes from the end as Cottee strikes to secure a victory for West Ham which had at no previous stage appeared to be on the cards.

Another late defensive lapse has left Villa in a mediocre eighth place in the league as Newcastle are to race away with maximum points from their six games.

On an afternoon of few plusses Ron Atkinson is again enthusiastic about the contribution of Ugo Ehiogu who has dealt calmly with the threat of second-half substitute, bustling Lee Chapman.

"Our three Bulgarian players were on view today," says Atkinson with black humour. "Couldov, Wouldov and Shouldov..."

Ugo Ehiogu – a positive display

Wednesday 21st September 1994 • Villa Park • 7.45pm

ASTON VILLA 5 WIGAN ATHLETIC 0

Half-time 2-0 • *Attendance* 12,433

Referee Gerald ASHBY (Worcester)

Linesmen D.N. CAMPBELL and A.J. MARTIN

Claret Shirts with Blue Stripes, White Shorts		Goals
13	Mark BOSNICH	
2	Earl BARRETT	
16	Ugo EHIOGU	
4	Shaun TEALE	
15	Phil KING	
12	Nii LAMPTEY	73
14	Garry PARKER	
11	Andy TOWNSEND †	
18	Dwight YORKE	4
9	Dean SAUNDERS	70
10	Dalian ATKINSON	26, 85

Substitutes

1	Nigel SPINK	
19	Graham FENTON †41	
3	Steve STAUNTON	

Black and Blue Striped Shirts, Black Shorts		Goals
1	Simon FARNWORTH	
2	Paul RENNIE	
3	Joe JAKUB	
4	Greg STRONG	
5	John ROBERTSON	
6	Ian KILFORD	
7	David CAMPBELL	
8	Neil MORTON	
9	Pat GAVIN	
10	Neill RIMMER	
11	Matthew CARRAGHER	

Substitutes

gk	Mark STATHAM	
12	David McKEARNEY	
14	Brendan ORMSBY	

FACTFILE

Nii Lamptey scores on his Villa debut as Villa hit Wigan for five... former Villa defender Brendan Ormsby is on the subs bench for Wigan... Ugo Ehiogu takes over the captain's role from the absent Kevin Richardson... Dalian Atkinson scores his first goals of the season...

Nii Lamptey – delighted with his goal

Aston Villa Review 1995

Lamptey signs in with 'a smasher'

After two successive defeats, albeit one of them with honour in Milan, the arrival at Villa Park of the Endsleigh League Division Three's bottom club offers some welcome light relief.

It also gives Ron Atkinson the chance to introduce the Ghanaian Nii Lamptey for his full first-team competitive debut and to re-introduce Graham Fenton to the squad as substitute.

Crowd-wise the tie is distinctly not a major attraction and the attendance of a mere 12,433 produces a fairly low-key atmosphere which badly needs warming up a shade.

Goals are the way to do it and among the five rattled past Wigan to make safe passage to the next round a mere formality is one for the onlookers to cherish.

The scorer of it, in the 74th minute, is the 19-year-old debutant who had, pre-match, vowed to mark his English debut with a goal, though no-one could have predicted the solo excellence of it.

Lamptey collects the ball on the edge of his own penalty area, not a point to which Wigan have penetrated very often. But nor is it the likeliest launching pad for a goal at the other end. The Ghanaian international sets off on what starts as a delivery from danger but develops into a one-man attacking foray as opponent after opponent is cut out of contention.

Only one defensive ploy remains as Lamptey bears down on the visiting goal, but before the referee can award a penalty for Paul Rennie's foul challenge the grounded Villa man sweeps out his foot to jab it over the line.

Even after that Lamptey is aware that he has to continue to be patient, Ron Atkinson having stressed as much many times.

Last season he scored 16 for PSV Eindhoven on loan from Anderlecht and he tells reporters afterwards: "Some of the goals I scored last season were better than that. But I know I have to be patient."

Atkinson describes the do-it-yourself strike as 'a smasher' but it is more taken with the 'professional performance' of the entire team.

"The onus was on us to get goals and we got them," he points out to dispel any suggestion that such a scoreline was automatic against demoralised inferior opposition.

The Villa team, which shows four changes from Upton Park, is captained by Ugo Ehiogu in Kevin Richardson's absence, a profound compliment to the 21-year-old.

Systematic demolition of outclassed Wigan as comprised of two goals from Dalian Atkinson and one each from Dean Saunders and Dwight Yorke, to provide a tantalising taste of what has been lacking against stronger challenges.

Fenton enjoys a brief return to the first-team scene as substitute for Townsend though he is unable to add to the scoreline.

Ahead of Villa, as the game arrives at its predictable conclusion is a far more testing programme with Blackburn Rovers away followed by Inter Milan and Newcastle at home.

Dalian Atkinson strikes home his first goal

Saturday 24th September 1994 • Ewood Park • 3.00pm

BLACKBURN ROVERS 3 ASTON VILLA 1

Half-time 1-0 • *Attendance* 22,694

Referee Martin BODENHAM (East Looe)

Linesmen J.P. ROBINSON and M.J. STODDART

Blue and White Halved Shirts, White Shorts		Goals	Claret Shirts with Blue Stripes, White Shorts		Goals
1	Tim FLOWERS		13	Mark BOSNICH ❑	
20	Henning BERG		2	Earl BARRETT ❑	
2	Tony GALE		16	Ugo EHIOGU	90
5	Colin HENDRY		5	Paul McGRATH	
6	Graeme LE SAUX		4	Shaun TEALE †	
7	Stuart RIPLEY †		18	Dwight YORKE ❑	
4	Tim SHERWOOD		6	Kevin RICHARDSON	
22	Mark ATKINS		11	Andy TOWNSEND ❑	
11	Jason WILCOX		3	Steve STAUNTON ❑	
9	Alan SHEARER	pen 17, 72	10	Dalian ATKINSON	
16	Chris SUTTON	56	9	Dean SAUNDERS	
	Substitutes			*Substitutes*	
13	Bobby MIMMS		1	Nigel SPINK	
24	Paul WARHURST †75		12	Nii LAMPTEY †63	
25	Ian PEARCE		19	Graham FENTON ‡84	

BEFORE		P	W	D	L	F	A	pts	AFTER		P	W	D	L	F	A	pts
2	Blackburn	6	4	2	0	13	2	14	2	Blackburn	7	5	2	0	16	3	17
8	Villa	6	2	3	1	7	5	9	9	Villa	7	2	3	2	8	8	9

FACTFILE

Ugo Ehiogu scores his first goal for Villa... the first Blackburn concede at home in the Premiership (four games)... Nii Lamptey makes his Premiership debut, substituting for Teale... 100th Villa league appearance for Earl Barrett... Villa gunned down by the SAS.

Shearer, Sutton show the way

The names 'Shearer and Sutton' loom large on Villa's horizon not merely because they are a worrying threat, which they emphatically are, but their names prompt a spot of self-analysis.

In this Ewood Park encounter, and the next two games, at home to Inter Milan and then Newcastle United, Villa are to be confronted by the kind of consistent strikers whom they, themselves, painfully lack.

After Shearer and Sutton will come Bergkamp and Sosa followed by Cole and Lee. Who are Villa's most potent strike pair? Impossible to say judging on the undeniable yardstick of goals in the opposition net.

Dean Saunders and Dalian Atkinson are the two given the challenge of attempting to match the Blackburn duo who, at £8m the pair, collectively cost a sizeable chunk of the club owner Jack Walker's considerable fortune.

So far this season Atkinson has not scored in the League, nor has he done so since his pair against West Ham in January, while Saunders has got three Premiership goals this campaign.

A posse of Inter spies are present, though they will have difficulty in making judgements on this particular Aston Villa.

After only 17 minutes Ugo Ehiogu makes a rather panicky challenge on Sutton after a poor attempt to clear Graham Le Saux's centre and Shearer claims the penalty. "A mistake on my part," confesses Ehiogu afterwards. "A complete rush of blood."

It's not one-way traffic by any means and Kevin Richardson misses a chance to equalise when he thumps the ball over the bar from ten yards while a bending free kick by Steve Staunton requires an England-class save from Tim Flowers.

Eleven minutes into the second half another calamity arrives in the shape of a Sutton goal, pushed over the line from a well-forward position which looked suspiciously like off-side after Shearer's shot had bounced off Ehiogu.

Goals are badly needed now so it's time to give Nii Lamptey a look-in and the Ghanaian replaces transfer-seeking Shaun Teale, but instead of reducing the lead Villa fall further behind.

This time, in the 72nd minute, it is Shearer benefiting from a Sutton assist for one of those power drives which have become his hallmark and Villa are 3-0 down having looked vulnerable in front of Mark Bosnich's goal.

Villa are forced into a second substitution when Lamptey is stretchered off for stitches in a gashed face after a heavy collision with Colin Hendry

Time for Graham Fenton to come on as substitute for the injured substitute but by now it has long since become a lost cause from Villa's point of view though Fenton does whack a scoring attempt against an upright.

All that is left is a late show of defiance by Ehiogu who has not had the best of matches though in terms of his learning curve it's been a useful 90 minutes.

The Villa defender gets up into a dangerous position as Richardson's free kick drops into the goalmouth and his header beats Flowers for the consolation goal Villa, and especially Andy Townsend, have worked hard to achieve.

"I don't know what the Inter spies made of us," mused manager Atkinson. "Probably as confused as we were."

Graham Fenton – shot against upright

Thursday 29th September 1994 • Villa Park • 8.05pm

ASTON VILLA 1 INTERNAZIONALE 0

After extra time • Aggregate 1-1 • Villa win 4-3 on penalties
Half-time 1-0 • Attendance 30,533
Referee Joel QUINION
Linesmen D. COTREL and C. POULAIN
Officials from France

Claret Shirts with Blue Stripes, White Shorts	Goals	Black and Blue Striped Shirts, Black Shorts	Goals
1 Nigel SPINK		1 Gianluca PAGLIUCA	
2 Earl BARRETT		2 Giuseppe BERGOMI	
3 Steve STAUNTON		3 Gianluca FESTA	
4 Ugo EHIOGU		4 Giovanni BIA	
5 Paul McGRATH ❑		5 Mirko CONTE †	
6 Kevin RICHARDSON ‡		6 Massimo PAGANIN	
7 Ray HOUGHTON	41	7 Nicola BERTI	
8 Andy TOWNSEND		8 Andrea SENO ❑	
9 Dean SAUNDERS †		9 Dennis BERGKAMP ❑	
10 Dalian ATKINSON		10 Ruben SOSA ❑	
11 Phil KING		11 Darko PANCEV ‡	

Substitutes		*Substitutes*	
gk Michael OAKES		gk Luca MONDINI	
12 John FASHANU		13 Davide FONTOLAN †62	
14 Guy WHITTINGHAM †18		14 Pierluigi ORLANDINI ‡112	
15 Shaun TEALE		15 Marco BAROLLO	
16 Garry PARKER ‡98		16 Marco DEL VECCHIO	

PENALTY SHOOT OUT				**PENALTY SHOOT OUT**			
1 Garry PARKER	✓		1-1	1 Giovanni BIA	✓		0-1
2 Steve STAUNTON	✓		2-2	2 Dennis BERGKAMP	✓		1-2
3 Andy TOWNSEND	✓		3-3	3 Andrea SENO	✓		2-3
4 Guy WHITTINGHAM	✗	Saved	3-3	4 Davide FONTOLAN	✗	Missed	3-3
5 Phil KING	✓		4-3	5 Ruben SOSA	✗	Hit bar	3-3

My greatest result – says Ron

Even in global terms, fixtures don't come much bigger than this.

"It's the kind of match we want constantly at Villa Park," trumpets Ron Atkinson in welcoming Internazionale for the UEFA Cup showdown.

In the event it proves to be, not only a show-down, and a spine-tingler at that, but a shoot-out too. Football-wise, to the death...

On the eve of the game Inter have appeared a touch concerned at their Penns Hall press conference. "A 1-0 lead is nothing," said their grim-faced coach, Ottavia Bianchi. "We start level."

Dutch World Cup striker Dennis Bergkamp, the scourge of British teams at club and inter-national level, shows concern, too.

"If Villa get a goal first it will be some match," he told reporters.

Prophetic words. Very. "We will rock you..." reverberates around the newly re-vamped stadium as Inter players warm up pre-match. The fans are clearly going to play a part. They can't do it, San Siro-style, with flares and smoke but lungs are clearly in sound shape.

Villa quickly set the scene by going for the prize from the first whistle. Inter are quickly under pressure though, in a seventh minute break, Nicola Berti rattles a shot against the angle.

A change has to be made in 20 minutes when Dean Saunders is withdrawn with a hip injury and Guy Whittingham takes over, full of physical challenge.

For a spell Inter slow down the pace using their smooth ball skills and passing accuracy to rather worryingly threaten to run the game.

But Villa's resolve deepens as impressive indi-vidual displays take shape. Steve Staunton is inspirational with his running from midfield, Earl Barrett more defiant than ever, Andy Townsend fired up for action.

The revelation, though, is Ray Houghton. "The little man has never played better for me, maybe in his entire career," says the manager afterwards.

The Italian defence is, distinctly, not happy and it cracks two minutes from half-time. Kevin Richardson's lobbed pass deflects off Paganin to Bergomi and drops beautifully for Houghton to drive it home.

In the second half Inter have only one telling shot, by Bergkamp, which Spink hurries to save. By now Villa are in complete control with Inter looking a spent force.

There's a dreadful late miss by substitute Fontolan before two periods of extra-time in which Inter are never going to score.

It's now 10.15 pm, cocoa time back home, but a high-octane cocktail of penalties at Villa Park.

Bia first: 1-0. Garry Parker, 1-1. Bergkamp, 2-1. Staunton, 2-2. Seno, 3-2. Townsend 3-3. Then, bedlam...

Substitute Fontolan misses. Yes, again. Whit-tingham can grab the lead now. But, calamity, Pagliuca saves. Still 3-3.

Sosa's turn. He won't miss. But he does, rattling the bar. Still 3-3. Inter have had their five shots now. Who's got the bottle to be Villa's villain or hero?

It's Phil King. Untried in this situa-tion, yet there he is joking with shattered team mates. Strolls up. Shoots. 4-3. Easy. King? A monarch, indeed.

Phil, the Penalty, King

Saturday 1st October 1994 • Villa Park • 3.00pm

ASTON VILLA 0 NEWCASTLE UNITED 2

Half-time 0-0 • Attendance 29,960

Referee Dermot GALLAGHER (Banbury)

Linesmen G.M. LEE and M.L. SHORT

Claret Shirts with Blue Stripes, White Shorts		Goals	Black & White Striped Shirts, Black Shorts		Goals
1	Nigel SPINK		1	Pavel SRNICEK	
2	Earl BARRETT		12	Marc HOTTIGER	
5	Paul McGRATH		15	Darren PEACOCK	
16	Ugo EHIOGU ❏		6	Steve HOWEY	
15	Phil KING		3	John BERESFORD ❏	
7	Ray HOUGHTON ‡		27	Phillipe ALBERT	
14	Garry PARKER		5	Ruel FOX	
11	Andy TOWNSEND		11	Scott SELLARS	
18	Dwight YORKE		7	Robert LEE	65
19	Graham FENTON †		8	Peter BEARDSLEY †	
22	Guy WHITTINGHAM		9	Andy COLE	81
	Substitutes			*Substitutes*	
30	Michael OAKES		30	Mike HOOPER	
12	Nii LAMPTEY †75		28	Paul KITSON †75	
3	Steve STAUNTON ‡80		19	Steve WATSON	

BEFORE	P	W	D	L	F	A	pts	AFTER	P	W	D	L	F	A	pts
1 Newcastle	7	6	1	0	23	8	19	1 Newcastle	8	7	1	0	25	8	22
9 Villa	7	2	3	2	8	8	9	12 Villa	8	2	3	3	8	10	9

First full outings of the season for Whittingham and Fenton... Paul Kitson's Newcastle debut after signing from Derby County... Newcastle extend unbeaten run in Premiership to nine games... Lack of recognised goalscorer is costing Villa points and places.

Fine form but no finish

Ron Atkinson has laid it firmly on the line: leg-weariness will be no excuse for poor form once a player has vowed himself ready for more action.

As the danger of a reaction from the late-night heroics against Inter Milan looms the Villa manager looks for a professional response against the impressive Premiership leaders.

Any suggestions that the demands of Thursday night could be an excuse for a below-par display are waved aside. "We were just doing our job against Inter," he said.

"We are professionals. We will do the same against Newcastle," though he acknowledges Kevin Keegan's side to be 'the most exciting footballing team in the country just now'.

Dean Saunders and Kevin Richardson are out with the injuries which forced them to be withdrawn from the UEFA Cup-tie but Nigel Spink keeps his place in goal and Garry Parker, Guy Whittingham, Dwight Yorke and Graham Fenton are also in the starting line-up.

Quickly it becomes clear that the manager's instructions have been followed to the letter and, as the enterprising passing football flows, there is no hint of a European hang-over.

Newcastle, who themselves dismissed the fragile UEFA Cup challenge of Royal Antwerp without having to break sweat in mid-week, are under the whip virtually from the start.

There are reports afterwards of a rocket or two fired in the Newcastle dressing room at half-time as Villa dominate but fail to consolidate.

Then, in the 65th minute, calamity. Robert Lee, to be named 48 hours later in Terry Venables' England squad for Rumania, fires the lead from outside the box with Spink stranded.

Psychologically it could not have been worse for Villa whose morale drops at the feeling of sheer injustice, though truthfully failure to convert openings into goals is again the root cause.

Almost predictably a second Newcastle goal arrives and almost predictably the supplier this time is Andy Cole, fed by Paul Kitson, the expensive new signing from Derby County.

Ron Atkinson describes the first-hour of form as better than against Inter Milan, though the inability to score goals must again be a nagging problem.

John Fashanu undergoes achilles tendon surgery on Monday though his previous presence has not made a marked impact, while the missing Saunders and Dalian Atkinson (rested) may not have made the necessary difference, either.

The outcome is a fall to twelfth place in the Premiership with only two wins in eight starts and a position which will only be remedied by a significant increase in the goals supply.

Two statistics say it all. Villa have scored eight goals in eight games. Leaders Newcastle have netted 25.

Nice try, Guy!

Wednesday 5th October 1994 • Springfield Park • 7.30pm

WIGAN ATHLETIC 0 ASTON VILLA 3

Half-time 0-1 • Attendance 2,633

Referee Peter JONES (Loughborough)
Linesmen D. PUGH and R. SUTTON

Black and Blue Striped Shirts, Black Shorts	Goals	Claret Shirts with Blue Stripes, White Shorts	Goals
1 Simon FARNWORTH		30 Michael OAKES	
2 Matthew CARRAGHER †		15 Phil KING	
4 Greg STRONG		3 Steve STAUNTON	
5 John ROBERTSON		4 Shaun TEALE	
3 Joe JAKUB		5 Paul McGRATH	
7 David CAMPBELL		14 Garry PARKER	
6 Andy FARRELL		19 Graham FENTON	
8 Ian KILFORD		18 Dwight YORKE	
10 Neill RIMMER		12 Nii LAMPTEY ❏	43, 85
11 Andy LYONS ‡		22 Guy WHITTINGHAM	60
9 Pat GAVIN		21 David FARRELL	

Substitutes		*Substitutes*	
13 Mark STATHAM		13 Mark BOSNICH	
12 Paul RENNIE †79		2 Earl BARRETT	
14 Neil MORTON ‡84		11 Andy TOWNSEND	

First team debut for goalkeeper Michael Oakes... Dave Farrell makes only his second ever senior appearance and his first of the season...Villa go through with 8-0 aggregate score... Third round draw is made live on TV from Villa Park next morning... a rare home cup draw for Villa.

FACTFILE

Dave Farrell and Nii Lamptey

Aston Villa Review 1995

Second string show Cup paces

In the thick of such an over-crowded programme in three competitions, several first-team fringe players are given the opportunity of steering the club safely through to the third round.

Most notable change is the introduction of third-choice goalkeeper Michael Oakes, son of the former Manchester City player, Alan Oakes and an England Under-21 squad man.

Mark Bosnich and Nigel Spink are thus made aware that another 'keeper has entered the arena should either or both of them suffer a form decline.

Lamptey and winger Dave Farrell are also in the much-changed team which enjoys the comfort of a five-goal cushion from the first leg.

Before a crowd of fewer than 3,000, and the outcome a foregone conclusion, the return leg is short of a touch of natural motivation, though Wigan work hard at restricting Villa's supply of chances which they achieve effectively.

The first break arrives a couple of minutes before half-time when Farrell throws the home defence into disarray with a run from the half-way line before feeding Lamptey 15 yards out.

The Ghanaian, scorer of that spectacular goal in the first leg, gratefully accepts the chance to increase the tie's aggregate to 6-0 in Villa's favour.

Fenton, playing in midfield, works as hard as ever to get things moving more freely and, to be fair, the scoreline would have been more emphatic in the first hour but for Guy Whitting-ham twice slamming efforts against the woodwork. The ex-Pompey striker's reward for constant persistence arrives in the 61st minute when Lamptey's feed falls just right for him and he gobbles up the chance of making it 2-0.

By now Wigan are struggling to hold on against far superior opposition and look forward to the luxury of a warm shower. Just one more indignity awaits them as Lamptey fires yet another reminder to the manager that he would like a Premiership place. The home goalkeeper Simon Farnworth has left his charge wide open with a foolhardy surge well off his line and Lamptey is able to knock the ball in untroubled for an 8-0 combined score.

Oakes has been largely a spectator on his first-team, competitive debut but when a weighty shot from Andy Lyons threatens he touches it safely over the bar.

There is one hiccup from Villa's point of view when Graham Fenton is carried off a couple of minutes from time after a heavy tackle by David Campbell.

Next day the third round draw is made live on GMTV direct from Villa Park at 7.20 am and it's Bryan Robson's Middlesbrough at Villa Park. The 'easy rides' are over.

Now for a far stiffer test against the Endsleigh Division One pacesetters managed by Ron Atkinson's former Manchester United skipper.

Michael Oakes - his first team debut

Saturday 8th October 1994 • Anfield • 3.00pm

LIVERPOOL 3 ASTON VILLA 2

Half-time 2-1 • *Attendance* 32,158

Referee Keith BURGE (Tonypandy)

Linesmen T.A. ATKINSON and E.G. HANNAH

Red Shirts, Red Shorts		Goals	Green, Black and Red Striped Shirts, Black Shorts		Goals
1	David JAMES		13	Mark BOSNICH	
12	John SCALES		2	Earl BARRETT	
25	Neil RUDDOCK	20	5	Paul McGRATH	
6	Phil BABB		16	Ugo EHIOGU	
2	Rob JONES		3	Steve STAUNTON	90
17	Steve McMANAMAN		18	Dwight YORKE	
14	Jan MOLBY		14	Garry PARKER	
10	John BARNES		11	Andy TOWNSEND ❑ †	
20	Stig BJORNEBYE		7	Ray HOUGHTON ‡	
9	Ian RUSH †		22	Guy WHITTINGHAM	37
23	Robbie FOWLER	26, 57	9	Dean SAUNDERS	
	Substitutes			*Substitutes*	
13	Michael STENSGAARD		1	Nigel SPINK	
7	Nigel CLOUGH		15	Phil KING †30	
15	Jamie REDKNAPP †78		12	Nii LAMPTEY ‡74	

BEFORE		P	W	D	L	F	A	pts	AFTER		P	W	D	L	F	A	pts
5	Liverpool	7	4	2	1	16	5	14	3	Liverpool	8	5	2	1	19	7	17
12	Villa	8	2	3	3	8	10	9	14	Villa	9	2	3	4	10	13	9

FACTFILE

A fourth successive Premiership defeat for Villa... Dwight Yorke's 100th league appearance... Guy pulls one back... Villa ease off and pay the price... Stan's injury time goal is too little too late... Manager Atkinson shows his displeasure.

Slide continues at Anfield

The problem of blending an effective strike pair fills Ron Atkinson's thoughts in advance of the trip to Anfield with a fourth successive league defeat threatened.

"I can't remember losing four league games on the trot before," declares the Villa manager as he wrestles with the contrast between Cup and Premiership results.

Two pairs of strikers are taken to Liverpool with the object of maybe ringing the changes from the subs bench though his feelings are that Guy Whittingham is due for his first extended run.

In the event it is Whittingham and Dean Saunders who are paired up front with Mark Bosnich returning in goal and the regulars recalled after the re-shaped line-up at Wigan, though skipper Kevin Richardson is still out injured.

As the action unfolds it proves to be a similar affair to the previous week against Newcastle with Villa's passing and general approach play impressive but no effective finish.

Having survived an opening onslaught by Liverpool unscathed Villa join in a sparkling match, full of inventive attacking football. Yet just when Villa seem able to hold their own a Liverpool team revitalised under Roy Evans' management, plunders a two-goal lead.

Ironically, having fretted about lack of goal-scoring consistency, Atkinson now has cause to ponder defensive slackness. "We certainly weren't as solid at the back as usual," he was to say later.

A mistake by Andy Townsend followed by a desperate attempt to redeem himself results in an indirect free-kick for Liverpool from which

Neil Ruddock blasts a 20th minute home lead. Six minutes later a shot by England cap Rob Jones is blocked by Paul McGrath but the ball rebounds invitingly for Rob Fowler to supply a two-goal Liverpool lead.

Immediate action has to be taken if an embarrassing scoreline is to be avoided and happily Whittingham's selection is justified in the 37th minute when he reduces the deficit to 2-1.

One of Villa's many neat build-ups sees Whittingham exchange passes with Dwight Yorke before directing the ball past David James as he loses his balance. Townsend has left the field injured and Phil King is on as sub.

Atkinson had voiced uncertainty before the kick-off as to whether Whittingham and Saunders can hit it off as a pair. Just before half-time there is an encouraging sign as the ex-soldier feeds a pass through to his strike partner but the Welsh striker's finish lacks power.

Deano also heads an ideal Steve Staunton centre over the crossbar, so Villa could have been 2-2 or even 3-2 by this time. In the event, early in the second half, they go 3-1 down as a lapse by Bosnich enables Fowler to strike again.

This latest blow visibly drains some of Villa's resolve and though Steve Staunton gets a second Villa goal in injury time the players are lambasted afterwards for their final half-hour's play during which time Nii Lamptey was replaced Ray Houghton.

"I didn't like the way we eased off when I felt there were more goals to be had," said Atkinson afterwards. More food for thought as the Premiership position deteriorates.

Guy Whittingham

Saturday 15th October 1994 • Villa Park • 3.00pm

ASTON VILLA 1 NORWICH CITY 1

Half-time 0-0 • Attendance 22,468

Referee Alan WILKIE (Chester-le-Street)
Linesmen G.K. HEGLEY and J. McGRATH

Claret Shirts with Blue Stripes, White Shorts		Goals	Yellow Shirts, Green Shorts		Goals
13	Mark BOSNICH		1	Bryan GUNN	
2	Earl BARRETT		16	Carl BRADSHAW ‡	
5	Paul McGRATH		3	Rob NEWMAN	
16	Ugo EHIOGU		14	Spencer PRIOR	
15	Phil KING		2	Mark BOWEN	
18	Dwight YORKE		20	Darren EADIE	
6	Kevin RICHARDSON ❑		8	Mike MILLIGAN	50
14	Garry PARKER		4	Ian CROOK	
3	Steve STAUNTON †		6	Neil ADAMS	
9	Dean SAUNDERS	62	22	Mike SHERON	
10	Dalian ATKINSON ‡		9	Mark ROBINS †	
	Substitutes			*Substitutes*	
1	Nigel SPINK		24	Andy MARSHALL	
7	Ray HOUGHTON †75		26	Ade AKINBIYI †58	
22	Guy WHITTINGHAM ‡75		32	Johnny WRIGHT ‡74	

BEFORE		P	W	D	L	F	A	pts	AFTER		P	W	D	L	F	A	pts
8	Norwich	9	4	3	2	7	7	15	9	Norwich	10	4	4	2	8	8	16
14	Villa	9	2	3	4	10	13	9	15	Villa	10	2	4	4	11	14	10

FACTFILE

The Black Sea beckons... Richardson returns... Townsend out... Villa minds are elsewhere as they struggle to overcome mediocre opposition... Where are the goals coming from?... Off nine points at last – but only just... Bossie blunder lets in the Canaries.

Saunders strikes to make point

The usual pre-Europe instruction is in the air, namely 'forget Turkey and concentrate on Norwich', but realistically next week's UEFA Cup trip to the Black Sea is in everyone's minds. The morning newspapers are full of reports, extracted from *Claret & Blue magazine*, that a daunting reception awaits the party in Trabzon on Monday.

Team-wise the news is that Kevin Richardson is back, the Irish contingent and Dean Saunders, who missed mid-week internationals are OK, but Andy Townsend is out with a groin strain.

Ron Atkinson spells out the dangers of a fifth successive league defeat in explicit terms. "We have to get off nine points," he emphasises. "Another defeat and we get sucked right into it." meaning the long-range danger zone.

Public reaction to this particular fixture is a lukewarm attendance of 22,468, though this could be partly down to the heavy programme of home games ahead.

As the moderate action unfolds it tends to match the cool atmosphere with little to encourage the feeling that a Premiership upsurge is on the way.

Writing in the Birmingham Post, Adrian Milledge pointed out that the return match with Norwich was scheduled to be the final fixture of the season. And he added: *"The first half resembled what next May's encounter at Carrow Road will probably turn out to be, a meaningless, mid-table end-of-the-season affair."*

Norwich present little threat to Villa's goal while, at the other end, enough chances are created to establish a clear lead, but are wasted. There's a general shortage of zest suggesting, perhaps, an unconscious psychological preoccupation with Trabzonspor.

Both Saunders and Dalian Atkinson, the latter without a Premiership goal since last January, ought to have done better than allow Bryan Gunn to make saves.

The second-half livens up noticeably, suggesting some half-time soul searching, and Norwich inherit Villa's 'missed chance' bug when Darren Eadie and Mike Sheron hit the woodwork.

In the 50th minute Norwich are ahead after Bosnich failed to deal decisively with a right-wing centre by Mark Robins. "It was totally his fault," said Ron Atkinson afterwards. "A Comic Cuts goal. Bosnich should have got both hands to it but he didn't touch it at all."

Mike Milligan is allowed to head Norwich into the lead and this, with the horror of that fifth successive league defeat threatening, does at least spread urgency through the ranks.

This upsurge in application brings the equaliser in a matter of 12 minutes, thanks to the alertness of Dwight Yorke and a splendid headed finish by Saunders.

The West Indian's quickly-taken corner, rolled to Garry Parker, enables the Welsh international to cruise in confidently to steer the resulting near-post cross to perfection wide of Gunn.

Saunders and Yorke, the team's two most energetic and industrious players are both close in the dying moments to conjuring what would have been a most welcome victory. Off nine points... but only as far as 10 from 10 games.

**Dean Saunders –
put Villa back on level terms**

Tuesday 18th October 1994 • Avni Aker Stadium • 8.00pm

TRABZONSPOR 1 ASTON VILLA 0

Half-time 0-0 • *Attendance* 30,000

Referee M. PIRAUX (Belgium)

Linesmen G.J. VERWOORT and R.P. METZ

White Shirts with Claret and Blue Sash, Light Blue Shorts	Goals		Claret Shirts with Blue Stripes, White Shorts	Goals
1 Victor GRICHKO			1 Nigel SPINK	
2 LEMI Çelik ❑			2 Earl BARRETT	
3 OGÜN Termizkanoglu			3 Steve STAUNTON ❑	
4 KEMAL Serdar ❑			4 Ugo EHIOGU	
5 TOLUNAY Kafkas			5 Paul McGRATH	
6 ABDULLAH Ercan			6 Kevin RICHARDSON	
7 CENGIZ Atilla			7 Ray HOUGHTON	
8 ONAL Karaman			8 Dean SAUNDERS	
9 SONER Boz			9 Guy WHITTINGHAM	
10 HAMI Mandirali †			10 Andy TOWNSEND	
11 ORHAN Kaynak ‡	77		11 Phil KING	

Substitutes			*Substitutes*	
gk NIHAT Tümkaya			gk Michael OAKES	
13 OSMAN Özköylü			12 Garry PARKER	
14 ENDER Tras			14 Graham FENTON	
15 HAMDI Aslan †89			15 Dalian ATKINSON	
16 KATCHARAVA Kakhaber ‡90			16 Shaun TEALE	

A hot reception for Villa and Steve Staunton in Turkey.

Late goal sets second leg task

The party which jetted by charter out of Birmingham airport yesterday had on board Villa's own chef and food supplies, with nothing left to chance in the Turkish outpost on the edge of the Black Sea.

Predictably the decrepit, compact Avni Aker stadium is packed to its capacity of approaching 30,000 with others clinging to trees and various vantage posts around the ground, anywhere in fact, to get a glimpse of the game and a possible Euro upset.

Their excitable nature produces an atmosphere which is quite as daunting and intimidating as anticipated though, mercifully, free of violence. The beating of drums and the sound of exploding firecrackers adds to the pressure on Villa.

Certainly the decision to cancel the proposed charter trip of fans was a wise one in the circumstances as illustrated by the heavy guard ringing the few claret-and-blue followers who have travelled with the official party.

Andy Townsend, given until the very last moment to recover from a groin strain is safely installed in midfield while Guy Whittingham has the striking role in place of Dalian Atkinson alongside Dean Saunders.

The opening stages are played to the background of almost hysterical support from Trabzonspor, but this fades gradually as Villa make it clear they are not intending to be overwhelmed.

Long before half-time the atmosphere has cooled considerably as Villa keep possession, play the ball around sweetly and deny the Turks the opportunity they need to take control.

Villa should have taken the lead when Steve Staunton and Saunders linked up to supply Whittingham with an ideal shooting chance but he hurries his shot and strikes it against the bar before failing to capitalise on the rebound.

Ray Houghton then gets a favourable opening, again inspired by Saunders and Staunton, but hits his shot straight at goalkeeper Viktor.

Now it's Saunders' turn to attempt a valuable away goal but his header from Earl Barrett's centre is off-target, all very disappointing in the light of Villa's impressive share of the possession play.

By half-time Villa look well capable of taking home at least the 'intact' scoreline Ron Atkinson has demanded but it is all to change after the interval when it is Trabzonspor's time to dictate the play.

The warning signs flash as Hami penetrates a suddenly unsure defence to thunder a rising shot against the bar to inspire a renewed outburst of drum-beating hysteria.

Even so the final quarter of the tense 90 minutes arrive with the scoreline still 0-0 and a well-satisfied immediate flight home beckoning invitingly. Come the 76th minute, however, and hopes are dashed.

A high ball into a crowded goalmouth lures Orhan to rise menacingly to head past Spink for a similar situation to that suffered in San Siro and a nerve-wracking home leg.

"We were excellent in the fist half and could have been two or three goals up," confirms a disconsolate Ron Atkinson. "But in the second half they were considerably better and we were considerably worse..."

He added graciously: "I thought it was a great atmosphere, electric. The crowd was terrific. They made lots of noise but they weren't hostile."

From the so-called hell-hole, which was never that, back to the airport and a five-hour flight through the night back to Birmingham fretting once again on the misery of good chances missed.

Saturday 22nd October 1994 • Villa Park • 3.00pm

ASTON VILLA 0 NOTTINGHAM FOREST 2

Half-time 0-1 • *Attendance* 29,217
Referee Keith COOPER (Pontypridd)
Linesmen P.A. ELWICK and A.R. LEAKE

Claret Shirts with Blue Stripes, White Shorts	Goals	Blue Shirts, Green Shorts	Goals
1 Nigel SPINK		1 Mark CROSSLEY	
2 Earl BARRETT ❏		18 Alf Inge HAALAND	
5 Paul McGRATH		4 Colin COOPER	
16 Ugo EHIOGU		5 Steve CHETTLE	
15 Phil KING ‡		3 Stuart PEARCE	pen 2
7 Ray HOUGHTON		11 Steve STONE	70
19 Graham FENTON †		7 David PHILLIPS	
11 Andy TOWNSEND		9 Lars BOHINEN ❏	
3 Steve STAUNTON ❏		14 Ian WOAN	
9 Dean SAUNDERS		10 Stan COLLYMORE	
18 Dwight YORKE		22 Bryan ROY †	

Substitutes		*Substitutes*	
30 Michael OAKES		23 Malcolm RIGBY	
14 Garry PARKER †ht		12 Jason LEE †65	
22 Guy WHITTINGHAM ‡72		17 Kingsley BLACK	

BEFORE	P	W	D	L	F	A	pts	AFTER	P	W	D	L	F	A	pts
2 Forest	10	7	3	0	23	11	24	2 Forest	11	8	3	0	25	11	27
16 Villa	10	2	4	4	11	14	10	16 Villa	11	2	4	5	11	16	10

FACTFILE

Villa's strike force fire blanks for a fifth game this season... Kevin Richardson is dropped for the first time in his Villa career... Ron Atkinson raises the subject of relegation at the post-match press conference... Ray Houghton's 100th appearance in Villa colours...

Villa fail to put out Forest fire

The arrival of Nottingham Forest, impressively-placed among the Premiership leaders has an ominous look about it in view of Villa's poor league results.

Forest, having been steered back to the big stage in one season by Brian Clough's replacement, Frank Clark, are clearly hungry for points.

What's more they have in Stan Collymore and Brian Roy the kind of in-form strike duo so agonisingly lacking, on current form, at Villa Park.

Ron Atkinson, still unable to find that crucial chemistry required for consistent goalscoring, tries another team re-shuffle. This time skipper Kevin Richardson loses his place for the first time, when fit, and Graham Fenton is brought in. Paul McGrath and Phil King have recovered sufficiently from heavy colds, but a similar ailment keeps Mark Bosnich out.

Dwight Yorke is up front with Dean Saunders while Guy Whittingham returns to the bench and a performance takes shape of similar dimensions to the home defeat by Newcastle.

The ingredients are much the same: Villa attack incessantly, construct smooth-looking passing moves and keep the opposition under such constant pressure that Clark is moved to criticise his side afterwards.

But here again the end-product is missing, there is no clinical finish, no confidence in accepting the prize when it beckons.

There is an essential difference, however, in that Forest have capitalised on what was for them

the heaven-sent start. As Roy races through he is surprisingly upended by Earl Barrett for a second-minute penalty, perfect fodder for dead-ball specialist Stuart Pearce.

Thus, the visitors can afford to defend in depth and attack on the break which they do to frustrating effect. As it becomes increasingly obvious that Villa are not going to score Forest claim a second through Stone after 70 minutes.

The break is made by Collymore who forces a corner and Ian Woan's flag kick is headed out to the Forest midfielder. By now Fenton has been injured in a collision with McGrath and Garry Parker is on against his former club.

But, first Pearced and now Stoned, Villa are heading for their sixth league game without a win and only one point from a possible 18.

Ray Houghton works industriously, Fenton has a promising header saved, Steve Staunton's drive is a shade too high, Yorke's close-range attempt is turned for a corner and Saunders heads just off target.

It's a familiar, discouraging tale that prompts Ron Atkinson to mention the dreaded 'R' word afterwards, though he pledges that it won't happen. During the weekend Dalian Atkinson, left out of the squad again, complain s that he has 'not been given a fair chance'.

Having not scored a Premiership goal since January despite league appearances running into double figures it seems, to fans, a remarkable claim when goalscorers who don't score goals have become the root cause of the club's slide down the table.

That and defensive mistakes which repeat themselves all too often.

Ray Houghton – century maker

Wednesday 26th October 1994 • Villa Park • 7.45pm

ASTON VILLA 1 MIDDLESBROUGH 0

Half-time 1-0 • Attendance 19,254
Referee Kelvin MORTON (Bury St Edmunds)
Linesmen B.L. POLKEY and R.A. SMITH

Claret Shirts with Blue Stripes, White Shorts	Goals	Green and Black Striped Shirts, Black Shorts	Goals
13 Mark BOSNICH		1 Alan MILLER	
2 Earl BARRETT		2 Neil COX ❑	
3 Steve STAUNTON		3 Curtis FLEMING ❑	
16 Ugo EHIOGU ❑		4 Steve VICKERS	
5 Paul McGRATH		5 Derek WHYTE ❑	
11 Andy TOWNSEND ❑	30	6 Clayton BLACKMORE	
7 Ray HOUGHTON		7 Andy TODD †	
14 Garry PARKER		8 Jamie POLLOCK	
9 Dean SAUNDERS		9 Paul WILKINSON	
22 Guy WHITTINGHAM †		10 John HENDRIE	
18 Dwight YORKE		11 Alan MOORE	
Substitutes		*Substitutes*	
gk Nigel SPINK		gk Ben ROBERTS	
6 Kevin RICHARDSON		12 Craig HIGNETT †78	
12 Nii LAMPTEY †82		14 Tommy WRIGHT	

FACTFILE

Villa march on in their bid to retain the Coca-Cola Cup... a return to Villa Park for former defender Neil Cox... Andy Townsend captain's Villa – and scores... Bosnich sports a drastic haircut – as a bet!... Villa travel to Selhurst Park to meet Crystal Palace in the next round.

Cup hopes are raised again

The arrival of the team managed by Ron Atkinson's favourite ex-pupil, Bryan Robson, has been trumpeted as a major challenge. In the event the continuing successful defence of the Coca-Cola Cup is completed without a hitch.

Due no doubt to the build-up of home games plus, perhaps, disappointment over the club's poor home record in the League, the gate is mediocre, but the new Holte End is taking shape impressively.

Ron Atkinson has resisted the temptation to play Nii Lamptey from the start but he's there, on the bench, waiting to sprint into the action.

Once again skipper Kevin Richardson is left out, surprisingly many feel, and Andy Townsend has the captain's armband.

A 4-4-2 formation comes quickly into play with Ray Houghton and Dwight Yorke the wide men of a midfield featuring Townsend and Garry Parker and with Guy Whittingham and Dean Saunders up front.

The first half sees Villa sometimes under pressure but mostly dictating the play with neatly-controlled inter-passing football though clear chances are few by comparison with the amount of possession.

A lead is offered when Townsend feeds in a nicely-weighted ball from the right but it arrives in the path of Saunders a few inches too far back for him to connect solidly and his dragged shot swings wide of the upright. At this stage there is a slight fear that Boro might sneak a lead, chiefly because of the aggressive forward play of Hendrie who is only a fraction off target after 20 minutes.

What proves to be the decisive goal arrives in the 29th minute following a corner on the right of the Holte End. As the dead-ball kick is half-cleared Ray Houghton sends over a cross to the far post. There, Whittingham does well to win an aerial duel and knock the ball down for Townsend to fire in a volley which takes a deflection off a defender on its way in.

Villa remain in command to half-time and are close to making it two when Ugo Ehiogu dives to meet a Houghton delivery which he heads a touch off-target. Ugo is clearly anxious to make up for a clumsy-looking tackle on the talented young Irishman Alan Moore, which earned him a 25th minute booking.

The quality of Villa's passing is the feature of the second half, with 'Boro forced to chase the game though again the feeling persists that the end-product does not match the build-up.

Saunders races clear down the right, but seems to shoot hurriedly at too narrow an angle and hits the side netting, while Townsend twice slices high and wide.

Dwight Yorke has given Neil Cox a hard time down Boro's right and the ex-Villa defender is booked for an ill-tempered tackle on his former team mate.

Whittingham is then injured in a challenge by Cox who also intimidates his replacement, Lamptey, when the Ghanaian is allowed to unveil his speed and close control for the last seven minutes.

The scoreline does not in any way reflect the extent to which Villa have shown their superiority and Robson, watching from the dug-out, is left in no doubt that he is still some way behind his former boss.

**Andy Townsend –
volleyed home Villa's winner**

Saturday 29th October 1994 • Loftus Road • 3.00pm

QUEENS PARK RANGERS 2 ASTON VILLA 0

Half-time 1-0 • *Attendance* 16,073

Referee Robert HART (Darlington)

Linesmen K.J. HAWKES and P.M. ROBERTS

Blue and White Hooped Shirts, White Shorts	Goals	Green, Black and Red Striped Shirts, Black Shorts	Goals
13 Sieb DYKSTRA		13 Mark BOSNICH	
2 David BARDSLEY		2 Earl BARRETT	
3 Clive WILSON		16 Ugo EHIOGU ❏	
4 Steve YATES		5 Paul McGRATH	
6 Alan McDONALD		3 Steve STAUNTON	
8 Ian HOLLOWAY †		12 Nii LAMPTEY ❏	
14 Simon BARKER		14 Garry PARKER ❏	
25 Steve HODGE		6 Kevin RICHARDSON ❏ †	
24 Danny DICHIO	36	11 Andy TOWNSEND	
20 Kevin GALLEN ❏ ‡		18 Dwight YORKE	
11 Trevor SINCLAIR		9 Dean SAUNDERS	
Substitutes		*Substitutes*	
1 Tony ROBERTS		1 Nigel SPINK	
16 Danny MADDIX ❏ †74		19 Graham FENTON †80	
12 Gary PENRICE ‡89	90	15 Phil KING	

BEFORE		P	W	D	L	F	A	pts	AFTER		P	W	D	L	F	A	pts
16	Villa	11	2	4	5	11	16	10	17	QPR	12	2	4	6	17	22	10
20	QPR	11	1	4	6	15	22	7	18	Villa	12	2	4	6	11	18	10

FACTFILE

Twenty points dropped out of 21... Nii Lamptey's league debut... Wimbledon's Sunday win pushes Villa into the bottom four... Former Villa striker Gary Penrice scores in injury time – a minute after coming on as substitute... Dichio celebrates his QPR debut with a goal...Steve Hodge makes his QPR debut.

Alarm bells start to ring

Squeezed in between Coca-Cola Cup victory over Middlesbrough and the next European challenge, the trip to Loftus Road never looks an appetising prospect. The fact that QPR are lying third from bottom having won only one of their five home games gives rise to little comfort in the light of Villa's own recent form.

There is no disguising the reality of the situation, namely that another defeat would push the club firmly into the danger zone and set alarm bells ringing.

Ron Atkinson takes his players off to London on Friday morning for afternoon training, reversing the usual practice which is to depart after lunch.

Left behind are the injured strikers John Fashanu and Guy Whittingham and now Dalian Atkinson has joined them in the treatment department.

The out-of-favour Atkinson has a groin strain, otherwise he might well have been under consideration for a return, despite recent complaints that the manager had not given him a fair chance. This general goal-scoring crisis makes the way for Nii Lamptey to make his full league debut.

Another injury problem has appeared to complicate selection possibilities, particularly with next Tuesday's UEFA Cup visit of Trabzonspor in mind. Defender Shaun Teale now has his arm in plaster following a domestic accident with a fish tank leaving him with a badly gashed arm.

A change of direction is urgently required after the disturbing run of six Premiership games which has produced only a single point, but it is not to be. What has become regarded as a typical league performance unfolds and once more the manager is left, afterwards, to lament about destructive errors in defence and the all-too-familiar tale of chances wasted up front, rapidly becoming a cocktail of despair.

As Mike Ward described it in the Birmingham Post on the following Monday: "As ever Villa's rich tapestry of passing, movement and manufacture of chances was a delight to watch.

"But, just as typically, they displayed a cutting edge that could not have sliced through a sherry trifle. All the more galling was to see Villa ripped apart by their own defensive errors as grotesque as any to unfold before Match-of-The-Day cameras this season..."

The most significant of these blunders arrives in the 36th minute when Paul McGrath fails to clear a harmless-looking ball from Ian Holloway and as Mark Bosnich hesitates, Daniele Dichio is allowed the freedom to advance past the goalkeeper and score.

"A stupid goal," an angry Atkinson tells the media in the post-match press conference. Villa's only shot on target in the first half is a 31st minute 30-yarder by Andy Townsend which Syb Dykstra deals with confidently.

Villa make and miss opportunities to square it thoughout a second half which they dominate, but there is more trauma ahead in injury time.

Earl Barrett misses a forward pass by David Bardsley with Bosnich off his line in no-man's-land. With the goal at his mercy ex-Villa man Gary Penrice, on as sub, is able to move in unchallenged for another 'stupid goal' conceded.

"We're in deep trouble, now" Atkinson concedes.

Nii Lamptey – League debut

Tuesday 1st November 1994 • Villa Park • 8.05pm

ASTON VILLA 2 TRABZONSPOR 1

Aggregate 2-2: Trabzonspor win on away goals

Half-time 1-0 • Attendance 23,858

Referee J. H. ULINBERG

Linesmen G.J. VERWOORT and R.P. METZ

Officials from Holland

White Shirts, White Shorts with Claret Trim	Goals	Claret and Light Blue Striped Shirts,Claret Shorts	Goals
1 Nigel SPINK		1 Victor GRICHKO	
2 Earl BARRETT		2 HAMDI Aslan	
3 Steve STAUNTON		3 OGÜN Termizkanoglu ■	
4 Ugo EHIOGU	90	4 KEMAL Serdar	
5 Paul McGRATH		5 TOLUNAY Kafkas	
6 Kevin RICHARDSON †		6 ABDULLAH Ercan	
7 Ray HOUGHTON		7 CENGIZ Atilla ❏	
8 Andy TOWNSEND		8 ONAL Karaman	
9 Dean SAUNDERS		9 SONER Boz	
10 Dalian ATKINSON	77	10 HAMI Mandirali	
11 Phil KING		11 ORHAN Kaynak	90

Substitutes		*Substitutes*
gk Michael OAKES		gk NIHAT Tümkaya
12 Garry PARKER †70		13 OSMAN Özköylü
14 Graham FENTON		14 ENDER Tras
15 David FARRELL		15 MEHMET Yener
16 Chris BODEN		16 KATCHARAVA Kakhaber

FACTFILE

Dalian Atkinson makes his 100th appearance in a Villa shirt...and has a seemingly good goal ruled out for offside... then scores... late, late drama with two goals in last minute... same old story for Villa.

The goal that put Villa out of the UEFA Cup.

A freak result – says stunned Ron

Time to forget, for a short time, the worries of a lowly league position and to concentrate on earning the boost of a further European adventure.

Just as in the previous round against Inter Milan the task is a formidable one in terms of needing 1-0 for extra time and penalties or a two goal margin to go straight through.

The dilemma of needing at least one goal while not conceding that precious away goal leave nerve ends exposed and creates a Villa Park atmosphere of hypnotic intensity.

How will Ron Atkinson's men set about it, with a patient attitude of safety first or an attempt to overrun the opposition from the start?

From the very first whistle the second approach is more the case as Villa use their superior pace, power and physical presence in an attempt to dominate.

Along with this, however, there is the occasional hint of living dangerously and the end-product is another edge-of-the-seat occasion as a thouand Turks in a 24,000 crowd help to whip up an electric atmosphere.

There is an early hint that Villa's increasing unease in front of goal is to undermine their attacking efforts yet again when Andy Townsend, clear through in the 10th minute, fails to connect with a wonderful scoring opportunity.

Incidents then pile up in bewildering fashion and Villa almost concede an own goal from a deflection before Nigel Spink conjures three superb stops, two of them in an acrobatic double-save.

By now Villa's first stroke of sheer bad luck has seen the Dutch referee inexplicably decline

a clear penalty when Andy Townsend is barged down from behind by Cenzig. It's not going to be Villa's night. You can feel it in your bones.

An inflammatory incident or two flares up with some reckless Turkish challenges and a spot of play-acting and as Villa continue to press goalkeeper Victor dives to keep out a Saunders free kick.

When half-time arrives at 0-0 the feeling persists that Villa have failed to capitalise on chances created from their greater share of the forward play.

Misfortunes quickly take a hand again early in the second half when Steve Staunton's free kick takes a deflection to rebound off the bar and Paul McGrath wildly blazes the ball over the top.

After an hour a bizarre scoring chance arrives as the Turkish 'keeper handles a back pass. Villa have a free kick near the six-yards line but Staunton is unable to blast his shot past a line of defenders shoulder-to-shoulder on the goalline.

Ugo Ehiogu misses with a header from eight yards as Garry Parker replaces Kevin Richardson and Saunders, with only the goalkeeper to beat, shoots straight at him.

Villa are to pay dearly for such misses although they take the lead at last after 77 minutes when defender Ogun concedes a penalty and he is sent off for deliberately handling Dalian Atkinson's drive.

Staunton's penalty is charged out, Ehiogu's return shot is scrambled away, possibly after it has crossed the line but then Atkinson smashes the aggregate equaliser.

No penalty shoot-out this time but more unforgettable drama. Right on 90 minutes a Turkish break sees Orhan drive into the net when surrounded by Villa defenders.

With seconds left Villa now need two more and get just one when Ehiogu storms upfield to earn a frustrating 2-1 scoreline which takes the Turks into the next round.

Sunday 6th November 1994 • Villa Park • 4.00pm

ASTON VILLA 1   MANCHESTER UNITED 2

Half-time 1-0 • *Attendance* 32,136

Referee Philip DON (Hanworth Park)

Linesmen K.J. Hawkes and P.M. ROBERTS

Claret Shirts with Blue Stripes, White Shorts		Goals	Black Shirts, Black Shorts		Goals
1	Nigel SPINK		13	Gary WALSH	
2	Earl BARRETT		16	Roy KEANE	
16	Ugo EHIOGU		4	Steve BRUCE ❑	
5	Paul McGRATH ❑		6	Gary PALLISTER	
15	Phil KING		3	Denis IRWIN	
7	Ray HOUGHTON ‡		14	Andrei KANCHELSKIS	51
6	Kevin RICHARDSON		19	Nicky BUTT †	
11	Andy TOWNSEND		8	Paul INCE	44
3	Steve STAUNTON †		11	Ryan GIGGS	
9	Dean SAUNDERS		7	Eric CANTONA	
10	Dalian ATKINSON	29	24	Paul SCHOLES ‡	
	Substitutes			*Substitutes*	
13	Mark BOSNICH		25	Kevin PILKINGTON	
18	Dwight YORKE †58		9	Brian McCLAIR †6	
14	Garry PARKER ‡79		31	Keith GILLESPIE ‡78 ❑	

BEFORE		P	W	D	L	F	A	pts	AFTER		P	W	D	L	F	A	pts
6	Man Utd	12	8	1	3	21	19	25	3	Man Utd	13	9	1	3	23	10	28
19	Villa	12	2	4	6	11	18	10	19	Villa	13	2	4	7	12	20	10

FACTFILE

Earl Barrett's 300th start in league football... Dean Saunders' 400th... Nigel Spink keeps his place in goal... Dalian Atkinson's first Premiership goal of the season... Villa denied late penalty appeal... Performance and goal attempts not reflected in result... just one point from 24 keeps Villa in the relegation zone.

United corner all the lucky breaks

In his pre-match briefing Ron Atkinson reminds everyone that, while admittedly going out of European competition in mid-week, the game against Trabzonspor was actually won.

United, in contrast, were heavily defeated by Barcelona in Spain, watched by the Villa manager who was in the Nou Camp stadium as a TV analyst.

Taking a positive line Atkinson sticks to last Tuesday night's line-up which, he points out, has played together only twice, against Inter Milan and the Turks and had won both times.

This confines the slightly unfortunate Dwight Yorke to the subs bench along with Garry Parker and Mark Bosnich as a 32,000 crowd flocks to Villa Park for what is always a plum fixture.

The fact that it is live on Sky has no adverse affect on attendance with all seats sold well in advance of the day which, for November, is surprisingly sunny and mild.

Although Atkinson has wisely attempted to play down the team's goalscoring problems, while giving his support solidly to his quality squad of players there can be no doubt that tensions are creeping in.

This is demonstrated in the very opening minute when Steve Staunton, put in possession by a Gary Walsh mistake, blazes his scoring attempt wide of an open goal.

A feeling of 'here-we-go-again' is inevitable among supporters but, to their credit, the players do not allow themselves to be affected and conjure a 29th minute lead.

Atkinson is facing away from the United goal when fed by Kevin Richardson some 25 yards out but he turns to fire in an impulse drive which cannons of Steve Bruce's boot, lifts over Walsh and finds the net.

If there was a modicum of good fortune about that goal then not only was it well over-due but it was the last Villa were going to get with an hour's play still remaining.

United are lacking their usual passion and creating very little danger until they equalise a minute before half-time. Ugo Ehiogu had firmly headed a defensive clearance well away from the goal but Paul Ince, 25 yards out, chests the ball down and blasts it past Nigel Spink who is temporarily unsighted.

The Villa 'keeper is again blocked out in the 51st minute when Denis Irwin's centre from the left finds Andrei Kanchelskis whose disguised shot passes through Phil King's legs into the net.

Frustratingly for Villa, whose methodical approach play dominates the flow of the game virtually throughout, this was only United's third shot at goal and, it is to prove, their last.

Villa are left to continue sweet-passing their way forward, mounting pressure on the United goal and failing to capitalise on it, despite a spirited half-hour from substitute Yorke. Villa force corner after corner and see Walsh make half-a-dozen good saves but fail to acquire that desperately needed equaliser.

Nothing more is going to go their way as illustrated by Bruce's late challenge on Paul McGrath which ought to have been a penalty but which the World Cup referee surprisingly declines.

Ron Atkinson doesn't mince his words afterwards. "One point from three is a worry. One from eight is a disaster," he said. "I suppose soon they will call for changes in personnel, be it me or the players."

**Earl Barrett –
300th League game**

Wednesday 9th November 1994 • Selhurst Park • 7.45pm

WIMBLEDON 4 ASTON VILLA 3

Half-time 1-2 • *Attendance* 6,221

Referee David ELLERAY (Middlesex)

Linesmen S. BENNETT and P. VOSPER

Dark Blue Shirts with Yellow Trim, Dark Blue Shorts		Goals	Claret Shirts with Blue Stripes, White Shorts		Goals
1	Hans SEGERS		13	Mark BOSNICH ❑	
2	Warren BARTON	pen 8	2	Earl BARRETT	
15	Alan REEVES		16	Ugo EHIOGU ❑	
28	Andy THORN ❑		5	Paul McGRATH	
12	Gary ELKINS		15	Phil KING ❑	
18	Steve TALBOYS		7	Ray HOUGHTON †	
4	Vinnie JONES	83	14	Garry PARKER	19
35	Oyvind LEONHARDSEN	90	11	Andy TOWNSEND ■	
26	Neal ARDLEY	65	18	Dwight YORKE	
9	Efan EKOKU		9	Dean SAUNDERS ‡	38, 50
7	Andy CLARKE		10	Dalian ATKINSON	
	Substitutes			*Substitutes*	
23	Neil SULLIVAN		1	Nigel SPINK	
6	Scott FITZGERALD		6	Kevin RICHARDSON †ht	
25	Mick HARFORD ❑		19	Graham FENTON ‡80	

BEFORE		P	W	D	L	F	A	pts	AFTER		P	W	D	L	F	A	pts
18	Wimbledon	13	3	3	7	20	21	12	16	Wimbledon	14	4	3	7	24	24	15
19	Villa	13	2	4	7	12	20	10	19	Villa	14	2	4	8	15	24	10

Villa surrender 3-1 lead to stay entrenched in the relegation zone... Norwegian signing, Oyvind Leonhardsen, scores winner on his Wimbledon debut... Bosnich and Yorke return to the side... Unfortunate dismissal for Andy Townsend for foul on Ardley... Deano back on the goal trail – his first double of the season...

Defeat ends Ron's reign

Away games with Wimbledon are always a potential banana skin but, for Ron Atkinson, this trip to Selhurst Park is to prove more like a cresta run down which he is to slide unchecked.

The final 26 minutes of a remarkable game in which Villa slump from 3-1 in the lead to a 4-3 defeat stretch the depressing Premiership run to 26 points lost out of 27.

This is to prove the end for chairman Doug Ellis and his board as events slide inexorably towards Big Ron's sensational dismissal.

Yet, such are the vagaries of football that, well into the second half, it had seemed that the corner had been turned as Villa, at 3-1 up, were heading for a victory at last.

Changes have been made from the team which lost at home to Manchester United on Sunday with Dwight Yorke re-instated along with Mark Bosnich and Graham Fenton.

There is an early feeling of 'not again!' when the Dons are awarded an 8th minute penalty against Ugo Ehiogu for what looks a perfectly-timed tackle on Efan Ekoku in front of goal.

This enables Warren Barton to drive home what seems an unjustified penalty but, to the team's credit, they simply get their heads down and fight back to retrieve the situation.

Villa's football is, once again, of the highest order and by the 18th minute it has produced an equaliser. An Andy Townsend pass finds the ever-probing Dwight Yorke whose delivery is tapped in by Garry Parker.

Hans Segers, in the Wimbledon goal, is under increasing pressure with Dalian Atkinson among the

Villa men threatening to force a lead.

After 36 minutes the tide deservedly turns Villa's way as the industrious Parker sees a shot palmed down by Segers right into the path of Dean Saunders who gratefully ends his barren spell.

Going in at 2-1 up there would have been a mood of optimism in the Villa camp except for an incident five minutes before half-time when Townsend is sent off for a tackle on Neil Ardley which looked no more than a yellow card offence.

Refereee David Elleray is not the most popular guy in the claret-and-blue half of the ground but, to be fair, he has simply interpreted this season's new code as he saw it when the tackle went in.

The stunned ten resume the second half with their mood of defiance heightened and in three minutes seemingly push the scoreline out of the Dons' reach when Saunders makes it 3-1 with his second of the night.

This one is the opposite type of goal to Villa's usual intricate-passing style as Bosnich's long clearance is flicked on by Atkinson for Deano to crack Wimbledon's off-side tactic.

That, effectively, is to prove the end of Ron Atkinson's three-and-a-half-year reign as the rot sets in with disaster after disaster.

Ardley heads in Elkins's cross (64), Vinny Jones' 81st minute long shot takes a deflection off Paul McGrath's boot and two minutes from time the game is lost.

On his debut, Wimbledon's Norwegian signing Oyvind Leonhardsen thumps a loose ball into the net when unmarked a few yards out and Villa's world comes crashing down in the most morale-crushing defeat of many.

**Garry Parker –
scored Villa's first goal**

Saturday 19th November 1994 • White Hart Lane • 3.00pm

TOTTENHAM HOTSPUR 3 ASTON VILLA 4

Half-time 1-3 • *Attendance* 26,899

Referee Paul DURKIN (DORSET)

Linesmen W.J. NORBURY and M. STOBBART

Whie Shirts, Navy Blue Shorts	Goals	Claret Shirts with Blue Stripes, White Shorts	Goals
13 Ian WALKER		13 Mark BOSNICH	
22 David KERSLAKE †		2 Earl BARRETT	
5 Colin CALDERWOOD		16 Ugo EHIOGU	
6 Gary MABBUTT		5 Paul McGRATH	
23 Sol CAMPBELL		15 Phil KING	
9 Darren ANDERTON		7 Ray HOUGHTON	
4 Gica POPESCU ❑		14 Garry PARKER	
15 David HOWELLS		6 Kevin RICHARDSON	
20 Darren CASKEY ‡		19 Graham FENTON ❑	21, 27
18 Jürgen KLINSMANN❑ pen 53,71		9 Dean SAUNDERS	90
10 Teddy SHERINGHAM	40	10 Dalian ATKINSON †	8
Substitutes		*Substitutes*	
30 Chris DAY		1 Nigel SPINK	
14 Stuart NETHERCOTT †ht		12 Nii LAMPTEY †53 ❑	
7 Nick BARMBY ‡46		24 Chris BODEN	

BEFORE		P	W	D	L	F	A	pts	AFTER		P	W	D	L	F	A	pts
13	Tottenham	13	5	2	6	21	26	17	15	Tottenham	14	5	2	7	24	30	17
19	Villa		14	2	4	8	15	24	10	19	Villa		15	3	4	8	19	27	13

> **FACTFILE**
>
> *First game since Ron Atkinson's dismissal... Andy Townsend has started a six-match suspension... Nine-match sequence without a win ends... Graham Fenton's first goals of the season... Jim Barron takes charge of the team in the absence of a manager... Nii Lamptey comes off the subs bench for a rare Premiership outing.*

Caretaker Jim stakes a claim

Time, for one day at least, for the guessing game to pause and the action to re-start as managerless Villa take on Spurs who are under Gerry Francis's leadership for the first time.

All week the pundits have played the Manager Game with Ron Atkinson's former post still open, Francis moving from Loftus Road to White Hart Lane and Ray Wilkins returning to Queen's Park Rangers.

No-one knows yet who will permanently replace Atkinson though the Leicester City former Villa trio of Brian Little, Allan Evans and John Gregory are the favourite forecast.

All this has put a heavy burden on the backroom staff at the Bodymoor Heath training ground where the former No. 2 Jim Barron and coach Dave Sexton are temporarily in charge while wondering if they will soon be out of work.

Steve Staunton has returned injured from the Irish Republic's mid-week European Championship qualifier with Northern Ireland and the subsequent re-shuffle sees Graham Fenton restored to an important midfield role.

The inevitable air of expectancy humming around the ground is quickly justified as a Dalian Atkinson header in the 8th minute sets alight a spectacular seven-goal thriller.

By mid-way through the half Fenton has signed in with two superb goals for a 3-0 Villa lead (21 mins, 27 mins).

The young Geordie shows the power and pace which marked his Wembley show last March as he moves into

the Spurs area and places his shot past Mike Walker. Then, with adrenalin still flowing, he closes in on the Spurs goal to find the same corner of the net with another fine finish.

Now the action is moving into classic dimensions as Spurs set about proving to their new boss that they are made of sterner stuff.

The defensive wobbles which had undermined Ron Atkinson's rule are manifest once more as Teddy Sheringham (40) and Jürgen Klinsmann (53 penalty and 71) stun the travelling Villa hordes with a 3-3 scoreline.

Briefly another 'Wimbledon' looks on the cards with a two-goal lead lost, but well into injury-time Dean Saunders adds a stunning finale to a superb game of football.

Garry Parker, whose passing and prompting have been exceptional, takes a pass from Phil King mid-way out on the left-hand touchline. He controls the ball deftly and weights a dream of a pass into forward space for Deano to chase.

The Welshmen defies Gary Mabbutt's attempts to intervene and lashes his decisive strike past the Spurs 'keeper to unleash a torrent of relief and joy in the claret-and-blue ranks.

At last that elusive silver lining said to embellish every cloud has revealed itself. For the moment Villa can ignore the fact that nine goals have been conceded in the last three Premiership games and that the overall defensive record away from home is the worst in the Premiership.

It will be the next manager's task to dwell on those statistics.

Graham Fenton – two goals in six minutes

Sunday 27th November 1994 • Villa Park • 4.00pm

ASTON VILLA 1 SHEFFIELD WEDNESDAY 1

Half-time 1-0 • *Attendance* 25,082

Referee Graham POLL (Tilehurst)
Linesmen D.C. MADGWICK and D.M. HORLICK

Claret Shirts with Blue Stripes, White Shorts		Goals	Blue and White Striped Shirts, Blue Shorts		Goals
13	Mark BOSNICH		1	Kevin PRESSMAN	
2	Earl BARRETT		2	Peter ATHERTON	57
16	Ugo EHIOGU		12	Andy PEARCE	
5	Paul McGRATH		17	Des WALKER	
15	Phil KING		3	Ian NOLAN	
7	Ray HOUGHTON		5	Dan PETRESCU ❑	
14	Garry PARKER		16	Graham HYDE ❑	
6	Kevin RICHARDSON		11	John SHERIDAN	
19	Graham FENTON		15	Andy SINTON	
9	Dean SAUNDERS		14	Chris BART-WILLIAMS	
10	Dalian ATKINSON †	20	20	Gordon WATSON †	
	Substitutes			*Substitutes*	
1	Nigel SPINK		23	Lance KEY	
22	Guy WHITTINGHAM †80		4	Ian TAYLOR †82	
24	Chris BODEN		7	Adem PORIC	

BEFORE		P	W	D	L	F	A	pts	AFTER		P	W	D	L	F	A	pts
16	Wednesday	15	4	5	6	16	22	17	16	Wednesday	16	4	6	6	17	23	18
20	Villa	15	3	4	8	19	27	13	20	Villa	16	3	5	8	20	28	14

FACTFILE

Brian Little's first game as Villa manager... Fifth home game in succession without a win... Only seven points gained in eight home games... Dalian scores against his old club... Wednesday's Ian Taylor samples the Villa Park atmosphere as a substitute – later to join Villa in a swap deal for Guy Whittingham...

Little learns a lot on Day One

New manager, same old story as Brian Little signs in, live-on-Sky, amid a clicking of press cameras and thrusting microphones.

Seventeen days of behind-the-scenes activity to replace Ron Atkinson were completed on Friday evening with Little and coach John Gregory's appearance at a Villa Park press conference.

But the controversial story of the managerial change-over has not yet fully run its course. A Sunday newspaper has revealed that Leicester City attempted to obtain a High Court injunction on Friday to prevent Little moving to Villa Park.

Although refused they are still pursuing their case as Little sends out a team unchanged from the one, selected by Jim Barron, which won at White Hart Lane eight days earlier.

Barron has now left, along with Dave Sexton, but the imperturbable Little looks untroubled by the disruption, waving in a relaxed manner as he is cheered to his touchline seat preceded by a phalanx of photographers.

Villa set the new era rolling with a surge of adrenalin-fuelled action, anxious to impress upon their new boss that they're not lacking in appetite for work.

"Players always seem to raise themselves when a new manager arrives," said Wednesday boss Trevor Francis prophetically before the kick-off.

His team are quickly under pressure and in the 16th minute Villa go ahead as Garry Parker's corner creates havoc in the visiting penalty area. Dean Saunders' header is touched away by the diving Kevin Pressman and the ball lands beautifully for Dalian Atkinson to tuck it neatly away.

On the half-hour Villa are agonisingly close to a 2-0 lead when Graham Fenton swivels stylishly to connect with a volley which looks a goal all the way until Pressman reaches the ball with a daring dive to touch it against the post and to safety as it rebounds against his flying body.

This it transpires, is to be Villa's last chance of pushing the scoreline beyond Wednesday's reach as all that early promise oozes away.

Early in the second half Dan Petrescu misses maddeningly for Wednesday as the wide-open target looms briefly and by now there is the ominous feeling that an equaliser is on its way.

Sure enough, aided by indisciplined defending, Peter Atherton is allowed to strike an awesome 57th minute equaliser from 30 yards.

Kevin Richardson gives a careless back-pass to Mark Bosnich whose badly struck clearance goes weakly to the unmarked ex-Coventry City player.

"I'm sure he didn't hear me but I shouted 'hit it' the moment the ball reached him,' said Francis. Twenty years ago, in the days when he was the rival star to Brian Little in Villa-Blues derbies, he would have been proud of that shot himself.

From that moment on Villa's crisis of confidence at Villa Park is on show once again as, result-wise, they go into terminal decline.

Guy Whittingham replaces Atkinson with no apparent effect and a Ugo Ehiogu error goes unpunished when Chris Bart-Williams declines a gift of a chance.

"Nine marks out of ten in the first half," says Little. "Five or six in the second. I'll do what I have to do to improve things."

New boss Brian Little

Wednesday 30th November 1994 • Selhurst Park • 7.45pm

CRYSTAL PALACE 4 ASTON VILLA 1

Half-time 0-1 • *Attendance* 12,653

Referee Gary WILLARD (Worthing)

Linesmen A.J. WEBB and D. DOWNS

Red Shirts with Blue Stripes, Red Shorts	Goals	Green, Black and Red Striped Shirts, Black Shorts	Goals
1 Nigel MARTYN		13 Mark BOSNICH	
2 John HUMPHREY		2 Earl BARRETT	
14 Richard SHAW		16 Ugo EHIOGU ■	
6 Chris COLEMAN		5 Paul McGRATH	
3 Dean GORDON		15 Phil KING	
11 John SALAKO		18 Dwight YORKE	
23 Ricky NEWMAN		7 Ray HOUGHTON	
4 Gareth SOUTHGATE	58, 76	14 Garry PARKER	
15 Bobby BOWRY		21 Dave FARRELL ‡	
9 Chris ARMSTRONG	48, 88	9 Dean SAUNDERS	
18 Andy PREECE		10 Dalian ATKINSON †	32
Substitutes		*Substitutes*	
13 Rhys WILMOT		1 Nigel SPINK	
16 Darren PITCHER		19 Graham FENTON †37	
24 George NDAH		22 Guy WHITTINGHAM ‡70	

Ehiogu – sent off

Villa's reign as Coca-Cola Cup holders ends with heaviest defeat since April loss against Southampton... give up four second-half goals... 12 in past four outings... First ever sending-off for Ehiogu... Farrell makes only second senior appearance of the season... Atkinson's early goal his fifth in six consecutive games... substituted five minutes later with pulled hamstring... Palace await the outcome of the match between Manchester City and Newcastle United for their next-round opponents...

High Court win but Cup KO

Brian Little finds himself, in bizarre fashion, awaiting two important results during one of the most remarkable days of his life.

Due to a delay in the proceding High Court case yesterday, Leicester's City's appeal for an injunction to prevent their ex-manager working for Villa has been put back a day.

This leaves him, along with the team in a London hotel, waiting for news from the court as to whether he will be legally allowed to take charge at Selhurst Park. Mercifully the Leicester case is thrown out and it's all systems go for Little to get on with the job of attempting to guide Villa into calmer waters.

As the night progresses, however, the news deteriorates almost by the minute from an encouraging start.

Winger Dave Farrell has been introduced as a means of attempting to inject some of the wing pace Little has constantly outlined as one of the team's weaknesses.

The new manager saw the Coca-Cola Cup won at Wembley last March and is deeply aware of how much its defence means to supporters, especially those who have travelled to South London.

But, just as in the 4-3 defeat by Wimbledon at the same ground three weeks earlier, their world is turned upside down with a player sent off and the lead surrendered.

Ugo Ehiogu is the red card victim this time as, in the 26th minute, a poor clearance by Mark Bosnich puts Chris Armstrong dangerously in possession and Ehiogu's challenge from behind is adjudged a 'professional' foul.

Despite this, and waves of Palace attacks, Villa recover bravely and a neat and tidy 32nd minute passing move ends with Dwight Yorke feeding Dalian Atkinson for a right-footed blast

past Nigel Martyn. But, the chapter of disasters begins within minutes as Atkinson pulls up with a hamstring strain and is replaced by Fenton. Villa's lead survives until the break but then the roof falls in.

A couple of minutes after half time Phil King floors Armstrong who then turns John Salako's free kick past Bosnich who ends up with a nightmare of a match.

Just inside the hour Gareth Southgate shoots past Bosnich from less than ten yards when Armstrong feeds the ball in from the left. Then the out-of-touch Australian punches weakly at Salako's 76th minute corner, knocking the ball straight to Southgate for number three.

Still the traumatic turn of events is not over as, a couple of minutes from time, the ever-troublesome Armstrong, beats both Paul McGrath and Dwight Yorke to fire the fourth and final Palace goal.

Villa, having won the trophy in such professional fashion, have now surrendered it with a shambles of a display bordering on farce.

"It was one of those occasions when almost everything went wrong," confessed Little at the end of his day of such mixed emotions. "We lost our skipper (Kevin Richardson) with a back spasm on the way down, then had a defender sent off and lost our goalscorer through injury."

If there was any consolation after a dismal second half it was that the priority of avoiding relegation could now continue, at least until the FA Cup, without distractions.

Dalian Atkinson – gave Villa an early lead but left the game injured just five minutes later.

Saturday 3rd December 1994 • Filbert Street • 3.00pm

LEICESTER CITY 1   ASTON VILLA 1

Half-time 1-0 • *Attendance* 20,896

Referee Martin BODENHAM (East Looe)

Linesmen A.N. BUTLER and B. LOWE

Blue Shirts, Blue Shorts	Goals	Claret Shirts with Blue Stripes, White Shorts	Goals
33 Kevin POOLE		1 Nigel SPINK	
8 Mark BLAKE ❑		2 Earl BARRETT	
19 Colin HILL		16 Ugo EHIOGU ❑	
14 Nicky MOHAN		4 Shaun TEALE	
3 Mike WHITLOW		20 Bryan SMALL	
16 Franz CARR		7 Ray HOUGHTON	
17 Steve THOMPSON		19 Graham FENTON ‡	
10 Mark DRAPER ❑		14 Garry PARKER	
11 Ian ORMONDROYD †		15 Phil KING †	
20 David OLDFIELD		9 Dean SAUNDERS	
26 Phil GEE ‡	5	22 Guy WHITTINGHAM	61
Substitutes		*Substitutes*	
1 Gavin WARD		13 Mark BOSNICH	
7 Julian JOACHIM †67		24 Chris BODEN †83	
9 Iwan ROBERTS ‡79		5 Paul McGRATH ‡89	

BEFORE	P	W	D	L	F	A	pts	AFTER	P	W	D	L	F	A	pts
19 Villa	16	3	5	8	20	28	14	19 Villa	17	3	6	8	21	29	15
21 Leicester	16	3	3	10	17	29	12	21 Leicester	17	3	4	10	18	30	13

FACTFILE

Shaun Teale back after 10-game absence to replace Paul McGrath – on subs bench for first time in six-season Villa career... Premiership debut for Chris Boden, as substitute... Bryan Small makes first Villa appearance of the season... Gary Parker's 300th league appearance...

Little has the last laugh

Fate can be the cruellest conspirator of all as Brian Little will testify, with feeling, after returning to Filbert Street as Villa's manager 12 days after resigning from Leicester City.

Despite winning his High Court battle with his former chairman, Martin George, to avoid being prevented from continuing as Aston Villa manager, the controversy goes raging on.

A letter of resignation written by Little to Leicester City has been published in that morning's press, a seemingly mischievous stroke of timing, and his former supporters give him a hostile 'reception'.

To make it even more uncomfortable for him the match, played out in a highly-charged atmosphere, is less than five minutes old when Villa are a goal down in a few moments of disastrous defending.

Little had dropped Paul McGrath and Mark Bosnich, both for the first time when fit and available. Nigel Spink is back in goal with Shaun Teale at the heart of the defence alongside Ugo Ehiogu for the first time since he badly gashed his arm in a domestic accident with a fish tank.

Before the revamped defence can settle Leicester, fuelled by an extra dose of adrenalin, surge forward as Colin Hill hits a speculative ball from defence.

Spink chases off his line and into the no-man's-land beyond the penalty area and Phil Gee has merely to lob it over the keeper's head to send the home fans into their first celebration since the managerial controversy arose.

More of this and Villa would be returning home in deep depression with their relegation situation and their morale in severe decline.

But, to their credit and Little's relief, they settled down quickly to dictate the shape of the game with Garry Parker and Graham Fenton determined in midfield and Parker's passing a particular feature.

Just before half-time Parker exchanges passes with Bryan Small to fire in a cross-shot from the left-hand side of the penalty area which Kevin Poole does well to block.

By early in the second half Villa are totally in command and more than deserving of the equaliser which comes their way in the 62nd minute.

With the home defence consistently under the cosh Fenton crosses from the left and Guy Whittingham times his leap and header to perfection in placing the ball between Poole and his left-hand post.

After this there is the fleeting chance of Villa giving their manager the perfect answer to all the abuse he has suffered in terms of a possible winning goal but Parker is marginally off-target.

In the event, and at the end of an occasion which few could actually have enjoyed, the most 'diplomatic' result is posted.

"I felt we came back extremely well from our poor start," says Little, looking distinctly shell-shocked by the day's events.

"I felt that we were the better side and had a far more compact look about the way we played.

"Otherwise it's not often I wish away a day of my life but I shall be glad to go to bed tonight and go to sleep."

Shaun Teale – back in the side after missing 10 games

Saturday 10th December 1994 • Villa Park • 3.00pm

ASTON VILLA 0 EVERTON 0

Half-time 0-0 • Attendance 29,678

Referee Roger GIFFORD (Llanbradach)

Linesmen A.J. HILL and P.A. ROBERTS

Claret Shirts with Blue Stripes, White Shorts		Goals	White Shirts, Black Shorts		Goals
1	Nigel SPINK		13	Jason KEARTON ❏	
2	Earl BARRETT		2	Matthew JACKSON	
16	Ugo EHIOGU		5	Dave WATSON	
4	Shaun TEALE		26	David UNSWORTH	
20	Bryan SMALL		16	David BURROWS	
7	Ray HOUGHTON		17	Anders LIMPAR	
14	Garry PARKER		18	Joe PARKINSON	
6	Kevin RICHARDSON ❏		14	John EBBRELL	
15	Phil KING †		3	Andy HINCHCLIFFE	
19	Graham FENTON		9	Duncan FERGUSON	
22	Guy WHITTINGHAM		15	Paul RIDEOUT	
	Substitutes			*Substitutes*	
13	Mark BOSNICH		33	James SPEARE	
12	Nii LAMPTEY †59		19	Stuart BARLOW	
5	Paul McGRATH		8	Graham STUART	

BEFORE		P	W	D	L	F	A	pts	AFTER		P	W	D	L	F	A	pts
18	Everton	17	4	5	8	15	24	17	18	Everton	18	4	6	8	15	24	18
20	Villa	17	3	6	8	21	29	15	20	Villa	18	3	7	8	21	29	16

FACTFILE

Dean Saunders and Everton's Neville Southall on international duty with Wales... Villa's third consecutive Premiership draw under new manager Brian Little and best unbeaten league spell (4) since start of season (5)... Villa's first clean sheet in Premiership for almost three months... Guy Whittingham's last game for Villa.

A clean sheet, but no punch

With the traumatic events of his brief return to Filbert Street now behind him, Brian Little can concentrate on attempting to improve the worrying league position.

Since his arrival there has been non-stop media speculation about the likelihood of his moving on several of the over-thirties, but he insists he has no particular plans in this regard.

Paul McGrath's name has been widely mentioned as a likely departee though Little has assured the Irish centre back that he has no such immediate intentions.

For Little's second home game he continues to have selection problems with Dean Saunders on obligatory Welsh duty and Dwight Yorke and John Fashanu both injured.

Kevin Richardson returns to midfield after injury allowing Graham Fenton to move forward in Saunders' place.

Everton, revitalised under the recent arrival as manager of Joe Royle to replace Mike Walker, present a formidable challenge.

The Goodison Park side has won its previous three games while Little is looking for his first victory in four Cup and League attempts.

Anyone forecasting that it would be a tight, uncompromising affair with little adventurous football is proved to be spot-on as both sides are more concerned about avoiding defeat than going for glory.

Nigel Spink, forgiven for his rash few moments at Leicester last week, looks a shade shaky early on but recovers impressively to form a solid barrier with Shaun Teale and Ugo Ehiogu who are impenetrable in the heart of the defence.

Ehiogu deals superbly with the tall and dangerous Duncan Ferguson but there is less to applaud going forward. Villa create little of a tangible nature on the offensive and Everton's young central defender David Unsworth is allowed to be as impressive as Ehiogu.

The final whistle arrives as something of a relief. Since Villa have never looked likely to lock up all three points the sparse consolation is that the horror run of only one point from 27 is at last behind them.

In the absence of Andy Townsend (suspended), Steve Staunton and John Fashanu (injured) and Saunders on international duty there are no real complaints about the unbeaten league run of six points out of 12 since Ron Atkinson's departure.

Although left still third from bottom Villa remain in touch with those immediately above them and Little has time to regenerate the squad and get things moving.

The Holte End stand is now in an advanced stage of construction with every indication that the upper tier will be opening on schedule by the end of the month.

There is room for long-term optimism throughout the club but the short-term situation remains tense as Little surveys the transfer scene and gives hints that signings could be on the way.

Ugo keeps watch on Paul Rideout

Monday 19th December 1994 • The Dell • 8.00pm

SOUTHAMPTON 2 ASTON VILLA 1

Half-time 1-0 • *Attendance* 13,874

Referee Stephen LODGE (Barnsley)

Linesmen L.E. CABLE and D.C. MADGWICK

Red and White Striped Shirts, Black Shorts	Goals	Claret Shirts with Blue Stripes, White Shorts	Goals
1 Bruce GROBBELAAR		1 Nigel SPINK	
2 Jeff KENNA		2 Earl BARRETT ❏	
5 Richard HALL	9	5 Paul McGRATH	
6 Ken MONKOU		4 Shaun TEALE	
3 Francis BENALI ❏		20 Bryan SMALL	
21 Tommy WIDDRINGTON		7 Ray HOUGHTON	80
4 Jim MAGILTON		14 Garry PARKER ❏	
12 Neil HEANEY ❏		6 Kevin RICHARDSON ❏	
7 Matthew LE TISSIER	90	15 Phil KING †	
8 Craig MASKELL		8 John FASHANU	
24 Ronnie EKELUND †		9 Dean SAUNDERS ❏	
Substitutes		*Substitutes*	
13 Dave BEASANT		13 Mark BOSNICH	
18 David HUGHES †57 ❏		18 Dwight YORKE †77	
28 Paul TISDALE		19 Graham FENTON	

BEFORE	P	W	D	L	F	A	pts	AFTER	P	W	D	L	F	A	pts
15 Saints	18	5	6	7	25	30	21	12 Saints	19	6	6	7	27	31	24
20 Villa	18	3	7	8	21	29	16	20 Villa	19	3	7	9	22	31	16

FACTFILE

Fashanu returns after 19 game absence with Achilles injury... McGrath back to replace the suspended Ehiogu... and makes his 200th league appearance for Villa... Le Tissier's injury-time winner is his 6th goal against Villa in last four meetings... Garry Parker's final Villa game.

Southampton twist the knife

Given at extra 48 hours to prepare due to the fixture at The Dell being switched to Monday for live screening on Sky, Brian Little decides to recall John Fashanu for his first look at him in serious action.

The ex-Wimbledon striker has been out for three months having undergone Achilles tendon surgery and, due to the postponement of a mid-week Reserve game, has not had the match practice he would have liked.

Ideally Fashanu's come-back would have been delayed to give him a couple of lesser games but the situation is such that the new manager feels he has no choice.

Paul McGrath is also recalled to the centre of the defence to cover for Ugo Ehiogu who has a one-match suspension, while Dean Saunders is back from international duty with Wales.

At a venue where Villa traditionally struggle they start encouragingly enough with several corners enabling Fash to make his physical presence felt.

But this promise survives for a mere nine minutes when defender Richard Hall moves in to back up his forwards for a series of Saints corners.

From the third of these Matthew Le Tissier flights a superb cross which beats the assembled defenders to find Hall's head at the far post.

This is just the setback that Villa, already striving hard to re-build shattered confidence, didn't need. And it becomes, like in the previous away game at Leicester, yet another damage limitation exercise.

Gradually Villa do slowly begin to get some forward flow re-established and some promising moments materialise with Fashanu continuing to provide new options in attack.

Bruce Grobbelaar is called upon to make a save or two, notably two from Fash, a long-range blast followed by one from closer in which the Saints 'keeper touches over the top.

Le Tissier, who scored twice against Blackburn the previous weekend, parades his skills spasmodically and ominously but Villa's defence remains steadfastly defiant whenever Southampton press forward.

As Villa seek out that coveted equaliser Southampton defenders are upset by Fashanu's robust surges and in a series of minor upsets seven names go into the book.

After 80 minutes however, Villa's persistence pays off with Ray Houghton, appropriately, the scorer. The Irish Republic cap has been busy and aggressive throughout and well deserves the plaudits he receives from his colleagues as he cleverly controls a ball played out of defence by Shaun Teale before firing it past Grobbelaar.

A continuation of Little's unbeaten start as Villa manager is on the cards, it seems. But not, it proves, with Villa's arch-enemy, Le Tissier, in the opposition ranks.

Well into injury time the talented, England-capped forward, fires a 30-yard free-kick which pierces the defensive wall and finds the net off Nigel Spink's palms as the goalkeeper lunges to his left in a vain attempt to keep it out.

Just as at Villa Park early in the season, Le Tissier has plunged in the knife moments before the final whistle for yet another serious blow to morale.

John Fashanu – short on match practise following injury

Monday 26th December 1994 • Highbury • 12.00am

ARSENAL 0 ASTON VILLA 0

Half-time 0-0 • *Attendance* 34,452

Referee Kelvin MORTON (Bury St Edmunds)

Linesmen E.W. GREEN and P. WALTON

Red and White Shirts, White Shorts	Goals	Green, Black and Red Striped Shirts, Black Shorts	Goals
13 Vince BARTRAM		1 Nigel SPINK	
2 Lee DIXON		2 Earl BARRETT	
14 Martin KEOWN		16 Ugo EHIOGU	
12 Steve BOULD ❏		4 Shaun TEALE	
3 Nigel WINTERBURN		3 Steve STAUNTON	
23 Ray PARLOUR		7 Ray HOUGHTON ❏	
21 Steve MORROW		6 Kevin RICHARDSON ❏	
15 Stefan SCHWARZ		17 Ian TAYLOR	
29 Stephen HUGHES †		11 Andy TOWNSEND ❏ ■	
7 Kevin CAMPBELL		8 John FASHANU	
24 Paul DICKOV		9 Dean SAUNDERS †	
Substitutes		*Substitutes*	
26 Lee HARPER		13 Mark BOSNICH	
25 Mark FLATTS †76		5 Paul McGRATH †70	
5 Andy LINIGHAN		19 Graham FENTON	

BEFORE		P	W	D	L	F	A	pts	AFTER		P	W	D	L	F	A	pts
11	Arsenal	19	6	6	7	23	22	24	11	Arsenal	20	6	7	7	23	22	25
20	Villa	19	3	7	9	22	31	16	20	Villa	20	3	8	9	22	31	17

Four changes to Villa side... out go Small, McGrath, Parker and King... New signing Ian Taylor makes his debut... Steve Staunton returns after a seven-game absence through injury... Townsend back following six-game ban, but sent off again... Nigel Spink's 450th full appearance in goal for Villa.

Townsend is sent off on return

Following on to the last-ditch defeat at The Dell a week earlier this Boxing Day fixture represents another potential banana skin in Brian Little's sixth fixture.

A favourable set of festive season results is essential if Villa are to retain a reasonable hope of remaining in the Premiership, so freedom of expression must be buried in favour of sensible caution.

Little's first signing since he succeeded Ron Atkinson, midfielder Ian Taylor from Sheffield Wednesday, is given his debut and John Fashanu partners Dean Saunders up front.

The other apparent bonus is that Andy Townsend has now completed his six-match ban though this is to prove, almost unbelievably, merely a brief reprieve.

Villa, in contrast to Arsenal who are badly depleted with five internationals missing including Ian Wright, have virtually a full squad fit for the first time in weeks.

The Boxing Day fare proves to be dull and unappetising as neither side truly grasps the initiative nor takes any undue risks.

Just to add to the fragmented, disjointed feel about the game the referee is, perhaps, over- vigilant, in adhering to the letter of the law and taking names for what seem to be quite trivial offences.

In the opening stages three names are taken, including that of Andy Townsend, for a foul, only 12 minutes into his first game back. By half time there has been very little incident of note other than a good Nigel Spink save from Kevin Campbell.

This trend continues into the second half until, in the 54th minute, an Earl Barrett through ball sends Fashanu away but goalkeeper Vince Bartram narrows the angle and blocks Fash's shot with his legs.

Disaster then strikes for Villa as Townsend receives his second booking for another foul tackle, on Paul Dickov, and is sent off only one hour after his come-back from suspension.

Fortunately for ten-man Villa Arsenal are in very poor shape, offering very little of a dangerous attacking nature to threaten Villa's defence.

But Little virtually decides to settle for a point by withdrawing Saunders and replacing him with Paul McGrath to further strengthen the defence and deny Gunners the remotest sight of an unprotected goal.

And so the game fizzles out to its unentertaining conclusion with Villa slightly more satisfied than Arsenal with their point, though Little struggled to arouse much enthusiasm afterwards.

"I'm disappointed we didn't win," he confessed. "Your mentality changes when you have a guy sent off with an hour to go but in one sense it was a great point for us".

Ray Houghton has been Villa's outstanding player, especially in the first half, while Ian Taylor has shown his capacity for hard work on what must have been a difficult debut for him.

Nigel Spink – 450 full appearances for Villa

Wednesday 28th December 1994 • Villa Park • 7.45pm

ASTON VILLA 3 CHELSEA 0

Half-time 2-0 • *Attendance* 32,901

Referee Keith BURGE (Tonypandy)

Linesmen D.C. RICHARDS and M.R. SIMS

Claret Shirts with Blue Stripes, White Shorts		Goals	Royal Blue Shirts, Royal Blue Shorts		Goals
1	Nigel SPINK		1	Dmitri KHARINE	
2	Earl BARRETT ❏		2	Steve CLARKE	
16	Ugo EHIOGU		6	Frank SINCLAIR	(og 10)
4	Shaun TEALE		5	Erland JOHNSEN	
3	Steve STAUNTON †		15	Andy MYERS	
7	Ray HOUGHTON		12	Craig BURLEY †	
17	Ian TAYLOR	80	18	Eddie NEWTON	
6	Kevin RICHARDSON		17	Nigel SPACKMAN	
11	Andy TOWNSEND		10	Gavin PEACOCK	
18	Dwight YORKE	32	7	John SPENCER	
9	Dean SAUNDERS		8	Paul FURLONG ❏	
	Substitutes			*Substitutes*	
13	Mark BOSNICH		13	Kevin HITCHCOCK	
5	Paul McGRATH †75		9	Mark STEIN †ht	
19	Graham FENTON		21	David ROCASTLE	

BEFORE		P	W	D	L	F	A	pts	AFTER		P	W	D	L	F	A	pts
9	Chelsea	20	8	4	8	28	26	28	10	Chelsea	21	8	4	9	28	29	28
20	Villa	20	3	8	9	22	31	17	19	Villa	21	4	8	9	25	31	20

FACTFILE

First win under Brian Little's managership... Villa Park's biggest gate of the season to date... Upper Tier of new Holte End is opened... Ian Taylor scores his first goal for Villa, on his home debut... Only second Premiership home win of the season... Andy Townsend's 300th start in league football.

The goals arrive at last...

The new Holte End Stand, now with its fully-operational upper tier packed with fans, looks great as Villa go out in search of that first victory needed to kick-start the *Little Revolution*.

A sequence of four draws and just one defeat in five Premiership games has been OK in putting down a foundation and serving to stop the awful pattern of defeats which was taking shape before.

But drawn games will not keep Villa in the Premiership unless they are well-punctuated with three-pointers and the players know that just as clearly as the supporters.

Villa haven't won a league game at Villa Park since Ipswich on September 10, a record which has caused the worrying slump into the relegation-threatened bottom four. Time, then, to start winning as from now. Or else...

So, on this occasion, Villa go for the prize from the first whistle, not always finishing with conviction but never short of attacking ambition by the shortest route possible.

A tenth minute goal by Steve Staunton provides the morale uplift they need to inspire them to go for more and Chelsea simply can't cope with the ammunition thrown at them.

The Irish Republic defender's corner returns to him from the packed goalmouth and he meets it with a stunning cross-shot which deflects off a defender.

Less decisively both Dean Saunders and Kevin Richardson miss tempting chances to bury the opposition in the opening 20 minutes as wave after wave of Villa attacks swarm in.

Exhilarating stuff at last for the home supporters who warm to the industrious and aggressive home debut pieced enthusiastically together by Ian Taylor, once a Holte Ender in his non-League days with Moor Green.

The second goal arrives in the 32nd minute with the energetic Staunton again playing a key role. This time it is a left-side free-kick which unsettles the visiting defence as Andy Townsend flicks on from the near post for Dwight Yorke to nimbly apply the finishing touch.

The 2-0 scoreline could by now be 5-0 but although Villa continue to dominate the opposition with very little threat to Nigel Spink's goal, it is ten minutes from time before the third goal arrives.

When it does the wait has been well-worthwhile as the script is completed with a story-book finale.

A move right out of the Ron Atkinson text book of passing football is started by Taylor himself with a feed to Earl Barrett.

The £1m ex-Wednesday player, watched by a whole battery of his home-City supporters, then motors into the Chelsea penalty area to be positioned just right to meet Dwight Yorke's swinging centre with the firmest of headers past Dmitri Kharine.

In his earlier days as a terrace fan he must  have dreamed of doing that a hundred times. Now it was happening, with the third and final goal planted into the goal below where he used to stand.

"To merely scrape a win would have been pleasing enough," says Little. "But to do it with such style was just what we have needed."

Ian Taylor – headed Villa's third goal on his home debut

Saturday 31st December 1994 • Maine Road • 3.00pm

MANCHESTER CITY 2 ASTON VILLA 2

Half-time 1-0 • *Attendance* 22,513

Referee Joe WORRALL (Warrington)

Linesmen R. PEARSON and D. PUGH

Light Blue Shirts, White Shorts		Goals	Claret Shirts with Blue Stripes, White Shorts		Goals
25	Andy DIBBLE		1	Nigel SPINK	
29	John FOSTER		2	Earl BARRETT	
15	Alan KERNAGHAN		16	Ugo EHIOGU	
12	Ian BRIGHTWELL	(og 55)	4	Shaun TEALE	
3	Terry PHELAN		3	Steve STAUNTON ‡	
16	Nicky SUMMERBEE		7	Ray HOUGHTON	
21	Steve LOMAS		17	Ian TAYLOR	
10	Gary FLITCROFT		6	Kevin RICHARDSON	
11	Peter BEAGRIE		11	Andy TOWNSEND †	
8	Paul WALSH		18	Dwight YORKE	
28	Uwe RÖSLER	14, 54	9	Dean SAUNDERS	60
	Substitutes			*Substitutes*	
33	John BURRIDGE		30	Michael OAKES	
4	Maurizio GAUDINO		5	John FASHANU †80	
6	Michael VONK		8	Paul McGRATH ‡88	

BEFORE		P	W	D	L	F	A	pts	AFTER		P	W	D	L	F	A	pts
11	Man City	21	8	4	9	31	36	28	11	Man City	22	8	5	9	33	38	29
20	Villa	21	4	8	9	25	31	20	20	Villa	22	4	9	9	27	33	21

FACTFILE

Old year goes out on a high note... Heavy cold keeps Bosnich out of contention... Deano ends his goal drought... Fifth draw in seven league games... Rösler bags a pair, but Villa come back to share the points... new boy Taylor again influential.

New Year's Eve revivalists

Strange to be saying Auld Lang Syne and good riddance to a year in which the Coca-Cola Cup has been won and a return to Europe achieved. But that's the way it was with 1994.

The high's were very high but the low had 'beware, relegation' ominously written on it and the New Year HAS to be better than that.

Selection-wise Brian Little is still feeling his way, but after the thrilling 3-0 home victory over Chelsea two days ago he has few decisions to make for this one.

Optimism is on the up-and-up after that outstanding display but football never loses its capacity to rebound from success and deliver a kick where it hurts.

At Maine Road, thirsting to register their first away victory under the new boss's guidance, Villa are to receive two such body blows before the New Year's Eve celebrations begin in earnest.

The first half is only a tightly-contested opening 14 minutes old before the German Uwe Rosler delivers the first of two goals he has in store.

Villa's defence, under significant pressure, then holds on firmly to half-time with occasional promise of reprisals from the front men but eight minutes into the second half Rosler strikes again.

So, just thirty-seven minutes left, the home team firmly in control and Villa's festive programme, which began with a 2-1 defeat at Southampton, looks to be heading firmly back into depression.

However, there is a broad band of resolve running through this Villa performance with outstanding individuals bringing hope of a collective improvement.

New signing Ian Taylor, a quickly-established folk hero with his fine third goal against Chelsea is showing the basic qualities outlined by Little when he signed him.

His non-stop mobility and the capacity to make powerful runs into the opposition box add a new dimension to Villa's midfield which features Ray Houghton and Kevin Richardson both in rejuvenated form.

But the powerful Steve Staunton is the decisive figure as Villa pull a goal back within two minutes of Rosler's second.

Staunton's cross is touched on by Dean Saunders and cannons off the static Ian Brightwell to give Villa the springboard they need. City have, by now, perhaps decided too soon that they have pushed the scoreline beyond the visitors' reach. If so they are to be proved emphatically wrong.

It takes only another five minutes for Villa to level at 2-2 and to hold on for another invaluable point to see the old year out.

Dwight Yorke is fed by Shaun Teale and the West Indian's centre provided Taylor with a shooting chance which, though blocked by Andy Dibble, rebounds enticingly for Deano's first goal in seven games.

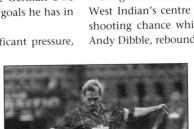

"It was always going to be a difficult fixture but I was very pleased with the way we fought on to the final whistle and earned our point," said the relieved Villa manager.

Kevin Richardson – rejuvenated form

Monday 2nd January 1995 • Villa Park • 3.00pm

ASTON VILLA 0 LEEDS UNITED 0

Half-time 0-0 • Attendance 35,038

Referee Paul DANSON (Leicester)
Linesmen T.A. ATKINSON and S.R. BRAND

Claret Shirts with Blue Stripes, White Shorts	Goals		White Shirts, Blue Shorts	Goals
1 Nigel SPINK			1 John LUKIC	
2 Earl BARRETT			2 Gary KELLY	
5 Paul McGRATH			6 David WEATHERALL ❑	
16 Ugo EHIOGU			12 John PEMBERTON ❑	
4 Shaun TEALE			15 Nigel WORTHINGTON	
7 Ray HOUGHTON †			27 Lucas RADEBE	
17 Ian TAYLOR			14 David WHITE	
6 Kevin RICHARDSON			10 Gary McALLISTER	
3 Steve STAUNTON			11 Gary SPEED ❑	
18 Dwight YORKE			26 Philomen MASINGA †	
9 Dean SAUNDERS			9 Brian DEANE ❑	

Substitutes			*Substitutes*	
30 Michael OAKES			13 Mark BEENEY	
8 John FASHANU †63			8 Rod WALLACE †73	
19 Graham FENTON			17 Mark TINKLER	

BEFORE	P	W	D	L	F	A	pts	AFTER	P	W	D	L	F	A	pts
7 Leeds	21	9	5	7	29	27	32	7 Leeds	22	9	6	7	29	27	33
20 Villa	22	4	9	9	27	33	21	19 Villa	23	4	10	9	27	33	22

FACTFILE

A vital point as Villa move up a place in the relegation zone... Paul McGrath makes only his second full start under Brian Little... It's the new manager's fifth draw in seven games... and Villa Park's biggest crowd of the season to date despite the bitterly cold weather...

A little more on the right track

Those who feel that English football inflicts many of its own wounds found plenty to complain about in this opening match of the 1995 programme.

This is Villa's fourth important fixture in eight days and has to be played on a frost affected surface which is more treacherous in some areas than others.

Although the attendance of 35,038 is the highest of the season they are not destined, it transpires, to be welcomed into 1995 with all guns blazing.

The only team change is the return of Paul McGrath to cover for Andy Townsend who has a minor injury. This apart Brian Little stays with the personnel and the playing style which has, at least, stopped the alarming run of defeats and which excited the crowd in the previous home game.

This time, unfortunately, the sheer volume of fixtures, the unpredictability of the pitch, the opposition's midfield and defensive strength combine to make Villa functional rather than fancy free. By the end of 90 dour minutes with little flair-ridden football and few goalmouth thrills it is time to pocket yet one more point, acknowledge that it was never going to be easy and hurry off into warmer surrounds.

For all the qualities contained in the strike pair of Dean Saunders and Dwight Yorke it would be acknowledged that height and power in the air is not part of their collective armoury.

Ranged against Leeds' centurion centre backs David Weatherall and John Pemberton, they spend an unproductive 90 minutes working hard to no avail.

To be fair, Villa start brightly enough by applying a fair degree of pressure in the opening ten minutes and keeping John Lukic on red alert.

After that the alarm bells in his goalmouth stop ringing and Nigel Spink has more cause for concern. The Villa 'keeper is relieved indeed when Ray Houghton proves to be well-placed on the line as a goal-bound Weatherall header beats him in flight.

Villa promise fleetingly just once to produce a second successive home victory. Kevin Richardson races through onto a Houghton pass but Lukic risks bruised limbs by clambering down to smother his shot ten minutes into the second half.

Moments like this are the best bits of a match which would not take up much space on a club video of the season's highlights. In the closing couple of minutes there is the hint of a chance of a Villa goal as Lukic saves volleys from Taylor and Staunton.

But, by the final whistle, realistically, it is Leeds who can claim that they were closest to breaking the chilly stalemate.

"Three draws is one too many," said Little of the post-Christmas quartet of games which was another way of saying that we needed to win this one.

"We would have been happy with two draws and two wins but I was pleased with many aspects of the performance because we kept another clean sheet defensively.

"The pitch was very tricky to play on and players were not keen to play long passes on it for fear of losing their feet. Also it was slippier in front of the main stand where it has had no sun."

**Paul McGrath –
first choice again**

Saturday 7th January 1995 • Oakwell • 3.00pm

BARNSLEY 0 ASTON VILLA 2

Half-time 0-0 • *Attendance* 11,469

Referee Lawrence DILKES (Mossley)

Linesmen A.R. LEAKE and R. INGHAM

Red Shirts, White Shorts		Goals	Green, Black and Red Striped Shirts, Black Shorts		Goals
1	David WATSON		1	Nigel SPINK	
6	Steve DAVIS		2	Earl BARRETT	
3	Gary FLEMING ‡		5	Paul McGRATH	
5	Adrian MOSES		16	Ugo EHIOGU	
2	Nicky EADEN		4	Shaun TEALE	
4	Danny WILSON †		18	Dwight YORKE	48
7	Brendan O'CONNELL		17	Ian TAYLOR	
8	Neil REDFEARN		11	Andy TOWNSEND	
11	Darren SHERIDAN ❑		3	Steve STAUNTON	
9	Andy PAYTON		9	Dean SAUNDERS	85
10	Andy LIDDELL		8	John FASHANU	
	Substitutes			*Substitutes*	
13	Lee BUTLER		13	Mark BOSNICH	
14	Martin BULLOCK †69		6	Kevin RICHARDSON	
12	Andy RAMMELL ‡72		7	Ray HOUGHTON	

FACTFILE

Only the second meeting in the FA Cup between the two sides... Villa extend their unbeaten record against Barnsley to 15 games... New signings Tommy Johnson and Gary Charles watch from the Oakwell stand... Dwight Yorke and Dean Saunders fight for places with important goals.

Johnson and Charles sign on for Villa

Easy route to fourth round

Immediate build-up to the Cup-tie has been monopolised by the signing of two new players on the eve of the game to give the competition for places a whole new impetus.

Winger Tommy Johnson and full-back Gary Charles, signed for a total of £2.9m, are at Oakwell knowing that if their new colleagues can get through, they will be challenging for a place in the fourth round.

This gives the mood among the players a new urgency adding credibility to the timing of Brian Little's second move into the market.

Both Kevin Richardson and Ray Houghton are on the subs bench, an indication of a new strength-in-depth created by Little's imports.

The post-Christmas league programme was no more than satisfactory, so a positive kick-off to the FA Cup campaign is needed to keep Little's mini-improvement moving along.

All the selection signs are good, Andy Townsend is back after missing the Leeds game through injury and Dalian Atkinson is also recalled to the fray.

The pre-match predictions suggest that Villa could be about to step on a banana skin, the last thing Little wants with the Coca-Cola and UEFA Cups having now passed Villa by.

A Villa Park replay appears to be the popular verdict, based on recent in-and-out form but from the very first whistle Villa show a determined desire to dominate proceedings.

Paul McGrath is a commanding figure in a defence which allows the First Division team to create almost nothing

of attacking significance from start to finish.

At the other end John Fashanu is equally uncharitable as his physical presence keeps Barnsley's defence constantly on the verge of collapse.

Although the first half ends 0-0 Villa are by now totally in command as Fash wins virtually every aerial ball and sees a diving 35th minute header disallowed for off-side, one of three such decisions in the 90 minutes.

The breakthrough comes three minutes into the second half as Dwight Yorke meets Steve Staunton's left-wing corner to perfection, heading in the opening goal which had so frustratingly evaded Fashanu.

Five minutes before the end another Staunton corner brings Villa's second goal, by Dean Saunders, as Townsend knocks the ball back in from the far post.

Deano's shot goes in through goalkeeper Dave Watson's legs, but it is enough to re-enforce Little's firm 'no' verdict when Everton boss Joe Royle subsequently makes a £2m bid for the Welsh international.

Ian Taylor, on his fourth appearance since his signing from Sheffield Wednesday, is unlucky to have a flag raised against him as he heads into the net after a surge from a deep position while Saunders slams one shot against the crossbar.

"Everyone who saw it would regard it as a thoroughly professional performance which we dominated throughout," said Little. 'Everyone' included Johnson and Charles who might just have wondered how they were going to get in to a side with so much commitment and ability.

Dwight Yorke – opened the scoring for Villa

Saturday 14th January 1995 • Villa Park • 3.00pm

ASTON VILLA 2 QUEENS PARK RANGERS 1

Half-time 1-0 • *Attendance* 26,578

Referee Alan WILKIE (Chester-le-Street)
Linesmen J. McGRATH and D.C. RICHARDS

Claret Shirts with Blue Stripes, White Shorts		Goals	Blue and White Hooped Shirts, Blue Shorts		Goals
13	Mark BOSNICH		1	Tony ROBERTS	
16	Ugo EHIOGU	76	2	David BARDSLEY	
5	Paul McGRATH		16	Danny MADDIX	
4	Shaun TEALE		4	Steve YATES ❑	88
2	Earl BARRETT		3	Clive WILSON	
17	Ian TAYLOR ❑		7	Andrew IMPEY	
18	Dwight YORKE		8	Ian HOLLOWAY	
3	Steve STAUNTON		25	Steve HODGE	
25	Tommy JOHNSON		22	Michael MEAKER	
8	John FASHANU	7	9	Les FERDINAND	
9	Dean SAUNDERS		20	Kevin GALLEN	
Substitutes			*Substitutes*		
30	Michael OAKES		13	Sieb DYKSTRA	
7	Ray HOUGHTON †80		18	Alan McCARTHY †89	
22	Gary CHARLES		10	Bradley ALLEN	

BEFORE	P	W	D	L	F	A	pts	AFTER	P	W	D	L	F	A	pts
14 QPR	22	7	6	9	34	38	27	15 QPR	23	7	6	10	35	40	27
19 Villa	23	4	10	9	27	33	22	18 Villa	24	5	10	9	29	34	25

FACTFILE

Villa out of the bottom four... Tommy Johnson makes his Villa debut... Gary Charles, Villa's other new signing, has to be content with a place on the bench... John Fashanu scores his first goal since the opening game of the season at Goodison... Mark Bosnich back with mixture of the brilliant and the bizarre...

Out of bottom four, at last

Brian Little is blessed with a whole new set of selection options as a result of the £2.9m import of the Derby County pair Tommy Johnson and Gary Charles and now available for their club debuts.

Although both Kevin Richardson and Andy Townsend are out suspended there is an impressive-looking squad from which to choose.

This gives the Villa manager the chance to introduce a playing style he favours, namely a 3-4-3 formation with a trio of centre backs in Ugo Ehiogu, Paul McGrath and Shaun Teale.

Earl Barrett keeps his place, but on the right side of a revised midfield forcing Charles to begin his claret-and-blue career on the bench. Mark Bosnich is back in goal to replace flu-victim Nigel Spink.

The new system gets off to an encouraging start in terms of a 7th minute opening goal by John Fashanu though there are clearly 'teething problems' ahead for the team, in terms of style re-adjustment, as well as for the robust striker.

A free kick on the edge of the centre circle by Teale leads to Dean Saunders putting Fashanu in possession near the 18-yard line and his curving shot beats goalkeeper Tony Roberts off the post.

Once ahead, however, Villa struggle to hold on as Ian Taylor and Dwight Yorke have difficulty in establishing a midfield control. Ahead of them Johnson has the task of forging a partnership with Saunders ann Fashanu and an understanding in terms of positional play clearly will not come easily.

QPR look the more controlled side and Villa have to battle to stay ahead, which they do with rare application and comforted by the three centre backs looking far more at ease than the front men.

Fashanu is involved in a series of physical challenges for possession and, just on the hour, leaves the field with two cracked front teeth, the legacy of a firm contact with Danny Maddix's elbow.

Ray Houghton replaces the target man, enforcing a further alteration in style and though QPR continue to look unfortunate to be behind, a second Villa goal arrives after 75 minutes.

Steve Staunton, playing an attacking role on the left of midfield, swings over one of his inviting corners and Ehiogu beats Roberts with a six-yard header.

The result is virtually out of Ranger's reach now as Villa continue to dig in and defend what they have, but there is a late scare as Steve Yates scores when a corner pushed onto the bar by Bosnich falls invitingly in front of him.

QPR have hit the woodwork twice and Bosnich has made a mixed return combining brilliance with the odd dangerous 'rush of blood' but at least Villa have now won two and drawn three of their last five home games.

"It wasn't a great performance," Little confessed. "We would like to play with a little more style, but at the moment we are result-orientated.

"Normally you would use a whole pre-season to prepare a new system but we had hardly had time to practice it at all."

Mark Bosnich – a mixed performance on his return to the side

Saturday 21st January 1995 • City Ground • 3.00pm

NOTTINGHAM FOREST 1   ASTON VILLA 2

Half-time 0-1 • *Attendance 24,598*

Referee Keith COOPER (Pontypridd)
Linesmen P.A. ELWICK and A.S. HOGG

Red Shirts, White Shorts		Goals	Green, Black and Red Striped Shirts, Black Shorts		Goals
1	Mark CROSSLEY		13	Mark BOSNICH	
2	Des LYTTLE		2	Earl BARRETT	
5	Steve CHETTLE		5	Paul McGRATH ❑	
6	Carl TILER ❑		16	Ugo EHIOGU ❑	
18	Alf-Inge HAALAND		4	Shaun TEALE	
11	Steve STONE		25	Tommy JOHNSON ‡	
7	Steve PHILLIPS		17	Ian TAYLOR	
9	Lars BOHINEN ❑		18	Dwight YORKE †	
14	Ian WOAN		3	Steve STAUNTON	
10	Stan COLLYMORE	pen 53	9	Dean SAUNDERS	68
22	Bryan ROY		8	John FASHANU ❑	32
	Substitutes			*Substitutes*	
30	John FILAN		1	Nigel SPINK	
8	Scot GEMMILL		7	Ray HOUGHTON †75	
21	Gary BULL		22	Gary CHARLES ‡88	

BEFORE		P	W	D	L	F	A	pts
4	Forest	24	12	6	6	36	26	42
18	Villa	24	5	10	9	29	34	25

AFTER		P	W	D	L	F	A	pts
5	Forest	25	12	6	7	37	28	42
14	Villa	25	6	10	9	31	35	28

FACTFILE

Win takes Villa up four places and out of relegation zone... Best Premiership place since October... Gary Charles makes Villa debut, albeit as substitute with just a minute left in the game... Fashanu scores his second goal in consecutive games... Earl Barrett's 150th and last Villa game before his transfer to Everton.

Relegation fears are eased

Most of the pre-match conjecture has surrounded the question of whether John Fashanu will play after his confrontation with a QPR elbow last Saturday.

But one other episode has captured the headlines, namely Earl Barrett's proposed £1.7m move to Everton and the deal's sudden breakdown just in time for him to reclaim his place at the City Ground.

Fash has had dental surgery on a very painful mouth with one tooth broken off, one cracked and dislodged, and a nerve exposed.

Brian Little has grave doubts about including him, fearing that the fact that he is forced to wear a protective tooth brace will inhibit his normal aggressions.

Fash is so insistent, however, that the Villa manager agrees to his giving it a go and this proves to be a brave and match-winning decision on the part of manager and player.

Forest manager Frank Clark, who has been rewarded with a new contract for his magnificent work for pulling the club around after relegation and Brian Clough's departure is destined to have his celebrations cut short.

About to impressively unfold is Villa's first away victory under Little's leadership, easily the best performance of his dozen in charge and a reassuring demonstration of the intention to climb the Premiership table.

Little's regular instruction to his players is to go out and dominate the opposition from the first whistle by pushing them back onto the defensive and forcing them to stay there.

The players follow his orders to the letter by defending well forward of their goal and, as a result, Forest find themselves under pressure from the start with little respite.

An important feature of Little's three-centre-back plan is that Steve Staunton is granted the freedom to advance almost at will down the left flank to fire in his armoury of powerful crosses from a variety of angles.

This attacking option proves decisive in the 32nd minute as Fashanu gets himself in the right place at the right time to skilfully deflect the ball wide of Mark Crossley.

Forest can conjure no such scoring ploy in response, though Stan Collymore has two or three attempts to unsettle a solid defence, but either misses the target or is smartly dispossessed.

Although it is Villa who seem more likely to score than Forest Collymore gets an equaliser from a fiercely-disputed penalty after a 53 minute tackle by Ugo Ehiogu on Brian Roy.

The Villa defender is so adamant that he tackled the Dutchman fairly that he gets a yellow card for his protests.

For a while it seems that Forest are to be blessed with a point which they distinctly do not deserve but Villa then open up a vast well of determination.

Unlike earlier in the season when they were prone to discard their advantages they go all out to regain the lead and are rewarded for their admirable resolve in the 69th minute.

Another Staunton ball fed menacingly in enables Dean Saunders, who has characteristically already rattled Crossley's bar, to apply the finishing touch with an accurately applied header. "It was a good result which we well deserved," said Little. "I can't remember Mark Bosnich really having a shot to stop."

John Fashanu – another game, another goal

Wednesday 25th January 1995 • Villa Park • 7.45pm

ASTON VILLA 1 TOTTENHAM HOTSPUR 0

Half-time 1-0 • Attendance 40,017

Referee Robert HART (Darlington)
Linesmen B.M. RICE and P. WALTON

Claret Shirts with Blue Stripes, White Shorts		Goals	White Shirts, Dark Blue Shorts		Goals
13	Mark BOSNICH ❏		13	Ian WALKER	
2	Earl BARRETT		2	Dean AUSTIN	
5	Paul McGRATH		5	Colin CALDERWOOD	
16	Ugo EHIOGU		6	Gary MABBUTT	
4	Shaun TEALE		3	Justin EDINBURGH	
18	Dwight YORKE ‡		9	Darren ANDERTON	
17	Ian TAYLOR		23	Sol CAMPBELL	
11	Andy TOWNSEND		4	Gheorghe POPESCU	
3	Steve STAUNTON		7	Nick BARMBY	
9	Dean SAUNDERS	17	18	Jürgen KLINSMANN †	
25	Tommy JOHNSON †		10	Teddy SHERINGHAM	
	Substitutes			*Substitutes*	
1	Nigel SPINK		28	Chris DAY	
7	Ray HOUGHTON †75		20	Darren CASKEY †26	
22	Gary CHARLES ‡89		14	Stuart NETHERCOTT	

BEFORE		P	W	D	L	F	A	pts	AFTER		P	W	D	L	F	A	pts
6	Tottenham	24	11	6	7	41	35	39	6	Tottenham	25	11	6	8	41	36	39
15	Villa	25	6	10	9	31	35	28	12	Villa	26	7	10	9	32	35	31

FACTFILE

Villa's revival continues as the team records first double of the season and ends Tottenham's 10-match unbeaten run... Win moves Villa up three places... A 'full house' at Villa Park brings record receipts... Brief home debut for substitute Gary Charles. Villa's best win sequence of the season (four games)...

Spurs fall to 'new' Villa

The game, which is described by Brian Little as 'a smashing fixture that the neutrals will want to see' has generated huge interest despite an all-day deluge.

Villa Park telephones have been jammed with inquiries on whether the match will be washed out by the incessant rainstorm. But those fearing the worst needn't have worried. The enormous black sheet protecting the pitch from such conditions has kept the surface in superb condition.

By kick-off time the stadium is virtually full for the first time since the completion of the Holte End stand as 40,000 people fill the magnificent arena with a hum of expectation.

There is one pre-match selection surprise in the absence of John Fashanu with a back problem which Little insists is not a 'convenient' injury to avoid a first confrontation with Gary Mabbutt, who was injured in the highly-publicised collision with Fash the Bash in his Wimbledon days.

Villa urgently need another victory to add growing credibility to the changes in attitude generated by Little's influence and they go for it with a will.

In the opening half-hour Villa play some storming attacking football based largely on Steve Staunton's power-house runs down the left and thunderously-struck balls into Spurs' penalty area. Half-way through this impressive spell of Villa domination Dean Saunders scores a memorable goal, inspired by the Irish Republic defender's drive and determination.

Gary Charles

A long, raking masterpiece of a pass down the left touchline sends Deano in successful pursuit of possession. The Welshman's speed takes him beyond Spurs' midfield players and forces the back four into anxious retreat.

Saunders sprints inside Dean Austin, by-passes Colin Calderwood and buries a cross-shot with such force and accuracy that one wonders why he hits the woodwork so often.

Spurs' have no cause to complain at being a goal down at this stage, especially to such a dynamic strike. But they have good cause to feel aggrieved a few minutes later and on the final whistle.

Their German mega-star, Jürgen Klinsmann, chases a ball played towards the Villa area and is carefully marshalled by Paul McGrath and Ugo Ehiogu.

Mark Bosnich is charging out to his 18-yard line but the ball will not carry that far. As Klinsmann goes for it Bosnich crosses the 18-yard line, makes an untidy leap forward and crashes into the German World Cup player who goes down and lies still.

Klinsmann is stretchered off and fans wait in dread for referee Robbie Hart's decision which proves to be, many feel, lenient in Bosnich's favour as the official's coloured cards remain in his pocket.

Spurs have to re-group with Darren Caskey on as sub but they gradually get their act back together again.

To Tottenham's credit they attack with such a will in the second half that it is Villa who are ultimately relieved to hear the final whistle with the lead still intact, though Ian Taylor might twice have scored with headers.

Klinsmann is found to have mild concussion and blows to the nose and back but recovers to play in Saturday's FA Cup-tie at Sunderland.

Bosnich subsequently gets booked near the end... for time-wasting! Based on the full 90 minutes Villa have played better many times, and lost.

Saturday 28th January 1995 • Maine Road • 3.00pm

MANCHESTER CITY 1 ASTON VILLA 0

Half-time 1-0 • *Attendance* 21,177

Referee Joe WORRALL (Warrington)
Linesmen D.R. CRICK and M.J. STODDART

Pale Blue Shirts, White Shorts		Goals
1	Tony COTON	
16	Nicky SUMMERBEE	
5	Keith CURLE	
6	Michael VONK	
18	David BRIGHTWELL	
12	Ian BRIGHTWELL	
4	Maurizio GAUDINO	
10	Gary FLITCROFT	
8	Paul WALSH †	7
28	Uwe RÖSLER	
11	Peter BEAGRIE	
	Substitutes	
25	Andy DIBBLE	
9	Niall QUINN †86	
29	John FOSTER	

Green, Black and Red Striped Shirts, Black Shorts		Goals
13	Mark BOSNICH	
2	Earl BARRETT	
5	Paul McGRATH	
16	Ugo EHIOGU	
4	Shaun TEALE	
18	Dwight YORKE †	
17	Ian TAYLOR	
11	Andy TOWNSEND	
3	Steve STAUNTON	
9	Dean SAUNDERS	
8	John FASHANU	
	Substitutes	
1	Nigel SPINK	
25	Tommy JOHNSON †78	
7	Ray HOUGHTON	

F A C T F I L E

First FA Cup meeting for 57 years... First defeat in nine games... and an end to a run of four successive victories... Third defeat in 14 games under Brian Little... Tommy Johnson makes way for John Fashanu... Earl Barrett's last game for Villa before moving to Everton.

**John Fashanu –
back after
injury, but to no
avail as Villa
make Cup exit.**

City put stop to winning run

Fourth round FA Cup day arrives with the mood of the club having undergone a dramatic change from 'will-we-stay-up?' to 'Wembley-here-we-come!'.

There seems little danger now of the revitalised squad allowing relegation to remain as a serious threat, but the sudden switch to FA Cup optimism proves to be premature, indeed.

With John Fashanu back to lead the attack Villa look good for a draw and a Villa Park replay at least, City having gone through a wretched spell of results.

In mid-week for instance, as Villa overcame Spurs, they were losing at home to bottom-club Leicester City though this proves to be a misleading form guide.

There is the usual high-profile Villa following at Maine Road ready to roar their team to its fifth win on the trot, vainly as it is to turn out.

City are ahead in only seven minutes and this is to prove the only goal of an exciting and entertaining tie which promises more but doesn't quite deliver. Match-winner for City is the darting and talented Paul Walsh who feeds greedily off a neat-and-tidy forward chip by Ian Brightwell.

Walsh well-respected for his pace and sharp reflexes, drives a shot waist-high wide of Mark Bosnich and safely inside the post for a lead which they never relinquish.

At this stage there seems ample time for Villa to claw themselves back into the game but that promise never materialises despite a good deal of possession and attacking play.

Although Villa play well enough City are the deserved winners of the fifth round prize as German international Maurizio Gaudino twice threatens to increase their lead.

One of these moments results from his finding his way through Villa's midfield and defence with a lengthy dribbling run which is finally negated by Bosnich diving at his feet.

As in Wednesday night's victory Villa's greatest promise of a goal arises from the positive aggression of Steve Staunton down the left side.

The presence of Shaun Teale behind him on that side of the defence gives the ex-Liverpool player the freedom to move forward whenever such a tactic is on and his firmly-driven balls into the box are fiendishly difficult for defenders to cut out.

The Staunton method is to vary the height and angle of his left-footed deliveries and few of them are floated in winger-style. Cross-shots, more like. Despite this attacking contribution by Villa, however, Tamworth-born Tony Coton has no more than four meaningful saves to make, one of them just before half-time from a Staunton stunner which this time is, indeed, a cross-shot rather than a centre.

One half-volley by Ian Taylor has threatened Coton's goal, as have a drive by Paul McGrath and a Fashanu header. Coton has dealt competently with each of these efforts to ensure that Villa are left with only Premiership placing to occupy their thoughts.

"It was an 'almost' day for us," admits Little at the end. "Everyone was about ten per cent down in their display."

Earl Barrett –
his last appearance for
Villa before transferring
to Everton

Saturday 4th February 1995 • Villa Park • 3.00pm

MANCHESTER UNITED 1 ASTON VILLA 0

Half-time 1-0 • *Attendance* 43,795

Referee David ELLERAY (Harrow)
Linesmen A. BATES and S.R. BRAND

Red Shirts, White Shorts	Goals	Claret Shirts with Blue Stripes, White Shorts	Goals
1 Peter SCHMEICHEL		13 Mark BOSNICH	
27 Gary NEVILLE ‡		22 Gary CHARLES	
4 Steve BRUCE		5 Paul McGRATH ❑	
6 Gary PALLISTER		4 Shaun TEALE	
3 Denis IRWIN		20 Bryan SMALL	
11 Ryan GIGGS †		18 Dwight YORKE ‡	
8 Paul INCE ❑		17 Ian TAYLOR	
9 Brian McCLAIR		11 Andy TOWNSEND	
5 Lee SHARPE		3 Steve STAUNTON	
17 Andy COLE	18	8 John FASHANU †	
24 Paul SCHOLES		9 Dean SAUNDERS	
Substitutes		*Substitutes*	
13 Gary WALSH		1 Nigel SPINK	
14 Andrei KANCHELSKIS †ht		25 Tommy JOHNSON †39	
12 David MAY ‡64		7 Ray HOUGHTON ‡61	

BEFORE	P	W	D	L	F	A	pts	AFTER	P	W	D	L	F	A	pts
2 Man Utd	26	16	6	4	47	20	54	2 Man Utd	27	17	6	4	48	20	57
12 Villa	26	7	10	9	32	35	31	14 Villa	27	7	10	10	32	36	31

Villa have won only twice at Old Trafford in 65 years... Gary Charles makes impressive full debut... Tommy Johnson impresses as Fashanu's sub... Villa's first defeat in nine Premiership starts... Andy Cole's first goal for his new club... Villa slip back two places in the table...

£7m Cole's first goal beat Villa

As Villa arrive for the potentially daunting trip to Old Trafford, Manchester United are still living in the tabloid headlines and claiming acres of newsprint space.

The after-effects of the Eric Cantona attack on a Crystal Palace fan and his suspension by United until the end of the season are still the big topic of debate.

Coming on top of the recent £7m signing of Andy Cole from Newcastle, who has yet to break his scoring duck, it has kept United's affairs firmly under the spotlight.

Brian Little has been forced to make changes with the sale of Earl Barrett to Everton and a two-match suspension for Ugo Ehiogu.

Barrett's departure means a full debut for Gary Charles while Bryan Small gets a recall as Shaun Teale moves from left back to join Paul McGrath in the centre.

United have their problems, too, with Roy Keane suspended and Mark Hughes, secured on a new contract to cover for Cantona's absence through injury, but the lead is theirs after only 18 minutes.

A Ryan Giggs corner sets up the chance and, as Gary Pallister heads it down into a dangerous position Cole thankfully gobbles up the goal he needed to get his United tally underway.

Villa's response is impressive but unrewarded as Charles reveals fine qualities in defence and attack and Ian Taylor strides back and forth confidently in midfield.

Just before half-time both sides lose a key player when John Fashanu and Ryan Giggs are in a crunching collision. Fashanu is stretchered off with injuries to his knee and shin while Giggs quickly follows after vainly attempting to recover from his shake-up.

The interval arrives with Villa looking the more dangerous in attack and this encouraging if misleading trend continues throughout much of the second half.

Apart from a first-half Lee Sharpe miss when he hit the post from a sound scoring position and a 78th minute Cole header which deflects onto the bar Mark Bosnich's goal is rarely under threat.

Peter Schmeichel, in contrast, finds his area persistently under siege as Villa press forward again and again using direct means of quickly getting the ball into dangerous areas.

A clear sign that United are under pressure arrives when Dwight Yorke is removed from action by a Paul Ince tackle on the hour which earns the England midfielder a booking.

Tommy Johnson, initially omitted but now on in place of Fashanu, begins to find a level of form previously lacking since his £2m signing with £900,000 Charles from Derby County. Along with Steve Staunton and Andy Townsend, Johnson is close to claiming an equaliser as Taylor remains impressively prominent in midfield and United struggle to hold on.

By the final whistle the memory is of United surviving a second-half blitz in which Villa's attacking football has left the home fans in a state of unending anxiety relieved only by the final whistle.

Villa are thus denied the draw which, at the very least, they deserve and United boss Alex Ferguson is forced to admit: "That was the sort of victory which wins titles," meaning, presumably, that it was clutched from the jaws of defeat.

Gary Charles – impressive debut.

Saturday 11th February 1995 • Villa Park • 3.00pm

ASTON VILLA 7 WIMBLEDON 1

Half-time 4-1 • Attendance 23,982

Referee Brian HILL (Market Harborough)
Linesmen D.M. HORLICK and R.A. SMITH

Claret Shirts with Blue Stripes, White Shorts		Goals	Dark Blue Shirts, Dark Blue Shorts		Goals
13	Mark BOSNICH		1	Hans SEGERS	
22	Gary CHARLES		37	Kenny CUNNINGHAM	
5	Paul McGRATH		15	Alan REEVES	(og 13)
4	Shaun TEALE		28	Andy THORN	
20	Bryan SMALL		12	Gary ELKINS	
18	Dwight YORKE	83	9	Efan EKOKU	
17	Ian TAYLOR		2	Warren BARTON	12
11	Andy TOWNSEND		4	Vinnie JONES	
3	Steve STAUNTON		35	Oyvind LEONHARDSEN	
25	Tommy JOHNSON	22, 26, 38	25	Mick HARFORD †	
9	Dean SAUNDERS	48, pen 67	10	Dean HOLDSWORTH ‡	
	Substitutes			*Substitutes*	
1	Nigel SPINK		23	Neil SULLIVAN	
6	Kevin RICHARDSON		36	Jon GOODMAN †73	
19	Graham FENTON		21	Chris PERRY ‡73	

BEFORE		P	W	D	L	F	A	pts	AFTER		P	W	D	L	F	A	pts
18	Wimbledon	26	10	6	10	31	40	36	9	Wimbledon	27	10	6	11	32	47	36
19	Villa	27	7	10	10	32	36	31	11	Villa	28	8	10	10	39	37	34

Club's highest League win for 33 years... Record win for Villa in the Premiership... equals Premiership record scores by Blackburn Rovers (v Norwich 3.10.92) and Newcastle United (v Swindon Town 12.3.94)... First Villa goals for Tommy Johnson... and a hat-trick... Kevin Richardson's final first team game.

Wimbledon jinx is truly crushed!

Being wise after the event it would have been tempting for any dedicated Villa-watcher to declare: "This one's been on the cards for months..."

'One of these days,' folks have said with a knowing nod 'some team somewhere is going to be hit by a Villa avalanche.

Such thoughts dated back to Ron Atkinson's days when Villa promised to deliver goals in plenty but rarely quite made it.

Under Brian Little's management the system has changed with a greater accent on getting forward quickly and this was to prove the occasion when all past frustrations were laid to rest under a barrage of goals unprecedented in recent times.

Behind the remarkable transformation in Villa's scoring record is the pairing of £2m Tommy Johnson with Dean Saunders in the absence of John Fashanu who will be out for, perhaps, the rest of the season for knee surgery.

Johnson and Saunders deploy stealth and speed to counter-act the loss of Fashanu's power and aggression and the ex-England centre forward's former club just cannot handle the pace and variety of Villa's attacks.

The one slightly sad feature of the day is that past memories of the notorious Wimbledon jinx has kept the attendance down below 24,000, the lowest since October. How the missing thousands must have yearned to be there as the goal flashes hit the airwaves and TV screens.

On the eve of the game Little lays heavy emphasis on the fact that Villa have gone an early goal down in the previous two games and that this time pre-match motivation must be right. Yet, oddly, the trend continues as Warren Barton volleys Dons ahead in the 12th minute to trigger the most remarkable league romp at Villa Park in decades.

The equaliser arrives within a few seconds as Dean Saunders' left wing centre deflects off Alan Reeves and away from Hans Segers' grasp. What follows can only be charted accurately goal-by-goal.

22 minutes: The lead arrives in dream-world fashion. Deano's through-ball finds the raiding Charles whose exquisite centre deceives defenders with its pace and height for Johnson to glide into the goalmouth for a glancing header placed to perfection.

26 minutes: Johnson's second, a low left-footer as Vinny Jones chases him in vain.

38 minutes: It's a hat-trick, a simple touch in when Shaun Teale blasts Steve Staunton's corner across goal.

48 minutes: A blockbuster of a shot from 25 yards by Saunders makes it 5-1 and fans revel in the experience of seeing their team rattling in their chances as never before.

67 minutes: The industrious Ian Taylor is tripped by Segers and Saunders raps in the penalty for 6-1 as Wimbledon are simply overwhelmed.

83 minutes: Dwight Yorke gets in on the act to sign off with a neatly-placed chip shot when fed by the irrepressible Saunders.

"We came to the wrong place at the wrong time," laments Dons manager Joe Kinnear. Villa outplayed us all over the park and the more we chased the more we got punished. It was their day and we hope they enjoyed it." Well, yes, actually. They did...

Tommy Johnson – a hat-trick.

Saturday 18th February 1995 • Hillsborough • 3.00pm

SHEFFIELD WEDNESDAY 1 ASTON VILLA 2

Half-time 0-2 • Attendance 24,063

Referee Dermot GALLAGHER (Banbury)

Linesmen D.M. HORLICK and R. PEARSON

Blue and White Striped Shirts, Blue Shorts		Goals	Claret Shirts with Blue Stripes, White Shorts		Goals
13	Kevin PRESSMAN		13	Mark BOSNICH	
3	Ian NOLAN		22	Gary CHARLES	
17	Des WALKER		5	Paul McGRATH	
2	Peter ATHERTON		16	Ugo EHIOGU	
29	Lee BRISCOE †		4	Shaun TEALE	
5	Dan PETRESCU		18	Dwight YORKE	
11	John SHERIDAN		17	Ian TAYLOR	
16	Graham HYDE		11	Andy TOWNSEND	
15	Andy SINTON ‡		3	Steve STAUNTON	
8	Chris WADDLE		25	Tommy JOHNSON	
10	Mark BRIGHT	71	9	Dean SAUNDERS	26, 44
	Substitutes			*Substitutes*	
1	Chris WOODS		1	Nigel SPINK	
19	Guy WHITTINGHAM †45		10	Dalian ATKINSON	
14	Chris BART-WILLIAMS ‡65		14	Franz CARR	

BEFORE		P	W	D	L	F	A	pts	AFTER		P	W	D	L	F	A	pts
8	Sheff Wed	28	10	9	9	37	36	39	8	Sheff Wed	29	10	9	10	38	38	39
11	Villa	28	8	10	10	39	37	34	9	Villa	29	9	10	10	41	38	37

FACTFILE

Villa make it five wins in six Premiership matches... and move to their highest place of the season... Deano's 100th league appearance for Villa... Ugo Ehiogu back after two-match suspension... A place on the bench for Dalian Atkinson after injury has kept him out of 14 games.

Double-strike by deadly Deano

How do you follow a seven-goal spectacular? Villa fans travel to Hillsborough with this pertinent query in mind and they depart after the final whistle thinking: "Just like that..."

While this is no repeat of those unique Wimbledon heroics it is just as satisfying in its way with three more points taking Villa into ninth place.

In the build-up to the game a fascinating new twist has been given to the Premiership's tail by Ron Atkinson's appointment to succeed the sacked Phil Neal, which sees Coventry City launch their own anti-relegation strategy.

Atkinson's first move is to sign Kevin Richardson as his own midfield motivator leaving Little with a gap in his squad to fill.

The final weeks of the season are destined to throw almost as much attention on the bottom end of the table as the top and the Villa boss insists that Villa are not yet clear of being dragged back in.

Little has demonstrated that sentiment plays no part in his team selection by leaving out Bryan Small, who played well last week, to recall Ugo Ehiogu after his two-match ban.

The fixture has a little extra spice for Ian Taylor who felt that he was never given enough chance by Trevor Francis to prove himself in his favourite centre midfield role.

The Birmingham-born former Port Vale player sets about motoring up and down the Hillsborough pitch to play a crucial role in another all-round display which bears visible testimony to the huge form transformation which has taken place.

Villa's football on the break is quick, penetrative and exhilarating to watch as illustrated most graphically in the first of two goals by Dean Saunders, in the 26th minute.

Dwight Yorke brings the ball through on the right-hand side to the half-way line before feeding Taylor who has backed him with a surge from a deep position.

Saunders reads the situation shrewdly and is moving into position perfectly as Taylor threads an angled ball in which requires merely some deftly-applied sleight-of-foot to beat Kevin Pressman.

But for a timely save by Pressman Yorke would have made it 2-0 before Saunders does just that a minute before half-time.

Wednesday's hopes of getting back on terms have been restricted to a mark Bright blast which rattles the crossbar and a Graham Hyde effort, brilliantly kept out by Mark Bosnich.

Yorke is once again behind the move for Saunders' second goal by switching the play from right to left with a crossfield pass to Steve Staunton.

The Irish cap, like Paul McGrath and Andy Townsend denied a full international in last Wednesday's disgrace in Dublin, powers in one of his searing centres for Saunders to find the net with a headed goal he will place high in his personal list of favourites.

Although Bright reduces the lead in the 71st minute Villa have largely snuffed out Wednesday's desperate attempts to swing the scoreline around. In further lethal counter attacks Saunders sees Pressman deny him a hat-trick while both Taylor and Tommy Johnson miss chances to build up the lead.

"The way we are playing now I expect to score in every game," says a beaming Dean Saunders after-the-game, while Taylor leaves Hillsborough feeling he has nothing left to prove.

Meanwhile Guy Whittingham, the man who joined Wednesday in part-exchange, can look back only at 45 minutes as second-half substitute and the feeling that his former club are distinctly upwardly mobile.

Wednesday 22nd February 1995 • Villa Park • 7.45pm

ASTON VILLA 4 LEICESTER CITY 4

Half-time 2-0 • *Attendance* 30,825
Referee Kelvin MORTON (Bury St Edmunds)
Linesmen A.N. BUTLER and D. PUGH

Claret Shirts with Blue Stripes, White Shorts		Goals	Blue Shirts, Blue Shorts		Goals
13	Mark BOSNICH		33	Kevin POOLE	
22	Gary CHARLES		2	Simon GRAYSON ❑	
5	Paul McGRATH		19	Colin HILL	
16	Ugo EHIOGU		4	Jimmy WILLIS	
4	Shaun TEALE		3	Mike WHITLOW †	
18	Dwight YORKE ‡	60	17	Steve THOMPSON	
17	Ian TAYLOR		34	Mike GALLOWAY	
11	Andy TOWNSEND		18	Garry PARKER	
3	Steve STAUNTON	37	10	Mark DRAPER ❑	
25	Tommy JOHNSON ❑ †	66	9	Iwan ROBERTS	77
9	Dean SAUNDERS	8	6	Mark ROBINS	61
	Substitutes			*Substitutes*	
1	Nigel SPINK		1	Gavin WARD	
10	Dalian ATKINSON †77		24	Neil LEWIS †28 ‡	
14	Franz CARR ‡87		25	David LOWE ‡53	80, 90

BEFORE		P	W	D	L	F	A	pts	AFTER		P	W	D	L	F	A	pts
9	Villa	29	9	10	10	41	38	37	9	Villa	30	9	11	10	45	42	38
21	Leicester	27	4	7	16	25	46	19	21	Leicester	28	4	8	16	29	50	20

FACTFILE

Villa give up a 4-1 lead as Leicester score three goals in final 13 minutes... coinciding with Dalian Atkinson's substitution and return to action after a long lay-off through injury... Franz Carr makes a brief Villa debut as substitute... sub Lowe hits two late goals for Leicester.

Fantasy football – for real!

In a year of conflicting fortunes, high peaks and low troughs, this is to prove the scoreline that is the most unpalatable to digest.

It will go down in memories as one of those 'do you remember when...' occasions which crop up whenever freak or fantastic events are being recalled. Like the previous game it will not be soon forgotten though for totally different reasons to the 7-1 win over Wimbledon.

Villa were once 4-0 down to Liverpool at Villa Park and fought back to a 4-4 draw. This is virtually the about-face of that oft-recalled fight-back, though 4-1 up was where it stands after 65 minutes.

The visit of Brian Little's former club to Villa Park is, with the exception of the odd abusive chant, a peaceful affair in contrast to the fixture at Filbert Street.

It's a marvel that the game is on at all, thanks once again to the pitch cover which keeps the surface in near-perfect shape while Coca-Cola Cup semi-finals and other Premiership games are succumbing to the downpour.

All seems well when Steve Staunton's ninth minute, long-range blast deflects off Dean Saunders for a 1-0 lead.

Leicester are always playing with promise but a second-goal by Staunton (37 mins) seems to put Villa on course for their sixth win in seven league games and a remarkable rise to seventh place.

A show-stopper of a goal it is, too, with Dwight Yorke delivering a 40-yard crossfield pass for the Irish Cap to collect and despatch into Kevin Poole's goal from 20 yards.

On the hour Yorke makes it 3-0 after Tommy Johnson's shot thunders back off the bar. There's a fleeting hint of Leicester's danger on the break as Iwan Roberts scores for Leicester straight from the kick-off but, in fact, Villa are then heading for their best spell.

Johnson upsets supporters by missing from a few yards out though quickly redeems himself with a 65th minute long-range lob over Poole's head for 4-1.

Exhibition time is here now, it seems, as Villa move the ball around sweetly and the crowd welcome each pass with a special 'olé'. And as Villa strut their stuff Leicester look demoralised and well-beaten. But appearances can be deceptive.

A 76th minute centre by Mike Galloway sees Roberts drag the score back to 4-2 inspiring Leicester into a whiplash finish and Villa into a mixture of confusion and panic.

A close-range hook by substitue David Lowe makes it 4-3 with ten minutes left, a very long ten minutes it is to prove. Villa fail to close the game down, go looking for more goals, leave inviting space for Leicester to play in and make a vital error as 90 minutes arrive, still at 4-3.

Near Mark Bosnich's right-hand post at the Holte End, the goalkeeper and Paul McGrath mix themselves up to concede a corner which should have been a safe clearance.

From that injury-time corner Lowe rattles in his second, Leicester's third in the space of 13 minutes and keep Villa pegged in a comfortable ninth place when, 25 minutes earlier they had looked set for two places higher.

"We went to sleep and switched off," admits Little, looking shell-shocked at the mind-numbing transformation. "It was a tough lesson, but we'll learn from it."

Steve Staunton celebrates his goal against Leicester.

Saturday 25th February 1995 • St James's Park • 3.00pm

NEWCASTLE UNITED 3 ASTON VILLA 1

Half-time 1-1 • *Attendance 34,637*

Referee Philip DON (Middlesex)
Linesmen J.P. DEVINE and A.J. HILL

Black and White Striped Shirts, Black Shorts		Goals	Claret Shirts with Blue Stripes, White Shorts		Goals
1	Pavel SRNICEK		13	Mark BOSNICH	
12	Marc HOTTIGER		22	Gary CHARLES	
15	Darren PEACOCK		5	Paul McGRATH	
6	Steve HOWEY ❏		16	Ugo EHIOGU	
3	John BERESFORD		4	Shaun TEALE †	
18	Keith GILLESPIE		18	Dwight YORKE	
2	Barry VENISON	31	17	Ian TAYLOR	
7	Robert LEE		11	Andy TOWNSEND	40
5	Ruel FOX		3	Steve STAUNTON	
8	Peter BEARDSLEY	55, 66	25	Tommy JOHNSON	
28	Paul KITSON		9	Dean SAUNDERS	
	Substitutes			*Substitutes*	
30	Mike HOOPER		1	Nigel SPINK	
4	Paul BRACEWELL		10	Dalian ATKINSON †75	
19	Steve WATSON		7	Ray HOUGHTON	

BEFORE		P	W	D	L	F	A	pts	AFTER		P	W	D	L	F	A	pts
3	Newcastle	28	14	9	5	47	30	51	3	Newcastle	29	15	9	5	50	31	54
9	Villa	30	9	11	10	45	42	38	11	Villa	31	9	11	11	46	45	38

FACTFILE

Fourth successive Premiership defeat for Villa by Newcastle and a 12-2 aggregate... The north-east club's biggest crowd of the season... Townsend's first Premiership goal of the season is a 25 yard stunner... a performance that deserved a better result... Beardsley is the difference.

Villa promise hit by Beardsley

Anyone assessing Villa's chances in their remaining fixtures would put this game down as a likely away defeat, so no-one is especially surprised by the outcome.

Newcastle away is not exactly the sort of fixture Villa need after their mid-week Villa Park experience of slumping from 4-1 up to 4-4 in the last 13 minutes.

Slack defending against dead-ball situations, namely one throw-in and two corners, are Brian Little's official reason for Villa's fade-out against Leicester City.

Despite that, he decides against any changes and fields an unchanged team at St James's Park.

A sell-out crowd of 34,637 is crammed into the ground and the pre-match atmosphere is electrifying as the Geordies fill the air with expectancy.

From the start there is every indication of a match worthy of that large crowd and, if anything, Villa have the upper hand in a fine display of attacking football.

"If Villa had gone 2-0 up in the first 20 minutes we could not have complained," Kevin Keegan, the Newcastle manager, is to confess afterwards.

No doubt one of these potential Villa goals Keegan has in mind is full back John Beresford's obvious fourth minute trip on his overlapping counterpart, Gary Charles, which looks every inch a penalty.

To Villa's annoyance and Newcastle's relief the referee Philip Don turns down the justified appeals of travelling supporters.

And worse is to follow in the 31st minute as Villa's admirable opening spell goes unrewarded. Barry Venison, who has not scored in almost three years, fires in a surprise shot from 20 yards which flies out of Mark Bosnich's reach.

A 1-0 deficit is rough justice, indeed, on a confident Villa side who have not been second-best at any stage and the truth of this is underlined five minutes before the interval with a deserved equaliser.

Andy Townsend is the provider by means of an even more spectacular shot than Venison's, a 25-yard left-footed drive for a well-merited half-time 1-1.

Villa have been the more impressive of two good sides in midfield with Ian Taylor churning back and forth and Dwight Yorke showing the capacity to beat defenders with his footwork.

Dean Saunders and Tommy Johnson have blended well as the strike force, using their skill and mobility to turn defenders this way and that, but the second-half is to see a different story unfold.

The opening 20 minutes belong almost exclusively to Peter Beardsley whose two goals settle the game and prove yet again the depth of his individual talent.

In the 55th and 66th minutes he contrives to worm his way into what look like tight corners in front of Villa's goal to push the scoreline out of reach.

"Two bits of Peter Beardsley magic was the difference between the two sides," agrees manager Little. "Up to then I thought that we were just the better team."

Keegan doesn't dispute his rival manager's verdict. "You get dizzy watching the ball between Peter's feet," said the admiring Newcastle boss. "No wonder he mesmerises defenders."

And on Villa, he adds: "I'm a big Ron Atkinson fan and I won't hear anything said against him, but this team of Brian Little's looks very good.

"In the first 20 minutes they did to us what we wanted to do to them."

Saturday 4th March 1995 • Villa Park • 3.00pm

ASTON VILLA 0 BLACKBURN ROVERS 1

Half-time 0-1 • *Attendance* 40,114

Referee Rodger GIFFORD (Llanbradach)

Linesmen J.F. COPELAND and P.A. ROBERTS

Claret Shirts with Blue Stripes, White Shorts		Goals	Blue and White Halved Shirts, Blue Shorts		Goals
13	Mark BOSNICH		1	Tim FLOWERS	
22	Gary CHARLES		20	Henning BERG	
5	Paul McGRATH		5	Colin HENDRY	12
16	Ugo EHIOGU		25	Ian PEARCE	
4	Shaun TEALE		6	Graeme LE SAUX	
18	Dwight YORKE ❑		4	Tim SHERWOOD	
17	Ian TAYLOR		22	Mark ATKINS	
11	Andy TOWNSEND †		7	Stuart RIPLEY	
3	Steve STAUNTON ❑		9	Alan SHEARER	
25	Tommy JOHNSON ❑ ‡		16	Chris SUTTON	
9	Dean SAUNDERS		11	Jason WILCOX	
	Substitutes			*Substitutes*	
1	Nigel SPINK		13	Bobby MIMMS	
7	Ray HOUGHTON †18		10	Mike NEWELL	
19	Graham FENTON ‡75		24	Paul WARHURST	

BEFORE		P	W	D	L	F	A	pts	AFTER		P	W	D	L	F	A	pts
1	Blackburn	30	20	6	4	63	26	66	1	Blackburn	31	21	6	4	64	26	69
11	Villa	31	9	11	11	46	45	38	11	Villa	32	9	11	12	46	46	38

FACTFILE

Pitch passed fit following early morning inspection and snow removal...Villa's best gate of the season to date... Villa denied late 'penalty'... Blackburn stay top but Manchester United close goals gap with Premiership record 9-0 win over Ipswich...

Villa miss out on penalty claims

The visit of Blackburn Rovers, bearing in mind their Premiership record against Villa, prompts the uncomfortable feeling that a daunting 90 minutes lie ahead.

And so it is to prove as a full-house 40,000 sees a game full of action which, realistically, Villa are never going to win and only fleetingly promise to draw.

Because of the requirements of Sky TV next Wednesday's scheduled match against Ron Atkinson's Coventry City has been brought forward 48 hours to Monday night, thus creating a high-pressure three-day spell with six valuable points at stake.

In the match programme for Blackburn's visit, Brian Little readily acknowledges their status as one of the two strongest teams in the Premiership while outlining some of the qualities which have put them there.

Once the action is under way these strengths quickly establish themselves as Villa have to battle hard to contain the well-organised opposition, a task which becomes more demanding after only 11 minutes.

As Stuart Ripley's right win corner swings towards the crowded far side of the goalmouth, central defender Colin Hendry steams in from a deep position to connect with a header which forces the ball through the pack and out of Mark Bosnich's reach.

Hendry is then to become the most commanding figure of the afternoon as Kenny Dalglish's team dig in for a deserved and hard-earned victory.

Although often content to concede space and possession to Villa Blackburn ruggedly keep their goal well-guarded while attacking with all the combined menace of Alan Shearer and Chris Sutton up front.

Bosnich is kept busier than Tim Flowers and Little tells his men at half-time: "We are allowing them to boss us around..."

Little's men get the message OK but their increased aggression brings scant reward as Hendry's tackles and clearances deny much hope of an equaliser.

Before the break Andy Townsend has been withdrawn with a back injury, enforcing Ray Houghton to be sent on as sub to take the wide-right role with the impressive Dwight Yorke moving inside.

By mid-way through the second half it is clear that Tommy Johnson is getting little scope to shine and he is replaced by Graham Fenton.

There is a late surge of hope as Villa pile in for a frantic finale and Flowers gets solidly behind an Ian Taylor drive. Two corners just before the final whistle prompt Bosnich to race upfield and he manages to get in a headed deflection.

This produces a shooting chance for Paul McGrath which strikes Hendry's upraised arm but furious claims for a penalty are rejected by Rodger Gifford who leaves the field to howls of protest from Villa fans.

"They allowed us some space and possession but showed us how to win a football match," concedes Little afterwards.

Dalglish is as downbeat and deadpan as ever as the news comes through that championship rivals Manchester United have beaten Ipswich 9-0. "They only get three points, same as us," he argues with simple logic.

"We were determined rather than spectacular today and there was always the chance that Villa would score."

Paul McGrath - penalty appeal.

Monday 6th March 1995 • Villa Park • 8.00pm

ASTON VILLA 0   COVENTRY CITY 0

Half-time 0-0 • *Attendance* 26,186

Referee Graham POLL (Berkshire)

Linesmen P.J. JOSLIN and M.J. STODDART

Claret Shirts with Blue Stripes, White Shorts	Goals	Sky Blue Shirts, Sky Blue Shorts	Goals
13 Mark BOSNICH		13 Jonathan GOULD	
22 Gary CHARLES		17 Ally PICKERING	
5 Paul McGRATH		2 Brian BORROWS	
16 Ugo EHIOGU ❑		5 David RENNIE	
4 Shaun TEALE ❑		29 David BURROWS	
18 Dwight YORKE		7 Sean FLYNN	
17 Ian TAYLOR		11 Willie BOLAND	
7 Ray HOUGHTON ‡		28 Kevin RICHARDSON ❑	
3 Steve STAUNTON		15 Paul COOK	
25 Tommy JOHNSON †		19 Dion DUBLIN	
9 Dean SAUNDERS		9 Peter NDLOVU	
Substitutes		*Substitutes*	
1 Nigel SPINK		30 John FILAN	
19 Graham FENTON †9 ❑		27 Mike MARSH	
14 Franz CARR ‡79		3 Steve MORGAN	

BEFORE	P	W	D	L	F	A	pts	AFTER	P	W	D	L	F	A	pts
11 Villa	32	9	11	12	46	46	38	10 Villa	33	9	12	12	46	46	39
12 Coventry	31	9	11	11	33	47	38	11 Coventry	32	9	12	11	33	47	39

The Monday Match for SKY TV... Ex-Villans Ron Atkinson and Kevin Richardson make a welcome return... Villa's unbeaten home record against Coventry still stands... Ray Houghton comes in for the injured Houghton... Two games in 48 hours takes its toll on both teams.

TV switch sees bore draw

A potentially embarrassing evening for Aston Villa as Sky TV cameras trace every step of Ron Atkinson's return, proves, in reality, to be something of a non-event.

Having been brought forward 48 hours from its scheduled slot on Wednesday evening and given an 8pm kick-off to satisfy Sky's programming, the actual match is to meander its way untidily to a sterile stalemate.

Just how badly the players' legs and appetites have been undermined by the loss of two days recovery time is impossible to judge, but the end-product is unsatisfactory for all concerned.

Brian Little has forecast in his match programme notes that the former Villa manager, dismissed three months earlier, will receive a warm 'welcome back' from fans, and so it proves.

Then, as one writer put it 'after the hype, the tripe'...

As the match unfolds it increasingly emerges that Atkinson's Sky Blues are a highly colourless collection, not matching their new boss's charisma and seemingly slightly over-awed by the occasion.

Unfortunately Villa are unable to make capital of the opposition's shortcomings in a fragmented display which lacks any continuity of playing style.

The home team's cause is not helped when, as early as the third minute, Tommy Johnson pulls a hamstring as he cleverly by-passes David Rennie to send a shot searing a fraction high.

Johnson is clearly in difficulties and is replaced within minutes by Graham Fenton.

Villa attempt to force the pace by moving the ball forward quickly and a Dwight Yorke effort hits the bar and Dean Saunders turns a shot wide.

Atkinson's knowledge of Villa has ensured that Steve Staunton's threat is quickly blocked off and after an uninspired first-half there is no sign of a lift in the second.

Jonathan Gould blocks a Yorke shot while Ugo Ehiogu heads over from a corner and Ray Houghton fires a long shot off target.

Coventry's nondescript efforts in attack, as ex-Villa man Kevin Richardson is as busy as ever in their midfield, are dealt with routinely as Paul McGrath reveals his undoubted class again and again.

"Is there anything to talk about," asks Brian Little with a wry smile as he joins the press afterwards.

"There were some pleasing things about our performance in terms of keeping a clean sheet and earning a point, but I can't remember us making any wide-open chances or missing any."

When Big Ron takes his press conference place his wise-cracking display is more entertaining than that of his team. But by now the general feeling is of relief that a mediocre affair is out of the way.

From Villa's point of view a potential banana skin had been avoided and, like Brian Little's even more controversial return to Filbert Street, Atkinson's Villa connection will never again upstage the actual game as the main event.

Together again – with Coventry City

Saturday 18th March 1995 • Villa Park • 3.00pm

ASTON VILLA 0 WEST HAM UNITED 2

Half-time 0-1 • *Attendance* 28,682

Referee Martin BODENHAM (East Looe)
Linesmen R. GOULD and D.C. RICHARDS

Claret Shirts with Blue Stripes, White Shorts		Goals	White Shirts with Claret Sleeves, Claret Shorts		Goals
13	Mark BOSNICH		1	Ludek MIKLOSKO	
22	Gary CHARLES		2	Tim BREACKER	
5	Paul McGRATH		4	Steve POTTS	
4	Shaun TEALE		8	Marc RIEPER	
2	Alan WRIGHT		3	Julian DICKS	
18	Dwight YORKE ‡		6	Martin ALLEN	
17	Ian TAYLOR		10	John MONCUR	11
11	Andy TOWNSEND		7	Ian BISHOP	
3	Steve STAUNTON		11	Matthew HOLMES †	
25	Tommy JOHNSON †		27	Tony COTTEE	
9	Dean SAUNDERS		26	Don HUTCHISON ‡	49
	Substitutes			*Substitutes*	
1	Nigel SPINK		30	Les SEALEY	
7	Ray HOUGHTON †ht		12	Keith ROWLAND †62	
16	Ugo EHIOGU ‡70		25	Jeroen BOERE ‡79	

BEFORE		P	W	D	L	F	A	pts	AFTER		P	W	D	L	F	A	pts
14	Villa	33	9	12	12	46	46	39	15	Villa	34	9	12	13	46	48	39
19	West Ham	33	9	7	17	31	44	34	18	West Ham	34	10	7	17	33	44	37

Ugo Ehiogu makes way for debut maker Alan Wright, Villa's recent £900,000 signing from Blackburn Rovers... A five-game run without a win... Three successive games without scoring a goal... Ray Houghton's final appearance in a Villa shirt.

Relegation fears return again

A critically important fixture for Villa arrives at the end of an unpleasant week for football when John Fashanu has been among five people questioned by police in connection with match-fixing allegations.

Fashanu, like the other four, including goalkeepers Bruce Grobbelaar (Southampton) and Hans Segers (Wimbledon) have been released without charge but the atmosphere in the game is uneasy.

Fashanu attends the game as a spectator amid media reports that his career could be over when he sees a specialist about his serious knee ligament damage three weeks hence.

Now the nightmare scenario for Villa, after a run of two draws and two defeats, is to lose at home to a team currently in the bottom four.

Such a prospect seemed unthinkable in the run-up to West Ham's visit, but as the downbeat 90-minute display unfolds it becomes an unpalatable fact.

The tempting reward for an emphatic, wholehearted display is self-evident in the formation of the bottom half of the Premiership.

Likewise, the penalty for failure stares back grimly from the table afterwards with Villa right back in the emotional spin drier instead of sitting in comparative mid-league safety.

Brian Little introduces his new £900,000 full-back Alan Wright, signed from Blackburn Rovers' reserves, and to make way for him creates a pre-match surprise by consigning Ugo Ehiogu to the subs bench.

Sadly for the manager things simply do not work out in what he himself describes afterwards as the team's poorest display of the 22 since he took control.

Things look ominous as early as the 11th minutes when a 25-yard strike from John Moncur pierces the defence and beats Mark Bosnich.

"The last thing we needed was to concede an early goal," says Little afterwards. "When we did we ran out of ideas."

This shortage of ideas sees Villa unable to make a telling response, as the crowd's obvious dissatisfaction spreads and the players display a clear lack of confidence.

Tommy Johnson's inability to make an impact up front makes him a target of supporters' frustration and, at half time, he is replaced Ray Houghton.

This is greeted by a similar setback to that suffered early in the first half when a poor Shaun Teale defensive clearance leads to Moncur setting up a far-post header for Hammers' second goal, by Don Hutchison.

In attack Villa are without conviction and are limited to a couple of close shots by Dean Saunders and a promising effort by Gary Charles which Ludo Miklosko does well to keep out.

Little makes a second substitution, sending on Ehiogu as a makeshift attacker in place of Dwight Yorke and though given a warm reception from the fans his energetic efforts do not bring the desired result.

After the disturbing scoreline is completed the Villa manager does not attempt to hide from the truth. "We have been sucked right back into trouble," he acknowledges. "It all started the night we gave away a 4-1 lead to Leicester.

"The honeymoon period is over for myself and I have to work as hard as the players to put it right."

Alan Wright – Villa debut

Saturday 1st April 1995 • Portman Road • 3.00pm

IPSWICH TOWN 0 ASTON VILLA 1

Half-time 0-0 • *Attendance* 16,710

Referee Joe WORRALL (Warrington)
Linesmen S.L. GAGEN and P.R. SHARP

Blue Shirts, Blue and White Shorts	Goals	Claret Shirts with Blue Stripes, White Shorts	Goals
1 Craig FORREST		1 Mark BOSNICH	
19 Frank YALLOP		16 Ugo EHIOGU	
5 John WARK		5 Paul McGRATH	
16 Chris SWAILES	(og 90)	4 Shaun TEALE	
3 Neil THOMPSON		22 Gary CHARLES	
17 Simon MILTON		17 Ian TAYLOR	
7 Geraint WILLIAMS		11 Andy TOWNSEND	
12 Claus THOMSEN		3 Steve STAUNTON	
21 Stuart SLATER		2 Alan WRIGHT	
33 Alex MATHIE		10 Dalian ATKINSON ‡	
10 Ian MARSHALL		9 Dean SAUNDERS †	
Substitutes		*Substitutes*	
13 Clive BAKER		1 Nigel SPINK	
11 Lee CHAPMAN		18 Dwight YORKE †45	
8 Gavin JOHNSON		19 Graham FENTON ‡75	

BEFORE		P	W	D	L	F	A	pts	AFTER		P	W	D	L	F	A	pts
16	Villa	34	9	12	13	46	48	39	13	Villa	35	10	12	13	47	48	42
21	Ipswich	33	6	5	22	31	75	23	21	Ipswich	34	6	5	23	31	76	23

FACTFILE

First of three successive away games after fixture shuffle... Villa left with full month without a home game... Own goal ends Villa's poor run... Dalian Atkinson's low-key come-back... Back injury forces Dean Saunders off at half-time... Ipswich go five consecutive games without scoring.

A little luck and a lot of relief

After a worrying sequence of five games without a win, this Portman Road visit coincides with the brink of the relegation chasm drawing dangerously close again.

Brian Little is torn between two contrasting lines of thought and if he follows the wrong one, and loses again, the effect on morale could be devastating.

Instinctively Little would go for an attacking policy as he repeatedly emphasised after replacing Ron Atkinson last November.

Such positive thought is fine when it works. But 13 points dropped from the last 15 has brought a sharp change in priorities.

With Tommy Johnson still out and Dean Saunders labouring under a back injury sustained when he scored for Wales against Bulgaria in mid-week the Villa manager opts for a safety-first policy and a five-man back line.

Dalian Atkinson, still insisting he's looking for a move abroad at the end of the season, returns after four months out through injury and joins Saunders up front.

But the supply to the front men is limited by a concentration on not conceding goals to a team below them in the Premiership.

The end-product is a tense, nervy and non-productive game though, fractionally, Villa do look the more likely of two sterile teams to sneak the one goal they both feel would be enough.

Atkinson, badly short of match fitness and sharpness, gets the best scoring chance during a tedious first half but he heads a nicely-weighted right wing centre by Saunders straight at the keeper.

At half-time Saunders has to succumb to his back problem, allowing Dwight Yorke on as sub while, later, Graham Fenton replaces Atkinson whose shortage of fitness is becoming more obvious.

The changes bring no improvement in attack and the major consolation for Little is that his packed defence is working to such perfection that almost an hour elapses before Mark Bosnich has his first shot to save.

Shaun Teale is particularly outstanding with his crisp tackles on any Ipswich forward threatening to break through the barrier. The reward for this looks to be the slender offering of a single point while extending the depressing run to six games without a win.

Then, football's equivalent of the huge finger of fortune which, according to TV commercials, sorts out a lottery millionaire each Saturday night points firmly at Villa.

A few seconds before the final whistle Gary Charles loops the ball into the goal area where defender Chris Swailes, on his Ipswich debut, heads the ball past goalkeeper Craig Forrest for an embarrassing own goal.

"Sometimes you need a lucky break and we got one today," confesses Little. "We now need eight points from the last seven games and I don't mind how we get them.

"I make no apologies for our tactics. We did not want to give anything away and we're happy to end the disappointing run we've just gone through."

As the other results come in it emerges that the extra two points have hauled Villa an extra four places up the table and five points clear of 19th position.

A lucky break, indeed...

**Dean Saunders –
back injury**

Tuesday 4th April 1995 • Selhurst Park • 7.45pm

CRYSTAL PALACE 0 ASTON VILLA 0

Half-time 0-0 • Attendance 12,606

Referee Keith COOPER (Pontypridd)

Linesmen W.J. NORBURY and M. STOBBART

Red Shirts with Blue Stripes, Red Shorts	Goals	Green, Black and Red Striped Shirts, Black Shorts	Goals
1 Nigel MARTYN		1 Mark BOSNICH	
22 Darren PATTERSON		22 Gary CHARLES	
14 Richard SHAW		16 Ugo EHIOGU	
5 Eric YOUNG †		5 Paul McGRATH	
6 Chris COLEMAN		4 Shaun TEALE	
20 Ray HOUGHTON		2 Alan WRIGHT	
4 Gareth SOUTHGATE		17 Ian TAYLOR	
16 Darren PITCHER		11 Andy TOWNSEND ❏	
11 John SALAKO		3 Steve STAUNTON †	
10 Bruce DYER ‡		10 Dalian ATKINSON ❏	
9 Chris ARMSTRONG		18 Dwight YORKE	
Substitutes		*Substitutes*	
19 Rhys WILMOT		1 Nigel SPINK	
3 Dean GORDON †52		19 Graham FENTON †75 ❏	
21 Ian COX ‡63		14 Franz CARR	

BEFORE	P	W	D	L	F	A	pts	AFTER	P	W	D	L	F	A	pts
13 Villa	35	10	12	13	47	48	42	11 Villa	36	10	13	13	47	48	43
19 Palace	33	9	10	14	25	35	37	19 Palace	34	9	11	14	25	35	38

FACTFILE

A valuable point towards safety... but Villa fail to score in last five league visits to Selhurst Park... Dean Saunders kept out with flu virus... Ray Houghton plays second game for Palace following recent transfer from Villa... Iain Dowie serves last of two-game suspension... Dalian Atkinson's 'goal' claim turned down.

'Perfect' goal is disallowed

In football, as in life, you sometimes get less than you deserve. This proves to be the case at Selhurst Park where, in the past, Villa's punishment has outstripped their deficiencies.

South London is not a happy hunting ground. This time there is never to be a danger of the kind of embarrassing slump suffered there on previous visits. But, equally, justified rewards for a far superior attacking display are not to be forthcoming.

Another three points, to add to those earned by a lucky late winner at Portman Road on Saturday, would provide another most welcome leg up the league. Not to be, it transpires.

An attacking change has been forced by the absence of Dean Saunders who, it emerges, left the field on Saturday suffering from a sickness bug, not his back injury, from which he has not recovered.

Gary Charles has also been affected by a similar ailment but has recovered in time to play in the same five-man defensive set-up as employed against Ipswich.

Unappealing though it may sound, Brian Little's priority has to be to a continued policy of giving nothing away, while painstakingly pursuing that 50-points target.

Palace, themselves more deeply in distress than Villa, have a Villa Park date against Manchester United on Sunday in the FA Cup semi-final – though this appears not to affect their wholehearted approach to the game.

The opening 20 minutes are so full of tension, however, that a rather uneventful stalemate begins to take shape. Then Steve Staunton delivers one of those explosive left-footed crosses for Dalian Atkinson to connect with a dynamic header.

Goalkeeper Nigel Martyn is powerless to intervene as the shot strikes the back of the bar, where it is connected to the net, and rebounds down for what even the most jaundiced of Palace fans believes is a goal.

Remarkably, however, as local radio reporters are proclaiming Villa's lead or bemoaning Palace's deficit, depending on their region, referee Keith Cooper waves play on.

Atkinson and Dwight Yorke follow up with menacing attacks as Villa swallow their disappointment but they fail to break through, just as speedsters Chris Armstrong and Bruce Dyer are unable to unhinge Villa's three centre-backs at the other end.

Ian Taylor is the next Villa forward to provide a fleeting glimpse of those three coveted Premiership points but his shot is saved by Martyn who is lucky, indeed, when a Yorke drive deflects to safety off his arm.

Right to the last gasp Villa look liable to conjure that one goal they need. But the adventurous Taylor, blessed with the best chance of the game as a Charles pass deceives Palace's offside trap, makes a mess of his intended shot and the last chance has been squandered.

Palace, apart from a Gareth Southgate effort which thumps against Mark Bosnich's upright have never threatened and a useful point is tucked away with the lingering feeling that it ought to have been three.

"I thought we played well," said Little with justification. "We weren't overly defensive. In fact at times we were very attack-minded."

**Ray Houghton –
a change of colours**

Saturday 15th April 1995 • Stamford Bridge • 3.00pm

CHELSEA 1 ASTON VILLA 0

Half-time 1-0 • Attendance 17,015

Referee Keith BURGE (Tonypandy)

Linesmen M.L. SHORT and M. TINGEY

Royal Blue Shirts, Royal Blue Shorts		Goals	Claret Shirts with Blue Stripes, White Shorts		Goals
1	Dmitri KHARINE		1	Mark BOSNICH	
2	Steve CLARKE		17	Ian TAYLOR	
4	Jakob KJELDBJERG		16	Ugo EHIOGU	
5	Erland JOHNSEN †		5	Paul McGRATH ❑	
6	Frank SINCLAIR		4	Shaun TEALE	
21	David ROCASTLE		18	Dwight YORKE	
25	David LEE		11	Andy TOWNSEND	
17	Nigel SPACKMAN		3	Steve STAUNTON	
10	Gavin PEACOCK		2	Alan WRIGHT ‡	
9	Mark STEIN ‡	41	9	Dean SAUNDERS	
8	Paul FURLONG		10	Dalian ATKINSON †	
Substitutes			*Substitutes*		
13	Kevin HITCHCOCK		1	Nigel SPINK	
27	Gareth HALL †27		25	Tommy JOHNSON †ht	
7	John SPENCER ‡81		19	Graham FENTON ‡75	

BEFORE		P	W	D	L	F	A	pts	AFTER		P	W	D	L	F	A	pts
12	Villa	36	10	13	13	47	48	43	14	Chelsea	37	11	12	14	43	50	45
16	Chelsea	36	10	12	14	42	50	42	16	Villa	37	10	13	14	47	49	43

Disappointing start to the Easter programme... form goes out of the window in a nervy game at the Bridge... Gary Charles a late illness victim... Staunton the driving force... crucial Saunders miss... Wright off – on a stretcher... Villa drop four places.

FACTFILE

Villa's worries continue

The two-fixture Easter week-end kicks-off with Villa almost desperate to take at least four points out of six as up to a dozen clubs fear for their future.

This visit to Stamford Bridge has taken on a new urgency as a result of Good Friday fixtures staged partially to satisfy Sky TV's demands.

Everton and Manchester City have beaten Newcastle and Liverpool respectively while Crystal Palace have drawn at home with Spurs. Little is going Villa's way and it's getting worse...

The mood of moderate optimism after taking four points from two away games is replaced by one of foreboding with defeat by Chelsea sucking Villa deeper into the relegation whirlpool and fixtures running out.

Brian Little again presents his three centre-back plan and a five-man midfield in which the wide players can be full-backs or wingers as the situation dictates. Ian taylor is on the right of midfield having replaced Gary Charles who has been forced to cry off through a virus infection.

Villa's tactics, and the pressure on both clubs to squeeze out precious points by whatever means suggest a game of high tension and low classical entertainment. So it is to prove.

In the Daily Telegraph Bryon Butler describes the action as 'a snarling combat' with two sides making each other 'suffer horribly in the name of sport' and claims that Stamford Bridge was 'full of pain'.

He did, however, con-cede that, with so much at stake and both sides committed to all-out effort, the script became exciting, even though it contained a disturbing conclusion for Villa.

The ultimate pain, that of defeat, was to be theirs as Southampton, Coventry and Arsenal join Chelsea in taking three points on a crucial Easter Saturday and the Premiership table takes on a sombre look to claret-and-blue eyes.

Expert analysis is not required to fathom the reasons. In the previous five games the only Villa goal has been the own goal at Ipswich and this trend continues.

Just before half-time the nimble and lethal Mark Stein cleverly pierces through Villa's defence to beat Mark Bosnich and, given Villa's current attacking deficiencies, it proves to be the match-winner.

Dean Saunders has been presented with a similar break to the one forged by Stein but misses his target, a typical example of the kind of lost opportunity which has constantly dragged the side down.

Steve Staunton works feverishly in a second-half Villa onslaught in search of an equaliser, but the necessary accuracy is never present in Villa's attacks and goalkeeper Dmitri Kharine deals capably with whatever flak comes his way.

Little withdraws the ineffective Dalian Atkinson to send Tommy Johnson on (75mins) and eight minutes from time the excellent Alan Wright is stretchered off following a dubious challenge from David Rocastle.

The final whistle is greeted by outpourings of relief from the home crowd... and a worried silence among the bulk of Villa sympathisers.

Alan Wright – carried off on a stretcher

Monday 17th April 1995 • Villa Park • 3.00pm

ASTON VILLA 0 ARSENAL 4

Half-time 0-2 • *Attendance* 32,005

Referee Kelvin MORTON (Bury St Edmunds)

Linesmen S.R. BRAND and M.R. SIMS

Claret Shirts with Blue Stripes, White Shorts	Goals	Red and White Shirts, White Shorts	Goals
1 Mark BOSNICH		1 David SEAMAN	
16 Ugo EHIOGU		2 Lee DIXON	
5 Paul McGRATH ❏		6 Tony ADAMS	
4 Shaun TEALE		12 Steve BOULD ❏	
3 Steve STAUNTON ❏		3 Nigel WINTERBURN	
10 Dalian ATKINSON		23 Ray PARLOUR †	
17 Ian TAYLOR		15 Stefan SCHWARZ ❏	
11 Andy TOWNSEND ❏		14 Martin KEOWN	
18 Dwight YORKE		10 Paul MERSON	
25 Tommy JOHNSON		16 John HARTSON	31, 87
9 Dean SAUNDERS		8 Ian WRIGHT ‡	33, pen 72

Substitutes	*Substitutes*
1 Nigel SPINK	13 Vince BARTRAM
22 Gary CHARLES	18 David HILLIER †75
19 Graham FENTON	31 Chris KIWOMYA ‡81

BEFORE		P	W	D	L	F	A	pts	AFTER		P	W	D	L	F	A	pts
10	Arsenal	38	12	10	16	46	46	46	10	Arsenal	39	13	10	16	50	46	49
16	Villa	37	10	13	14	47	49	43	16	Villa	38	10	13	15	47	53	43

FACTFILE

Injury sustained in previous match keeps out Alan Wright... They couldn't have picked a better time to play Arsenal but – Villa's heaviest home defeat in four years... Dean Saunders misses penalty... Wright shows how its done... seventh consecutive match a Villa player fails to score...

Gunners fire four past Villa

Fate in its most spiteful mood could not have fashioned a Bank Holiday Monday of more depressing dimensions than this as Villa's precarious position gets worse on a day it was meant to get better.

The large Easter gathering of the Villa faithful is looking for a fitting celebration of the first home game for a month with three points to re-balance the books after Saturday's defeat at Stamford Bridge. It proves a forlorn hope...

Despite having their European date against Sampdoria ahead Gunners' commitment to the Premiership is not being undermined, as illustrated in Saturday's 4-1 home win over Ipswich.

Much to Villa's discomfort the Highbury club also continues to display admirable resolve in surviving the controversy of George Graham's dismissal.

In short, Arsenal's game reveals itself to be in sound shape – in sharp contrast to Brian Little's team which is uncertain and lacking in confidence.

The foundation of Villa's destruction is put down with two first-half goals in a minute after half-an-hour's undistinguished play by Villa. For the first, John Hartson applies the finishing touch to a neat and tidy move involving Ian Wright and Paul Merson.

Before the gloom of that setback has dispersed, an Ian Wright breakaway and shot sees the ball slither agonisingly under Mark Bosnich's body for a half-time 0-2.

In the absence of injured Alan Wright Little has reverted to a more orthodox formation with Ugo Ehiogu at right back and Dalian Atkinson on the right of the attack.

A positive attacking performance is needed but it is simply not there. Promising moves are virtually non-existent and Villa are never going to overturn that deficit, even with the aid of a 60th minute penalty for a Steve Bould infringement on Ian Taylor.

Dean Saunders' spot kick is read correctly by David Seaman, the hero-to-be of Arsenal's European shoot-out against the Italians, for a save which ends any hope Villa might have had.

"When the penalty was missed the heads dropped and our discipline went," confirmed Little.

The contrast between the two sides is glaringly demonstrated after 76 minutes when it is the visitors' turn for a free shot from 12 yards after a foul tackle by Paul McGrath on Wright.

Placing a penalty out of the goalkeeper's reach is easier when the striker is in search of a bonus rather than a life-or-death necessity.

This much becomes clear as the England striker takes a quick, easy stride and dispatches his shot wide of Bosnich to send discontent seething through the claret-and-blue hordes.

By the time Hartson knocks in his second and Gunners' fourth three minutes from time the 'lack of discipline' Little talked of is self-evident in the defensive ranks.

"Time is running out but it has not run out," says Little in a sombre post-match press conference. "Two months ago I couldn't do anything wrong and picked up an award for winning football matches.

"In the last eight games I can't pick a team that can win a game of football." There is now a 12-day gap before playing Leeds, away. A very worrying 12 days, indeed...

Ugo Ehiogu – played as full-back.

Saturday 29th April 1995 • Elland Road • 3.00pm

LEEDS UNITED 1 ASTON VILLA 0

Half-time 0-0 • Attendance 32,955

Referee David ELLERAY (Harrow)
Linesmen A. BATES and A.R. LEAKE

White Shirts, White Shorts	Goals	Claret Shirts with Blue Stripes, White Shorts	Goals
1 John LUKIC		13 Mark BOSNICH ❑ ■	
2 Gary KELLY		22 Gary CHARLES	
6 David WEATHERALL ❑		16 Ugo EHIOGU	
12 John PEMBERTON		5 Paul McGRATH	
3 Tony DORIGO		4 Shaun TEALE	
8 Rod WALLACE		2 Alan WRIGHT	
4 Carlton PALMER ❑	90	9 Dean SAUNDERS	
10 Gary McALLISTER		17 Ian TAYLOR	
11 Gary SPEED		11 Andy TOWNSEND †	
9 Brian DEANE ❑		3 Steve STAUNTON	
21 Anthony YEBOAH		18 Dwight YORKE ‡	
Substitutes		*Substitutes*	
13 Mark BEENEY		1 Nigel SPINK ‡87	
15 Nigel WORTHINGTON		19 Graham FENTON †84	
19 Noel WHELAN		25 Tommy JOHNSON	

BEFORE	P	W	D	L	F	A	pts	AFTER	P	W	D	L	F	A	pts
6 Leeds	38	17	12	10	52	35	63	6 Leeds	39	18	12	10	53	35	66
16 Villa	38	10	13	15	47	53	43	17 Villa	39	10	13	16	47	54	43

FACTFILE

The goal drought continues – just one in eight games... Mark Bosnich sent off... and will be suspended for last game of season away to Norwich... just one defeat in 10 games for Leeds who steal points in injury time... Fellow strugglers Crystal Palace and Norwich City both loose... but West Ham beat Blackburn next day.

Late goal beats Villa again

If ever there could be an example of how fate can twist the knife to inflict yet more pain this Elland Road defeat is the ultimate.

With one, perhaps life-saving point, there frustratingly in Villa's grasp with the full 90 minutes virtually elapsed, it is suddenly and controversially snatched away in agonising fashion almost on the final whistle.

"Villa were magnificent..." says Leeds boss Howard Wilkinson in tribute to a battling Villa display which has denied his side a break-through until their final, fortunate throw of the dice.

In the event it is scant consolation to a Villa side now with only three games remaining to eke out enough points to keep their noses ahead of Crystal Palace and Norwich.

With points rather than quality of performance the one over-riding priority Brian Little fields a 5-4-1 formation with Dwight Yorke a lone raider, Dean Saunders in a five-man midfield and Tommy Johnson on the bench.

Playing with rugged determination and no mean cohesive skill Villa are the equal of high-flying Leeds until those fateful last few seconds. The foundation of defeat is put down just before the break when Mark Bosnich, who has had virtualy nothing to do, is booked for time-wasting as the crowd attract the referee's attention to his delaying tactics.

"Only five seconds before half-time," for heaven's sake," groans Little afterwards in protest at the referee's strict adherence to the letter of the law.

Villa continue to nullify all Leeds' best efforts in the second half with Shaun Teale winning everything in the air and on the ground and Ian Taylor motoring back and forth non-stop making a contribution at each end.

The one disturbing feature of the performance is that, while Leeds' attack is not allowed to function effectively, Villa create few scoring chances either, with the industrious Yorke well covered by the home defence.

By the final whistle Villa have gone through a 12-hour spell of football in which their only goal has been the own goal for victory at Portman Road. To dry up so dramatically at such a time is worrying, indeed.

In contrast other teams, such as Manchester City and West Ham have clawed their way in positive fashion towards safety.

The fatal blows for Villa are delivered just when a thoroughly well-deserved draw is looming. With two minutes to go Bosnich pushes Carlton Palmer in the chest after the Leeds man has fouled Teale.

His second caution for the push means a red card and substitute Nigel Spink is 'between the sticks' when Palmer's unstoppable shot leaves Villa on their knees.

"We're not blaming anyone," adds Little. "Bozzie was unlucky. It was the sort of push you see go unpunished all of the time. We played very well today, and got everything right except the result."

Mark Bosnich – sent off late in the game.

Wednesday 3rd May 1995 • Villa Park • 7.45pm

ASTON VILLA 1 MANCHESTER CITY 1

Half-time 1-0 • *Attendance* 30,133

Referee Steven LODGE (Barnsley)

Linesmen D.C. MADGWICK and A. STREETS

Claret Shirts with Blue Stripes, White Shorts		Goals	Light Blue Shirts, Light Blue Shorts		Goals
1	Mark BOSNICH		33	John BURRIDGE ❑	
22	Gary CHARLES		22	Richard EDGHILL	
16	Ugo EHIOGU ❑	9	5	Keith CURLE	
5	Paul McGRATH		15	Alan KERNAGHAN	
4	Shaun TEALE ❑		3	Terry PHELAN †	
2	Alan WRIGHT		16	Nicky SUMMERBEE	
17	Ian TAYLOR ❑		10	Gary FLITCROFT	
11	Andy TOWNSEND		19	Fitzroy SIMPSON	
3	Steve STAUNTON ❑		8	Paul WALSH	
18	Dwight YORKE		9	Niall QUINN	
9	Dean SAUNDERS		28	Uwe RÖSLER ‡	63
Substitutes			*Substitutes*		
1	Nigel SPINK		13	Martyn MARGETSON	
19	Graham FENTON		11	Peter BEAGRIE †ht	
25	Tommy JOHNSON		4	Maurizio GAUDINO ‡80	

BEFORE	P	W	D	L	F	A	pts	AFTER	P	W	D	L	F	A	pts
13 City	39	12	12	15	50	59	48	13 City	40	12	13	15	51	60	49
18 Villa	39	10	13	16	47	54	43	18 Villa	40	10	14	16	48	55	44

FACTFILE

Penultimate home game... Villa Park bathed in sunshine... a 30,000 plus crowd... its all set up for a heroic performance... plenty of effort, but little to show for it... Ugo takes a hand in the goal-scoring stakes... All to no avail... one bright spot – Palace lose at the Den.

Villa on top but point dropped

An early taste of summer with temperatures in the seventies is unable to put much sunshine into Villa's life as the relegation clouds continue to threaten.

The last two home games of the troubled campaign, in the space of four days, ought to offer the opportunity of six status-saving points to take the ultimate trauma out of the last-day trip to Norwich.

Unfortunately recent results do not inspire a belief that this will be the case and, by the end of a hard-working 90 minutes, such doubts are justified.

A point is welcome enough but, with Crystal Palace losing at Southampton, the chance of opening up a four-point safety margin slips away.

On a balmy spring evening the crowd tops 30,000 and, as the teams appear on the field, Land of Hope and Glory, echoes from the public address. Inspiring stuff, though it will suffice if hope can be realised. Glory will have to wait...

Every effort is made by the supporters to create an atmosphere of optimism and the players respond with a positive and encouraging opening 45 minutes.

The first Villa goal at Villa Park since the 4-4 draw with Leicester is scored by Ugo Ehiogu in the 10th minute with a suspicion of hand-ball as he goes for the kill.

Steve Staunton signals that his corner from the right, at the North Stand end, will be a short one. Dwight Yorke nips from centre goal and plays it back to the Irish defender who whips it into the goalmouth.

Shaun Teale deflects the ball with a header on the right side of the goal and Ugo goes for it, and connects, towards the far post and the ground erupts as it crosses the line.

Forty-three-year-old John Burridge, who played in Villa's goal 20-years earlier, is unable to keep it out but complains vehemently that the Villa goalscorer has handled.

Burridge is then bombarded with first-half shots by Yorke, Saunders and Staunton and defies his years of service to 16 clubs to deal competently with them all.

At this stage Villa appear to be on the way to that precious victory, with Niall Quinn kept quiet by the three centre halves and the darting Paul Walsh providing the main threat.

Predictably, however, City raise their own game after the break and Villa's nerve-ends begin to show through. Eighteen minutes into a tense and uncertain second-half when defensively Villa are made to look uneasy, the almost inevitable equaliser arrives.

Quinn evades a tackle by Teale and crosses from the right for Uwe Rösler to jab in from close range with Mark Bosnich caught off-balance by the centre.

There is a spate of bookings, a number of City scoring chances, a super save by Bosnich from substitute Peter Beagrie and a feeling of relief at the end that, one point, which might have been three or none, is safe.

"The commitment is fine at the moment and a point is better than nothing but we do need that win from somewhere," says Brian Little. Indeed. Desperately...

Ugo Ehiogu – put Villa into an early lead.

Saturday 6th May 1995 • Villa Park • 3.00pm

ASTON VILLA 2 LIVERPOOL 0

Half-time 2-0 • *Attendance* 40,154

Referee Robert HART (Darlington)

Linesmen R. GOULD and D.C. RICHARDS

Claret Shirts with Blue Stripes, White Shorts		Goals	Green Shirts, Green Shorts		Goals
1	Mark BOSNICH		1	David JAMES	
22	Gary CHARLES		12	John SCALES	
16	Ugo EHIOGU		5	Mark WRIGHT	
5	Paul McGRATH		22	Steve HARKNESS	
4	Shaun TEALE		16	Michael THOMAS	
2	Alan WRIGHT		15	Jamie REDKNAPP	
17	Ian TAYLOR		10	John BARNES	
11	Andy TOWNSEND ❏		11	Mark WALTERS ‡	
3	Steve STAUNTON †		17	Steve McMANAMAN	
18	Dwight YORKE	25, 35	23	Robbie FOWLER	
9	Dean SAUNDERS		9	Ian RUSH †	
	Substitutes			*Substitutes*	
1	Nigel SPINK		26	Tony WARNER	
19	Graham FENTON †75		7	Nigel CLOUGH †64	
25	Tommy JOHNSON		21	Dominic MATTEO ‡75	

BEFORE		P	W	D	L	F	A	pts	AFTER		P	W	D	L	F	A	pts
4	Liverpool	39	20	11	8	63	31	71	4	Liverpool	40	20	11	9	63	33	71
18	Villa	40	10	14	16	48	55	44	15	Villa	41	11	14	16	50	55	47

FACTFILE

Its do-or-die time for Villa in the summer sunshine... Dwight delivers the goods... another 40,000 plus crowd roars Villa on to victory... Liverpool never allowed to get going... Streaker comes on to show them the way to goal... Villa move up three places and things look slightly healthier.

Double Dwight puts it right

With just one more match, at Norwich in eight days time, to follow this final home game, the scoreline says it all in terms of what this heat-wave Saturday was about.

Brian Little sends his well-motivated team out with the stark message that only a win will do as the 'four-down' situation at the bottom reaches its 'pressure-cooker' last nine days.

Liverpool, in good form recently, look hardly the team you would want to face in such life-or-death circumstances but memories of a year ago inspire a dash of added encouragement.

In that final game of 1993-94, when the Holte End was used for the last time as a standing terrace, Dwight Yorke conjured two goals in the second half for a 2-1 win.

No-one seriously expects a re-run of that desirable state of affairs, yet there proves to be a revised version of it before half-time.

Little fields the same team that dropped two points to Manchester City in mid-week but looks for more attacking aggression through the 90 minutes rather than in the firt-half only.

Fired by the urgent need of those three points Villa, on a scorching hot day and in front of a full-house 40,000 gate, take charge of the game and never let go.

This time Yorke's two 'action replay' goals arrive in an eleven-minute spell mid-way through the first half.

An in-swinging Steve Staunton corner creates havoc in front of the Liverpool goal and goalkeeper David James finds his route to possession

blocked by the towering bulk of Ugo Ehiogu.

In that split-second of uncertainty Yorke is moving in sharply to send his header into the net. Liverpool complain that their goalkeeper was impeded but to no avail and while still burning at what they see as the injustice of it all a far more determined Villa make it 2-0.

This time Dean Saunders is the supplier for Yorke to pick his run and his spot to perfection for a 2-0 lead which is rarely to be threatened.

The West Indian is now at full-throttle having been blessed with fewer goals than he deserved throughout a difficult season. In the second half, searching for a hat-trick, he thunders a shot against the Liverpool crossbar.

In return the Anfield club, with a UEFA Cup place already achieved via their Coca-Cola Cup Final win over Bolton and Premiership position relatively unimportant, muster only a scoring attempt by Steve McManaman which Mark Bosnich collects without difficulty.

The appearance of a male streaker, who is duly arrested for his eccentricity, enlivens what has become a one-sided, non-contest which leaves Liverpool manager Roy Evans to offer his travelling contingent an embarrassed apology.

"We were on our holidays," he said. "The biggest losers were the fans. We should have signed the streaker... it was the most movement we saw all afternoon."

From a 'lofty' 15th position in the table Villa's Premiership position now looks a touch rosier in the late afternoon sunshine.

Dwight Yorke – another double strike against Liverpool.

Sunday 14th May 1995 • Carrow Road • 4.00pm

NORWICH CITY 1   ASTON VILLA 1

Half-time 0-1 • Attendance 19,374

Referee K. COOPER (Pontypridd)

Linesmen P.A. ELWICK and W.M. JORDAN

Yellow Shirts with Green Trim, Green Shorts		Goals	Claret Shirts with Blue Stripes, White Shorts		Goals
24	Andy MARSHALL		1	Nigel SPINK	
2	Mark BOWEN		22	Gary CHARLES	
4	Ian CROOK		2	Alan WRIGHT	
5	Jon NEWSOME		3	Steve STAUNTON	7
16	Carl BRADSHAW		4	Shaun TEALE	
10	John POLSTON ❏		5	Paul McGRATH	
15	Daryl SUTCH		16	Ugo EHIOGU	
7	Ashley WARD		19	Graham FENTON	
18	Robert ULLATHORNE		9	Dean SAUNDERS	
26	Ade AKINBIYI		18	Dwight YORKE	
11	Jeremy GOSS	56	11	Andy TOWNSEND	
	Substitutes			*Substitutes*	
34	Andy RHODES		30	Michael OAKES	
6	Neil ADAMS		15	Phil KING	
22	Mike SHERON		25	Tommy JOHNSON	

BEFORE		P	W	D	L	F	A	pts	AFTER		P	W	D	L	F	A	pts
15	Villa	41	11	14	16	50	55	47	18	Villa	42	11	15	16	51	56	48
20	Norwich	41	10	12	19	36	53	42	20	Norwich	42	10	13	19	37	54	43

FACTFILE

D for Destiny Day has arrived... it's Villa or Palace for the drop... just a draw will do... the big screen is up at Villa Park – 7,000 turn up who couldn't get tickets for Carrow Road... Staunton settles the nerves with an early header... Palace go three down at St James's Park and despite pulling two back Villa are safe!

Villa make the needed point

This is it, after nine increasingly disturbed months, the day of reckoning has arrived.

All Premiership final fixtures affecting the Championship and relegation have been put back to Sunday, kick-off 4pm, to provide TV coverage and uniformity.

Only four clubs now have their destiny undecided with Blackburn or Manchester United to become champions and either Villa or Crystal Palace joining Leicester City, Ipswich Town and Norwich City in the Endsleigh First Division.

Almost from the start of his Villa Park reign Brian Little has lived with the danger of it going 'right down to the wire' and the recent mid-week results have mischievously ensured this being the case.

Coventry City, West Ham and Everton have all won their penultimate games, leaving the simple but stark scenario: Villa still need one point to be sure of staying up should Palace pull-off a shock win at Newcastle.

The form book says that Villa should be OK. But who trusts form books when nerves and human frailty can turn strong men into wrecks?

Villa's traditional claret-and-blue army of loyalists have made the journey to East Anglia. Another 7,000 are at Villa Park watching events beamed back on a large screen.

Carrow Road is a haven of unrest with fans demonstrating against chairman Robert Chase and it is against this background, that Villa keep Little's vow that they will not simply go for the one point they need to stay up.

In an aggressive, attacking start Steve Staunton's pugnacious determination is rewarded with a seventh minute goal scored, though Villa are not to know it, at much the same time as Ruel Fox is scoring for Newcastle.

A quickly-taken short corner by lone front man Dwight Yorke is curled over by Andy Townsend for the Irish defender to relish the rare experience of a headed goal, from six yards out.

Now Norwich need two to put Villa down even if Palace stage a come-back at St James's Park. In the event they do, but far too late. At half time Palace are 3-0 in arrears and this means that a six-goal swing is required collectively in the two games to deprive Villa of their precious Premiership place.

For the most pessimistic among the claret-and-blue set there is a tremor or two as Palace score twice in the second half and Norwich just once, but there the danger ends.

Villa, typically perhaps, have missed several chances to increase their lead when a 57th minute Jeremy Goss shot, against the run of play, beats Nigel Spink who is deputising for the suspended Mark Bosnich.

Thirty-three minutes left, favourable score-lines still in place at both grounds and Norwich rarely attacking with enough zeal to create a real scare. Tommy Johnson, who has replaced the injured Dean Saunders at half time, is a lively addition to Villa's attacking armoury and both he and Staunton waste opportunities to restore the lead.

It matters not, however. The final minutes of a traumatic season drift by without further disasters as Palace are pegged at 3-2 and return to the Endsleigh First Division.

The mood is now one of relief rather than ecstatic celebration. Villa gratefully stay among 19 Premiership clubs, including automatically-promoted Middlesbrough, while one more place awaits the winner of the First Division play-offs to form next-season's newly-constituted 20-club division.

So Villa have survived, albeit it narrowly, football's most fraught, fear-ridden season. There is a lot of work to be done in the summer....

Tuesday 19th July 1994 • Bickland Park • 6.45pm

FALMOUTH TOWN 1 ASTON VILLA 3

Half-time 0-2 • Attendance 2,920

Referee Bruce TAYLOR (Heston)

Linesmen S. Lawry and S. Lawrence

Amber Shirts, Black Shorts	Goals	Claret Shirts with Blue Stripes, White Shorts	Goals
1 Dave PHILIP		1 Nigel SPINK ‡	
2 Dave BALL		2 Darren EVANS §	
3 Andy PARR		3 Chris BODEN	
4 Adrian STREET #		4 Bryan SMALL ∆	
5 Nigel ROWE †		5 Ugo EHIOGU	
6 Dave SWEET		6 Kevin RICHARDSON ††	
7 Andy STREET ‡		7 Dwight YORKE ‡‡	
8 Mark RAPSEY		8 Garry PARKER §§	35
9 Justin ASHBURN		9 Guy WHITTINGHAM ##	
10 Mark ROWE		10 Dalian ATKINSON †	13
11 Andy WADDELL	63	11 David FARRELL #	
Substitutes		*Substitutes*	
12 Ian GOSLING †57		12 Graham FENTON †19	
14 Sean HOOPER ‡		13 Michael OAKES ‡ht	
15 Graham HERD #68		14 Dennis PEARCE ∆75	
		15 Scott MURRAY #ht	88
		16 Gareth FARRELLY ††54	
		17 Trevor BERRY ‡‡61	
		18 Daniel WEST §ht	
		19 Neil DAVIS §§74	
		20 Stephen COWE ##73	

> **FACTFILE**
>
> *Jewson League side Falmouth field six new signings in this pre-season warm-up match... Villa's senior squad are based for six days at HMS Raleigh in Torpoint as part of their preparations for the new season... It's Villa's first visit to Cornwall since playing a County representative side in May 1947.*

Saturday 23rd July 1994 • Mill Field • 3.00pm

TORPOINT ATHLETIC 1 ASTON VILLA 9

Half-time 0-4 • Attendance 2,200

Referee Martin BODENHAM (East Looe)
replaced by I. Harris (Torpoint) at halftime
Linesmen I. HARRIS and F. KENT

Black and Gold Striped Shirts, Black Shorts	Goals		Claret Shirts with Blue Stripes, White Shorts	Goals
1 Gary TURNER #		1	Nigel SPINK †	
2 Wayne HILLSON †		2	Darren EVANS §§	
3 Darren REDDING ‡		3	Chris BODEN	
4 Steve WILLIAMS		4	Bryan SMALL	
5 Adie COXON		5	Ugo EHIOGU ‡‡	15
6 Gary WILLIAMS §		6	Kevin RICHARDSON #	
7 Nick HAIGH	48	7	Dwight YORKE ##	70
8 Tony CUSACK		8	Garry PARKER ‡	
9 Lee CANSFIELD		9	Dean SAUNDERS §	25
10 Justin NORMAN		10	Guy WHITTINGHAM ††	6, 35, 67
11 Darren NORTHCOTT		11	Scott MURRAY	80
Substitutes			*Substitutes*	
12 Mike DAVIDSON †ht		12	Trevor BERRY §63	
13 Mark GEARS #50		13	Michael OAKES †ht	
14 Terry JOURNEAUX §58		14	David FARRELL ‡ht	84
15 Paul STEPHENS ‡ht		15	Gareth FARRELLY #62	63
		16	Denis PEARCE ††67	
		17	John MURPHY ##80	
		18	Ian BROWN §§82	
		19	Daniel WEST ‡‡75	

FACTFILE

Villa's Irish contingent are on leave following their extended season playing in the World Cup Finals in America... Guy Whittingham snaps up a poacher's hat-trick...

Monday 1st August 1994 • Manor Ground • 7.30pm

OXFORD UNITED 3 ASTON VILLA 3

Half-time 1-0 • *Attendance* 4,620

Referee Dermot GALLAGHER (Banbury)

Linesmen J. McINTYRE and P. ISAACS

Red and Black Striped Shirts, Black Shorts		Goals	Claret Shirts with Blue Stripes, White Shorts		Goals
1	Phil WHITEHEAD †		1	Nigel SPINK	
2	Dave COLLINS		2	Phil KING	
3	Mike FORD	77	3	Steve STAUNTON †	
4	Mickey LEWIS		4	Bryan SMALL	
5	Kerry EVANS		5	Ugo EHIOGU	
6	Alex DYER		6	Kevin RICHARDSON	
7	Stuart MASSEY		7	Dwight YORKE ‡	
8	David SMITH		8	Garry PARKER ††	65
9	Paul MOODY		9	Dean SAUNDERS §	
10	John BYRNE	10	10	Dalian ATKINSON	
11	Chris ALLEN	85	11	David FARRELL	
	Substitutes			*Substitutes*	
13	Mark DEEGAN †72		12	Ray HOUGHTON ‡ht	
			13	Graham FENTON #ht	46
			14	Guy WHITTINGHAM §ht	48
			15	Darren EVANS †33	
			8	Dwight YORKE ††75	

Yorke was subbed at halftime and came back on again for Parker in the 75th minute.

FACTFILE

Ken Fish began his football career in South Africa and then went on to play centre-forward for Aston Villa, Port Vale and Young Boys of Berne in Switzerland. When his playing career ended he joined Birmingham City as a trainer and then later, Oxford United. In recent times, aged 79, he suffered a massive blood clot and was forced to have both his legs amputated. Ken now lives in Stoke-on-Trent.

Friday 5th August 1994 • Campo Municipal De A Malata, Ferrol • 8.30pm

ATLETICO MADRID 0 ASTON VILLA 0

Half-time 0-0 • Attendance 5,000

Referee Puente LEIVA (Colegio)

Villa won 3-1 on penalties

Red and White Striped Shirts, Blue Shorts	Goals	Green, Black and Red Striped Shirts, Black Shorts	Goals
ABEL Resino		1 Nigel SPINK	
TOMAS Reñones		2 Phil KING	
Roberto SOLAZABAL		3 Steve STAUNTON	
ROCHA		4 Ugo EHIOGU	
Antonio Muñoz 'TONI'		5 Paul McGRATH	
Manuel Sánchez 'MANOLO'		6 Kevin RICHARDSON	
Juan VIZCAINO		7 Ray HOUGHTON	
José Ignacio SOLER		8 Garry PARKER	
Francisco Jos Mori 'PIRRI'		9 Dean SAUNDERS	
Fransisco Narváez 'KIKO'		10 Dalian ATKINSON	
Roman KOSECKI		11 Dwight YORKE	
Substitutes		*Substitutes*	
		gk Michael OAKES	
		Dave FARRELL	
		Guy WHITTINGHAM	
		Graham FENTON	
		Bryan SMALL	

PENALTY SHOOT OUT

1	ROCHA	✓		1-0
2	VIZCAíNO	✗	missed	1-1
3	PIRRI	✗	saved	1-1
4	KOSECKI	✗	Saved	1-2

PENALTY SHOOT OUT

1	Dean SAUNDERS	✓		1-1
2	Steve STAUNTION	✗	saved	1-1
3	Garry PARKER	✓		1-2
4	Phil KING	✓		1-3

STEVE OGRIZOVIC TESTIMONIAL MATCH

Wednesday 10th August 1994 • Highfield Road • 7.45pm

COVENTRY CITY 1 ASTON VILLA 2

Half-time 1-0 • Attendance 7,500

Referee Peter WALKER

Linesmen P. WALKER and M.KAIRNS

Sky Blue Shirts, Sky Blue Shorts	Goals	Claret Shirts with Blue Stripes, White Shorts	Goals
1 Steve OGRIZOVIC		1 Nigel SPINK #	
2 Brian BORROWS		2 Phil KING	
3 Steve MORGAN		3 Chris BODEN §	
4 Willie BOLAND		4 Shaun TEALE	
5 David BUSST		5 Paul McGRATH †	
6 Phil BABB ‡		6 Kevin RICHARDSON ‡	
7 Sean FLYNN		7 Nii LAMPTEY	
8 Julian DARBY	35	8 Andy TOWNSEND	
9 David RENNIE		9 Guy WHITTINGHAM	87
10 Mick QUINN †		10 Graham FENTON	
11 Leigh JENKINSON #		11 Dwight YORKE	
Substitutes		*Substitutes*	
gk Jonathan GOULD		gk Michael OAKES #65	
12 Ally PICKERING		12 Garry PARKER ‡ht	79
14 Roy WEGERLE †63		15 David FARRELL §75	
15 Sandy ROBINSON ‡73		16 Ugo EHIOGU †ht	
16 John WILLIAMS #63			

An impressive debut in Villa colours by new signing Nii Lamptey – a Ghanaian striker signed from Anderlecht... Reserve defender Chris Boden is also given an opportunity to impress.

Nii Lamptey – impressive performance at start of season.

PRE-SEASON FRIENDLY MATCH

Friday 12th August 1994 • United Park • 8.00pm

DROGHEDA UNITED 0 ASTON VILLA 3

Half-time 0-1 • *Attendance* 4,000

Referee Oliver COONEY

Linesmen S. WARD and S. BREEN

Red and Black Striped Shirts, White Shorts | Goals

1 John GRACE §
2 Colm TRESSON
3 Sean BYRNE
4 Aaron O'CALLAGHAN
5 Mick DOOHAN
6 Anthony BRENNAN
7 Trevor CROLLY †
8 Gerd HAXHIU #
9 John RYAN
10 Brendan O'CALLAGHAN
11 David STAUNTON ‡

Substitutes

12 Michael HARTE †54
13 Tom SULLIVAN ‡54
14 Dave CONNELL #67
15 John CARROLL
gk Jody BYRNE §67

Green, Black and Red Striped Shirts, Black Shorts | Goals

1 Michael OAKES
2 Kevin RICHARDSON
3 Steve STAUNTON §
4 Ugo EHIOGU
5 Paul McGRATH †
6 Andy TOWNSEND
7 Ray HOUGHTON # 57
8 Garry PARKER
9 Dean SAUNDERS 20
10 Dalian ATKINSON
11 Dwight YORKE ‡

Substitutes

12 Shaun TEALE †ht
14 Nii LAMPTEY ‡ht 52
15 David FARRELL #58
16 Phil KING §67
gk Nigel SPINK

Steve Staunton returns to his home town and captains the Villa side... His brother, David, leads out Drogheda... United field a surprise signing for the new season, U21 Albanian striker, Gerd Haxhiu.

FACTFILE

Brothers David and Steve Staunton lead out the teams.

Monday 15th August 1994 • Bescot Stadium • 7.45pm

ASTON VILLA 8 RAPID BUCHAREST 0

Half-time 3-0 • Attendance 5,081

Referee Paul REJER

Linesmen A. BLACK and M. FLETCHER

Green, Black and Red Striped Shirts, Black Shorts	Goals		White Shirts, White Shorts	Goals
13 Mark BOSNICH ‡			1 Leontin TOADER	
2 Phil KING §			2 Nicolae STANCIV †	
3 Steve STAUNTON			3 Georgica VAMESU ‡	
4 Ugo EHIOGU #	8		4 Adrian MATEI	
5 Paul McGRATH			5 Bernard WHITE	
6 Kevin RICHARDSON			6 Florin MOTROC	
7 Ray HOUGHTON			7 Tira FANEL	
8 John FASHANU ‡			8 Ionel CHEBAC	
9 Dean SAUNDERS	34, 49		9 Ion VLADOIU	
10 Garry PARKER			10 Iulian CHIRITA	
11 Nii LAMPTEY	43		11 Rodin VOINEA #	
Substitutes			*Substitutes*	
gk Michael OAKES ‡ht			gk Dan DIAC	
12 Shaun TEALE #50			13 Adrian BOGOI †ht	
14 Dwight YORKE ‡ht 47,68,72,85			16 Ionel BUDACA ‡ht	
15 Graham FENTON §75			17 Romulus BEALCU #69	
16 David FARRELL				

FACTFILE

Romanians no match for Villa... News cameras are present to record John Fashanu's first outing for Villa since his £1.35m transfer from Wimbledon... The new signing impresses before disappearing at half time... However, substitute Dwight Yorke grabs the glory with four second-half goals... Only the Romanian goalkeeper Toader kept the score from reaching double figures... It's Villa's final warm-up game before the Premiership kick-off...

Tuesday 15th November 1994 • St Andrews • 7.30pm

BIRMINGHAM CITY 1 ASTON VILLA 1

Half-time 0-1 • Attendance 19,766

Referee Vic CALLOW (Solihull)

Linesmen M.L. MARKHAM and B. JEAVONS

Blue Shirts, Blue Shorts	Goals	Claret Shirts with Blue Stripes, White Shorts	Goals
1 Ian BENNETT		1 Mark BOSNICH †	
2 Gary POOLE		2 Earl BARRETT	
3 Chris WHYTE		3 Bryan SMALL #	
4 Mark WARD		4 Phil KING	
5 Richard DRYDEN		5 Paul BROWNE	
6 Gary COOPER		6 Kevin RICHARDSON	
7 Jonathan HUNT		7 Nii LAMPTEY	10
8 Paul TAIT		8 Dwight YORKE	
9 Steve McGAVIN	58	9 Ronald HOOP	
10 Louie DONOWA ‡		10 Garry PARKER	
11 Jose DOMINGUEZ †		11 Riccardo SCIMECA ‡	

Substitutes

gk Ryan PRICE

Kenny LOWE †ht

Neil DOHERTY ‡59

Miguel DESOUZA

George PARRIS

Paul MOULDEN

David HOWELL

Substitutes

Nigel SPINK †ht

Trevor BERRY ‡65

Dennis PEARCE #70

Chris BODEN

Stephen COWE

Shaun TEALE

Darren EVANS

FACTFILE *Inauguration of new Tilton and Kop stands at St Andrews... Villa field surprise Dutch trialist, Ronald Koop – a Ruud Gullit look-a-like... Scottish centre-half Phil Browne impresses in a first team debut... Jim Barron takes charge as caretaker manager... Villa under-strength due to International calls on players.*

Tuesday 9th May 1995 • Villa Park • 7.45pm

ASTON VILLA 2 BIRMINGHAM CITY 0

Half-time 1-0 • *Attendance* 12,014

Referee Mike READ

Linesmen P. REJER and T. STEVENS

Claret Shirts with Blue Stripes, White Shorts	Goals	Blue Shirts, Blue Shorts	Goals
13 Mark BOSNICH ‡‡		1 Ian BENNETT	
2 Gary CHARLES		2 Ian HENDON	
3 Alan WRIGHT ##		3 Gary COOPER	
4 Ugo EHIOGU		4 Mark WARD	
5 Paul McGRATH ††		5 Chris WHYTE	
6 Phil KING		6 Liam DAISH	
7 Ian TAYLOR †		7 Jonathan HUNT	
8 Dwight YORKE	49	8 Gareth HALL	
9 Riccardo SCIMECA #	33	9 Jose DOMINGUEZ	
10 Tommy JOHNSON §		10 Ricky OTTO	
11 Andy TOWNSEND ‡		11 Neil DOHERTY	
Substitutes		*Substitutes*	
1 Michael OAKES ‡‡75		1 Ryan PRICE †ht	
12 Franz CARR #ht		2 Scott HILEY ‡ht	
14 Bryan SMALL ††57		3 John FRAIN	
15 Graham FENTON †15		6 Paul CHALLINOR #ht	
16 Gareth FARRELLY ‡28		7 Paul HARDING ††ht	
17 David FARRELL ##ht		8 Ben SEDGEMORE §ht	
18 Nii LAMPTEY §ht		9 Andy SAVILLE ‡‡75	

FACTFILE

On the bright side: almost £100,000 goes to Paul McGrath's testimonial kitty...
On the dark side: Other Premiership results on the night mean Villa have to gain
a point from their final game of the season away to Norwich to avoid relegation...
Ian Taylor is doubtful for that game after damaging a hamstring against Blues.

Sunday 21st May 1995 • Queens Park Oval • 4.00pm

TRINIDAD & TOBAGO XI 2 ASTON VILLA 1

Half-time 1-0 • *Attendance* 18,000

Match Officials not named

White Shirts with Red Trim, White Shorts		Goals	Claret Shirts with Blue Stripes, White Shorts		Goals
22	Russ RUSSELL		1	Nigel SPINK	
4	Dexter FRANCIS		2	Gary CHARLES	
5	Peter LEWIS		3	Alan WRIGHT	
6	Marvin FAUSTIN	35	4	Ugo EHIOGU	
7	Terry ST LOUIS		5	Phil KING	
8	Angus EVE		6	Bryan SMALL	
9	Arnold IWARIKA		7	Graham FENTON	
10	Russell LATAPY	86	8	Dwight YORKE	
11	Gerren NIXON		9	Franz CARR †	
14	Alvin THOMAS		10	Gareth FARRELLY	
16	Richard THEODORE		11	Tommy JOHNSON	
Substitutes			*Substitutes*		
1	Haydn THOMAS		gk	Michael OAKES	
3	Serwyn JULLEN		12	David FARRELL †68	69
12	Shawn GARCIA		14	Paul BROWNE	
15	Dexter CYRUS				
18	Anthony ROUGIER				

> *Absent from the Villa tour party were Paul McGrath, Steve Staunton, Andy Townsend, Dean Saunders and Mark Bosnich, all on international duty for their respective countries. Shaun Teale remained behind to undergo an operation*

FACTFILE

Wednesday 24th May 1995 • National Stadium • 8.00pm

BARBADOS 3 ASTON VILLA 1

Half-time 1-1 • Attendance 3,500

Match Officials not named

Yellow Shirts, Yellow Shorts

Claret Shirts with Blue Stripes, White Shorts   Goals

Barbados line-up not available

Gareth Farrelly – the young midfielder was impressive in the two games he played in the Caribbean.

		Goals
1	Nigel SPINK	
2	Gary CHARLES	
3	Alan WRIGHT	
4	Ugo EHIOGU	
5	Phil KING	
6	Paul BROWNE	
7	Graham FENTON	12
8	Dwight YORKE	
9	Franz CARR †	
10	Gareth FARRELLY	
11	David FARRELL	
Substitutes		
gk	Michael OAKES †ht	
12	Bryan SMALL ‡70	

The first team squad line up with the new management team for a New Year's picture. Back Row (left to right): Ray Houghton, Earl Barrett, Steve Staunton, Paul McGrath, Shaun Teale, Bryan Small, Phil King. Middle Row: Paul Barron (Fitness Coach), Garry Parker, Gary Charles, Ugo Ehiogu, Nigel Spink, Mark Bosnich, Michael Oakes, John Fashanu, Ian Taylor, Graham Fenton, Jim Walker (Physiotherapist). Front Row: Kevin Richardson, Dalian Atkinson, Tommy Johnson, Allan Evans (Assistant Manager), Brian Little (Manager), John Gregory (First Team Coach), Dean Saunders, Dwight Yorke, Andy Townsend.

Big Ron makes way for Brian Little's return

November 1994 was a period of great turmoil at Villa Park and at the Bodymoor Heath training ground.

OUT... on Thursday November 10, went manager Ron Atkinson only hours after the 4-3 defeat by Wimbledon at Selhurst Park which left the club in 19th place.

IN... two matches later, for the home game with Sheffield Wednesday on November 27, came Brian Little along with John Gregory, another ex-Villa player from Leicester City, as his coach.

These appointments led almost inevitably to assistant manager Jim Barron, coach Dave Sexton, youth coach Colin Clarke and chief scout Brian Whitehouse also departing.

Soon Little was re-joined by his former

RON ATKINSON

Filbert Street No.2, Allan Evans, another ex-Villa player, while a fourth ex-Leicester City staffman arrived in youth coach Tony McAndrew.

Already, on the youth development side, the European Cup Final match-winner of 1982, Peter Withe, had succeeded Dave Richardson and thus a new managerial-coaching-scouting set-up was in place.

The only survivors of the former regime were physiotherapist Jim Walker and kit manager Jim Paul who simply carried on much as before.

Little was a folk-hero during his nine years as a Villa first-teamer and even before that. As a mere boy his innate flair, control and goalscoring panache had emerged in helping the club win the FA Youth Cup.

At the same time he was setting off on a senior career which subsequently helped Ron Saunders' famous team to promotion and two League Cups and earned him an England cap.

He looked set for a lengthy international run but Little's career was ended prematurely by knee and back injuries. By this time, in 1977-78, Evans had

JIM BARRON

DAVE SEXTON

COLIN CLARKE

PETER WITHE

begun an even more illustrious Villa career which led to the ultimate distinction of Championship and European Cup medals plus Scottish caps.

Gregory spent only two years at Villa Park but progressed to England appearances later in his career.

As a team-behind-a-team the trio had partially proved themselves by getting Leicester City, on limited potential, to three promotion play-offs and finally the Premiership.

At Bodymoor Heath they introduced a slightly different style both behind-the-scenes and on the park though, in the intensity of the battle, and with the fixture list constantly changed and disrupted it was not easy to achieve a sense of continuity.

There was no great upheaval in terms of personnel, though Little was committed to bringing down the average age of a squad which, some felt, had too many over-30s.

Kevin Richardson followed Ron Atkinson to Coventry City while Earl Barrett also returned to a former manager, namely Joe Royle, when he moved from Oldham to Everton.

BRIAN LITTLE

Little swopped Guy Whittingham for Sheffield Wednesday's Ian Taylor and allowed Garry Parker and Ray Houghton to go to clubs subsequently to be relegated in Leicester City and Crystal Palace.

In addition to Taylor, Villa's new boss brought in the Derby County pair Tommy Johnson and Gary Charles for a combined £3m, took Franz Carr in part exchange for Parker and signed Alan Wright from Blackburn Rovers.

Just before the deadline Brian Little gave a clue to his future ambitions by attempting, unsuccessfully at that time, to sign two England 'fringe' players in Mark Draper from Leicester and Stan Collymore from Nottingham Forest. Just before the end of the season chairman Doug Ellis flew to Rome in an attempt to sign Paul Gascoigne from Lazio.

And so, once relegation has been avoided Little's re-building work had to begin with the thought in mind that it had all been too close for comfort.

Plans for a new, successful era needed urgently to be put in place.

ALLAN EVANS   *JOHN GREGORY*   *TONY McANDREW*   *JIM WALKER*

The first team squad line up at the start of the 1994-95 season. Back Row (left to right): Dave Farrell, Ugo Ehiogu, Paul McGrath, John Fashanu, Shaun Teale, Andy Townsend, Garry Parker. Centre Row: Jim Walker (Physiotherapist), Graham Fenton, Guy Whittingham, Nigel Spink, Mark Bosnich, Michael Oakes, Bryan Small, Earl Barrett, Jim Barron (Assistant Manager). Front Row: Dwight Yorke, Nii Lamptey, Ray Houghton, Kevin Richardson, Ron Atkinson (Manager), Dean Saunders, Dalian Atkinson, Phil King, Steve Staunton.

The successful Purity League and League Cup winners. Back Row: Tommy Jaczeszun, Alan Lee, David Moore, Lee Collins, Adam Rachel, Andrew Mitchell, Marc Senior, Stuart Brock, Jamie Impey, Jonathan Miley, Richard Walker, David Hughes. Front Row: Richard Burgess, Ben Petty, Lee Hendrie, Lee Burchell, Darren Byfield, Alan Kirby, Leslie Hines.

DALIAN ATKINSON

Born Shrewsbury,
21st March 1968
Joined Villa July 1991,
from Real Sociedad,
£1.6m.
Villa debut v Sheff Wed,
Lge (a), 17/8/91. 1 goal.

The former Ipswich, Sheffield Wednesday and Real Sociedad striker had a most erratic season with periods of unfitness and difficulty in holding his place.

From those earlier days when he formed a lethal strike partnership with Dean Saunders he appeared to be at a crossroads and ended the season seeking a move abroad.

Although, for a player of such natural talents, it was a frustrating nine months, he revived hints of his former effectiveness in a six-match spell, while Little was replacing Ron Atkinson, when he scored five goals.

Nearer the end of the season, however, when he returned for four matches he was less prominent.

Career Record:

Season	Club	League Apps	Gls	Cups Apps	Gls
85-86	Ipswich T.	- (1)	-	-	-
86-87	Ipswich T.	3 (5)	-	1 (2)	-
87-88	Ipswich T.	13 (4)	8	1	-
88-89	Ipswich T.	33 (1)	10	5	3
89-90	Sheffield W.	38	10	7	5
90-91	Real Sociedad	29	12		
91-92	Aston Villa	11 (3)	1	3	-
92-93	Aston Villa	28	11	4	2
93-94	Aston Villa	29	8	15	7
94-95	Aston Villa	11 (5)	3	5	4
Villa record		*79 (8)*	*23*	*27*	*13*
TOTAL		195 (19)	63	41 (2)	21

★ *England 'B' International (1 cap)*

EARL BARRETT

Born Rochdale,
28th April 1967.
Joined Villa February
1992 from Oldham,
£1.7m.
Villa debut v Man City,
Lge (a), 29/2/92.

Transferred to Everton near the end of January after his original manager at Oldham, Joe Royle, had been appointed at Goodison Park.

Barrett had virtually been a regular from the start of the season until Everton's approach and Little's reluctant decision to part.

The former England squad player, capped on a US Tour, again showed his versatility by providing cover in other defensive roles.

Career Record:

Season	Club	League Apps	Gls	Cups Apps	Gls
84-85	Man. City	-	-	-	-
85-86	Man. City	1	-	-	-
(loan)	Chester City	12	-	-	-
86-87	Man. City	1 (1)	-	1	-
87-88	Man. City	-	-	-	-
	Oldham Ath.	16 (2)	-	-	-
88-89	Oldham Ath.	44	-	6	-
89-90	Oldham Ath.	46	2	19	2
90-91	Oldham Ath.	46	3	6	-
91-92	Oldham Ath.	29	2	7	-
	Aston Villa	13	-	-	-
92-93	Aston Villa	42	1	9	-
93-94	Aston Villa	39	-	13	1
94-95	Aston Villa	24 (1)	-	9	-
Villa record		*94 (1)*	*1*	*31*	*1*
TOTAL		313 (4)	8	70	3

★ *Full England international (3 caps). Also capped at 'B' and Under-21 levels.*

Born Wolverhampton, 13th October 1973. *Joined Villa* July 1990 as a trainee. November 1991 on professional forms. *Villa debut* sub v Leicester City, Lge (a) 3/12/94.

The young midfield player was on the bench for four matches and made a brief appearance in the 1-1 draw at Leicester in December.

With the competition for places tight in a difficult situation his possible progress was being blocked and, on transfer deadline day, he moved to Derby County.

Career Record:

Season	Club	League		Cups	
		Apps	Gls	Apps	Gls
91-92	Aston Villa	-	-	-	-
92-93	Aston Villa	-	-	-	-
93-94	Aston Villa	-	-	-	-
(loan)	Barnsley	4	-	-	-
94-95	Aston Villa	- (1)	-	-	-
Villa record		*- (1)*	*-*	*-*	*-*
TOTAL		4 (1)	-	-	-

Born Fairfield, Australia, 13th January 1972. *Joined Villa* February 1992 from Sydney Croatia. *Villa debut* v Luton Town, Lge (a) 25/4/92.

The popular Australian continued his progress as one of the league's best young keepers and the adversity of a relegation battle added to his experience.

He began the first few weeks of the season in a stop-go situation with Nigel Spink because of injury and form variations but enjoyed a 19-match unbroken sequence after Brian Little's arrival.

This was interrupted by suspension from the final game after a red card for two bookings at Leeds when Villa lost after he had left the field, thus creating a disappointing end to the season for him.

Career Record:

Season	Club	League			Cups		
		Apps	Gls	Ag	Apps	Gls	Ag
89-90	Man. United	1	0		-	-	
90-91	Man. United	2	2		-	-	
91-92	Aston Villa	1	1		-	-	
92-93	Aston Villa	17	12	1	0		
93-94	Aston Villa	28	28	12 (1)	11		
94-95	Aston Villa	30	44	4	5		
Villa record		*76*	*85*	*17 (1)*	*16*		
TOTAL		79	87	17 (1)	16		

★ *Australian international*

GOAL TIME GRAPH

● Villa ○ Opponents
V = Scored at villa Park

0-15 mins   16-30 mins   31-45 mins   46-60 mins   61-75 mins   76-90 mins

FRANZ CARR

Born Preston,
24th September 1966.
Joined Villa February 1994
from Leicester City, part
exchange for Garry Parker.
Villa debut as sub v
Leicester City, Lge (h),
22/2/95.

Signed from Leicester City as part of the
deal which took Garry Parker to Filbert
Street. Carr made a big impact in the
early days of his career with Nottingham
Forest but in subsequent moves never
quite lived up to his enormous potential.

A fast, exciting winger who performed
well for Little when the current Villa
manager was at Leicester City. After
arriving at Villa Park his involvement
was restricted to the subs bench.

Career Record:

Season	Club	League Apps	Gls	Cups Apps	Gls
84-85	Blackburn R.	-	-	-	-
85-86	Nottingham F.	23	3	1 (1)	1
86-87	Nottingham F.	36	4	6	3
87-88	Nottingham F.	22	4	3	1
88-89	Nottingham F.	18 (5)	3	12 (3)	-
89-90	Nottingham F.	10 (4)	1	2	1
(loan)	Sheffield W.	9 (3)	-	2	-
90-91	Nottingham F.	13	2	1	-
(loan)	West Ham U.	1 (2)	-	-	-
91-92	Newcastle U.	12 (3)	2	1	-
92-93	Newcastle U.	8 (2)	1	4 (3)	-
	Sheffield U.	8	3	4	-
93-94	Sheffield U.	10	1	-	-
94-95	Leicester C	12 (1)	1	-	-
	Aston Villa	- (2)	-	-	-
Villa record		- (2)	-	-	-
TOTAL		182 (22)	25	36 (7)	6

★ *Made 9 England appearances at U21 level*

GARY CHARLES

Born London,
13th April 1970.
Joined Villa January 1995
from Derby County, £1m.
Villa debut as sub v.
Nottingham Forest, Lge
(a), 21/1/95

Signed from Derby County in the £3m
deal which included Tommy Johnson
and quickly settled down to fill the right
back berth vacated by Earl Barrett.

With his Nottingham Forest and
England pedigree Charles emerged as a
quality player both in defence and as an
additional attacker down the wing.

He is the ideal type of full-back, with
his forward-running inclinations, to
blend in with the three centre-back
system which the manager often favours.

Career Record:

Season	Club	League Apps	Gls	Cups Apps	Gls
87-88	Nottingham F.	-	-	-	-
88-89	Nottingham F.	1	-	1	-
(loan)	Leicester City	5 (3)	-	-	-
89-90	Nottingham F.	- (1)	-	- (2)	-
90-91	Nottingham F.	9 (1)	-	7	1
91-92	Nottingham F.	30	1	12 (2)	-
92-93	Nottingham F.	14	-	1	-
93-94	Derby County	43	1	8 (1)	-
94-95	Derby County*	18	2	7	-
	Aston Villa	14 (2)	-	-	-
Villa record		14 (2)	-	-	-
TOTAL		134 (7)	4	36 (5)	1

* N.B. Cup figures for Derby Co. 94-95 only include Anglo-Italian and Coca-Cola Cup competitions

★ *Full England international (2 caps). Also capped at Under-21 level.*

UGO EHIOGU

Born Hackney, London, 3rd November 1972. *Joined Villa* July 1991 from West Bromwich Albion, £40,000. *Villa debut* v Arsenal, Lge (h), 24/8/91.

Ugo was off to a cracking start to the best season of his career so far missing only four games throughout, with one appearance as a substitute.

The England Under-21 international continued to press his claims for full honours with superb consistency in the heart of the defence.

Ehiogu took Shaun Teale's place when the latter was injured for the opening games and then kept him out until the change of management saw them frequently team up with Paul McGrath in a three centre-back formation.

His controversial headed goal against Manchester City, when the opposition claimed he handled the ball, earned a valuable home point in the tense finale to the relegation battle.

Career Record:

Season	Club	League Apps	League Gls	Cups Apps	Cups Gls
90-91	W.B.A.	- (2)	-	-	-
91-92	Aston Villa	4 (4)	-	1 (1)	-
92-93	Aston Villa	1 (3)	-	1	-
93-94	Aston Villa	14 (3)	-	- (2)	-
94-95	Aston Villa	38 (1)	3	9	1
Villa record		*57 (11)*	*3*	*11 (3)*	*1*
TOTAL		57 (13)	3	11 (3)	1

★ *England Under-21 international.*

DAVE FARRELL

Born Birmingham, 11th November 1971 *Joined Villa* January 1992 from Redditch United, £45,000. *Villa debut* As sub v Oldham, Lge (a), 24/10/92.

The local-born winger was restricted to only two full appearances, both in the unsuccessful attempt at defending the Coca-Cola Cup.

He played in the 3-0 win at Wigan and then in the 4-1 defeat by Crystal Palace, Brian Little's second match in charge.

Farrell is a fast and tricky forward who, because of difficult circumstances, has found it difficult to acquire the first team experience he needs.

Career Record:

Season	Club	League Apps	League Gls	Cups Apps	Cups Gls
91-92	Aston Villa	-	-	-	-
92-93	Aston Villa	1 (1)	-	-	-
(loan)	Scunthorpe	4 (1)	1	1	-
93-94	Aston Villa	4	-	-	-
94-95	Aston Villa	-	-	2	-
Villa record		*5 (1)*	*-*	*2*	*-*
TOTAL		9 (2)	1	3	-

JOHN FASHANU

GRAHAM FENTON

Born Kensington,
18th September 1963
Joined Villa August 1994
from Wimbledon, for
£1.35m.
Villa debut v Everton, Lge
(a), 20/8/94.

Born Wallsend,
22nd May 1974
Joined Villa July 1990 as
a trainee. February 1992
on professional forms.
Villa debut v Manchester
City, Lge (h), 22/2/94.

After being signed by Ron Atkinson in the summer of 1994 for £1.3m from Wimbledon, Fashanu went through a troubled season at Villa Park.

An Achilles tendon operation kept him out from September to the turn of the year and then, in early February at Old Trafford, he was wiped out for the rest of the season by serious knee ligament damage.

The North-Easterner went through rather a frustrating season after making such an impression in the 1994 Coca-Cola Cup Final at Wembley.

His seven full appearances and numerous selections as sub were spread across the season with his best run coming around the time of the managerial change-over.

Fenton's high-spot, ironically, was in scoring twice in the 4-3 victory at White Hart Lane between the reign of the two managers when Jim Barron was briefly in charge.

Leicester City were keen to sign Fenton before the deadline, when Brian Little bid for Mark Draper but Villa were reluctant to lose the powerful midfield player's potential.

Career Record:

Season	Club	League Apps	Gls	Cups Apps	Gls
79-80	Norwich City	-	-	-	-
80-81	Norwich City	-	-	-	-
81-82	Norwich City	5	1	-	-
82-83	Norwich City	2	-	-	-
83-84	Crystal Palace	1	-	1	-
	Lincoln City	22 (4)	7	3 (1)	-
84-85	Lincoln City	9 (1)	4	2	-
	Millwall	25	4	4	2
85-86	Millwall	25	8	11	5
	Wimbledon	8 (1)	4	-	-
86-87	Wimbledon	37	11	4 (1)	3
87-88	Wimbledon	38	14	11	7
88-89	Wimbledon	30	12	10	3
89-90	Wimbledon	24	11	4	3
90-91	Wimbledon	34 (1)	20	3	-
91-92	Wimbledon	38	18	5	2
92-93	Wimbledon	27 (2)	6	7 (1)	2
93-94	Wimbledon	35 (1)	11	9	1
94-95	Aston Villa	11 (2)	3	3	-
Villa record		11 (2)	3	3	-
TOTAL		371 (12)	134	77 (3)	28

Career Record:

Season	Club	League Apps	Gls	Cups Apps	Gls
92-93	Aston Villa	-	-	-	-
93-94	Aston Villa	9 (3)	1	1 (1)	-
(loan)	W.B.Albion	7	3	-	-
94-95	Aston Villa	7 (10)	2	1 (2)	-
Villa record		16 (13)	3	2 (3)	-
TOTAL		23 (13)	6	2 (3)	-

RAY HOUGHTON

Born Glasgow,
9th January 1962
Joined Villa July 1992
from Liverpool,
£900,000.
Villa debut v Ipswich,
Lge (a), 15/8/92.

The Irish Republic international played a high percentage of the first team games until his move to Crystal Palace on transfer deadline day.

He gave his usual, whole-hearted displays scoring the important goal against Inter Milan at Villa Park, to earn the penalty shoot-out.

Career Record:

Season	Club	League Apps	Gls	Cups Apps	Gls
79-80	West Ham	-	-	-	-
80-81	West Ham	-	-	-	-
81-82	West Ham	- (1)	-	-	-
82-83	Fulham	42	5	7	2
83-84	Fulham	40	3	5	-
84-85	Fulham	42	8	4	3
85-86	Fulham	5	-	-	-
	Oxford Utd.	35	4	14	3
86-87	Oxford Utd.	37	5	6	1
87-88	Oxford Utd.	11	1	2	-
	Liverpool	26 (2)	5	7	2
88-89	Liverpool	38	7	14	1
89-90	Liverpool	16 (3)	1	4 (1)	-
90-91	Liverpool	31 (1)	7	7	3
91-92	Liverpool	36	8	15	4
92-93	Aston Villa	39	3	9	1
93-94	Aston Villa	25 (5)	2	8 (3)	3
94-95	Aston Villa	19 (7)	1	5 (1)	1
Villa record		*83 (12)*	*6*	*22 (4)*	*5*
TOTAL		442 (19)	60	107 (5)	24

★ *Republic of Ireland full international (64 caps, 5 goals – up to 11/6/95)*

TOMMY JOHNSON

Born Newcastle,
15th January 1971
Joined Villa January 1995
from Derby County,
£1.9m.
Villa debut v QPR,
Lge (h), 14/1/95

It was a very mixed four-and-a-half months for Johnson after the England Under-21 forward was signed by Brian Little from Derby County along with Gary Charles.

After easing himself in for three full games and a couple of appearances as substitute he gave a magnificent performance against Wimbledon with a hat-trick in the astonishing 7-1 victory at Villa Park.

He scored again two games later in the 4-4 draw with Leicester City but injury intervened and his progress was stop-start after that as he virtually missed out on the crucial part of the successful relegation-saving spell.

Career Record:

Season	Club	League Apps	Gls	Cups Apps	Gls
88-89	Notts Co.	6 (4)	4	1 (1)	-
89-90	Notts Co.	34 (6)	18	9 (2)	2
90-91	Notts Co.	29 (8)	16	7 (3)	5
91-92	Notts Co.	31	9	7 (1)	3
	Derby Co.	12	2	2	1
92-93	Derby Co.	34 (1)	8	16	2
93-94	Derby Co.	31 (6)	13	7 (1)	6
94-95	Derby Co.	14	7	5	2
	Aston Villa	11 (3)	4	- (1)	-
Villa record		*11 (3)*	*4*	*- (1)*	*-*
TOTAL		202 (28)	81	54 (9)	21

* N.B. Cup figures for Derby Co. 94-95 only include Anglo-Italian and Coca-Cola Cup competitions

★ *England Under-21 international*

PHIL KING

Born Bristol,
28th December 1967
Joined Villa August 1994
from Sheffield
Wednesday, £250,000
Villa debut as sub v
Everton, Lge (a) 20/8/94

Ron Atkinson signing King was a regular until the managerial change and he then found himself out of the first-team reckoning.

It was a disappointing turnabout in fortunes for him since, only weeks earlier, he had been the hero in nervelessly driving in the decisive penalty in the shoot-out to beat Inter Milan.

King, a cheerful, happy-go-lucky character, is a useful squad player with ability both in defence and attack.

Career Record:

Season	Club	League		Cups	
		Apps	Gls	Apps	Gls
84-85	Exeter City	15 (1)	-	1 (1)	-
85-86	Exeter City	9 (2)	-	1	-
86-87	Torquay U.	24	3	5	-
	Swindon T.	20 (1)	-	-	-
87-88	Swindon T.	44	1	14	-
88-89	Swindon T.	34 (3)	2	7	-
89-90	Swindon T.	14	1	3	-
	Sheff Wed.	25	-	4	-
90-91	Sheff Wed.	43	-	13	-
91-92	Sheff Wed.	38 (1)	1	8	-
92-93	Sheff Wed.	11 (1)	1	3	-
93-94	Sheff Wed.	7 (3)	-	3	-
(loan)	Notts Co.	6	-	2	-
94-95	Aston Villa	13 (3)	-	7	-
Villa record		13 (3)	-	7	-
TOTAL		303 (15)	9	71 (1)	-

NII LAMPTEY

Born Ghana,
10th December 1974
Joined Villa July 1994,
on loan from Anderlecht
on loan
Villa debut v Wigan,
CCC 2/1, 21/9/94

The Ghanaian international was signed by Ron Atkinson on loan from Belgian club Anderlecht. The fee was to be £1m if he signed permanently or a vastly-reduced figure if he did not play enough games and returned to Anderlecht.

Lamptey showed flair and scoring ability in pre-season friendlies and scored in each leg of the Coca-Cola Cup against Wigan but failed to make a full Premiership break through.

Having not played enough games to gain a work permit renewal his loan arrangement was brought to an end.

Career Record:

Season	Club	League		Cups	
		Apps	Gls	Apps	Gls
89-90	Cornerstone U.	-	-	-	-
90-91	Anderlecht	11 (3)	7	-	-
91-92	Anderlecht	6 (9)	2	-	-
92-93	Anderlecht	- (1)	-	-	-
93-94	Anderlecht	-	-	-	-
(loan)	PSV	19 (3)	9	-	-
94-95	Anderlecht	-	-	-	-
(loan)	Aston Villa	1 (5)	-	2 (1)	3
Villa record		1 (5)	-	2 (1)	3
TOTAL		37 (21)	-	2 (1)	3

★ *Ghanaian full international*

PAUL McGRATH

Born Ealing, London, 4th December 1959. *Joined Villa* August 1989 from Man. United, £400,000. *Villa debut* v Nott'm F., Lge (a), 19/8/89.

Despite earlier misgivings about his fitness for a full season the Irish international missed few games and was as popular with the new manager as he had been with his predecessor.

Playing in a three-man barrier with Shaun Teale and Ugo Ehiogu he was as shrewd, economical and skilful as ever.

Was awarded a testimonial match against Birmingham City at the end of the season.

Career Record:

Season	Club	League Apps	Gls	Cups Apps	Gls
81-82	Man. United	-	-	-	-
82-83	Man. United	14	3	1 (1)	-
83-84	Man. United	9	1	3	-
84-85	Man. United	23	-	7	2
85-86	Man. United	40	3	8	1
86-87	Man. United	34 (1)	2	4 (1)	-
87-88	Man. United	21 (1)	2	2	1
88-89	Man. United	18 (2)	1	5 (1)	-
89-90	Aston Villa	35	1	12	-
90-91	Aston Villa	35	-	9	-
91-92	Aston Villa	41	1	7	-
92-93	Aston Villa	42	4	8	1
93-94	Aston Villa	30	-	14	-
94-95	Aston Villa	36 (4)	-	9	-
Villa record		219 (4)	6	59	1
TOTAL		378 (8)	18	89 (3)	5

★ *Republic of Ireland full international (76 caps, 7 goals – up to and including 11/6/95)*

MICHAEL OAKES

Born Northwich, 30th October 1973 *Joined Villa* July 1991 as a non-contract player, February 1992 on professional forms *Villa debut* v Wigan Ath., CCC (a), 5/10/94.

The England U21 keeper continued as third choice because of the presence of Mark Bosnich and Nigel Spink.

He made his Villa first-team debut in the Coca-Cola Cup-tie at Wigan and was on the bench a dozen times.

The 21-year-old son of ex-Manchester City player, Alan Oakes from the 1950s, continued to impress with his dedication and professionalism, keeping the two keepers ahead of him on their toes.

Although restricted in his first team football for Villa he patiently awaited his chances.

Made his full first-team debut this season, playing in the Coca-Cola League Cup competition.

Career Record:

Season	Club	League Apps	Gls	Cups Apps	Gls
91-92	Aston Villa	-	-	-	-
92-93	Aston Villa	-	-	-	-
93-94	Aston Villa	-	-	-	-
(loan)	Scarborough	2	-	-	-
(loan)	Tranmere	-	-	-	-
94-95	Aston Villa	-	-	1	-
TOTAL		2	-	1	-

★ *England Under-21 international*

GARRY PARKER

KEVIN RICHARDSON

Born Oxford, 7th September 1965. *Joined Villa* November 1991 from Nottingham Forest, £650,000. *Villa debut* v Oldham, Lge (a), 30/11/91.

The talented midfielder, who found it difficult to gain a regular place, was transferred to Leicester City in February.

Garry made 16 full appearances in the first six months of the season but was frequently on the subs bench. He played in Brian Little's first five games, but lost his place just before Christmas when Ian Taylor signed from Sheffield Wednesday.

Career Record:

Season	Club	League Apps	Gls	Cups Apps	Gls
82-83	Luton Town	1	-	-	-
83-84	Luton Town	13	2	1	-
84-85	Luton Town	13 (7)	1	4 (4)	1
85-86	Luton Town	4 (4)	-	1 (1)	-
	Hull City	12	-	-	-
86-87	Hull City	37 (1)	-	5	1
87-88	Hull City	33 (1)	8	6	-
	Nott'm. For.	1 (1)	-	-	-
88-89	Nott'm. For.	22	7	14 (1)	6
89-90	Nott'm. For.	36 (1)	6	13	1
90-91	Nott'm. For.	35 (1)	3	15	5
91-92	Nott'm. For.	5 (1)	1	4	-
	Aston Villa	25	1	5	1
92-93	Aston Villa	37	9	9	-
93-94	Aston Villa	17 (2)	2	4	-
94-95	Aston Villa	12 (2)	1	4 (2)	-
Villa record		91 (4)	13	22 (2)	1
TOTAL		303 (21)	40	81 (6)	15

★ *Capped at England Under-21, Under-19 and youth levels.*

Born Newcastle-upon-Tyne, 4th December 1962. *Joined Villa* August 1991 from Real Sociedad, £450,000. *Villa debut* v Sheff Wed, Lge (a), 17/8/91.

The former club skipper, troubled by injuries and variations in form, lost his place in Brian Little's team and was then Ron Atkinson's first signing at Highfield Road where he assisted in their relegation-saving campaign.

Having won championship honours with Everton and Arsenal he left Villa with a Coca-Cola Cup medal added to his collection.

Career Record:

Season	Club	League Apps	Gls	Cups Apps	Gls
80-81	Everton	-	-	-	-
81-82	Everton	15 (3)	2	1	-
82-83	Everton	24 (5)	3	3 (2)	-
83-84	Everton	25 (3)	4	11 (1)	3
84-85	Everton	14 (1)	4	3 (1)	-
85-86	Everton	16 (2)	3	7	1
86-87	Everton	1	-	1	-
	Watford	39	2	11	-
87-88	Arsenal	24 (5)	4	10 (1)	2
88-89	Arsenal	32 (2)	1	5 (1)	-
89-90	Arsenal	32 (1)	-	7	-
90-91	Real Sociedad	37	-		
91-92	Aston Villa	42	6	9	-
92-93	Aston Villa	42	2	9	1
93-94	Aston Villa	40	5	15	2
94-95	Aston Villa	18 (1)	-	4	-
Villa record		142 (1)	13	37	3
TOTAL		401 (23)	36	96 (6)	9

★ *Full England international (1 cap).*

DEAN SAUNDERS

Born Swansea, 21st June 1964. *Joined Villa* September 1992 from Liverpool, £2.3m. *Villa debut* v Leeds Utd, Lge (a), 13/9/92.

The cheerful Welsh international was again Villa's leading scorer with 15 goals.

It was a difficult season for Saunders as transfers, injuries and form fluctuations repeatedly changed his forward partners but he was still selected as the Supporters' Player of the Year.

Career Record:

Season	Club	League Apps	League Gls	Cups Apps	Cups Gls
82-83	Swansea C.	-	-	-	-
83-84	Swansea C.	14 (5)	3	- (1)	-
84-85	Swansea C.	28 (2)	9	4 (1)	-
(loan)	Cardiff City	3 (1)	-	-	-
85-86	Brighton	39 (3)	14	9	5
86-87	Brighton	27 (3)	6	5	-
	Oxford Utd.	12	6	-	-
87-88	Oxford Utd.	35 (2)	12	11 (1)	9
88-89	Oxford Utd.	10	4	2	2
	Derby Co.	30	14	6	1
89-90	Derby Co.	38	11	11	10
90-91	Derby Co.	38	17	8	4
91-92	Liverpool	36	10	18	11
92-93	Liverpool	6	1	1	1
	Aston Villa	35	12	9	4
93-94	Aston Villa	37 (1)	10	14	6
94-95	Aston Villa	39	15	9	2
Villa record		*111 (1)*	*37*	*32*	*12*
TOTAL		427 (17)	144	107 (3)	55

★ *Full international for Wales (49 caps, 16 goals – up to and including 7/6/95).*

BRYAN SMALL

Born Birmingham, 15th November 1971. *Joined Villa* June 1988 from FA School of Excellence as a trainee. July 1990 professional. *Villa debut* v Everton, Lge (a), 19/10/91.

The Birmingham-born defender had limited opportunity to earn a regular place in terms of five full appearances.

Three of these were in early December soon after Brian Little's arrival but the team was undergoing inevitable change and he had to wait until February for his next senior chance.

This came when Earl Barrett left and he played in the defeat at Old Trafford and the 7-1 home win over Wimbledon.

Small, who spent a spell on loan at St Andrew's, was subsequently kept out by the arrival of Alan Wright.

Career Record:

Season	Club	League Apps	League Gls	Cups Apps	Cups Gls
89-90	Aston Villa	-	-	-	-
90-91	Aston Villa	-	-	-	-
91-92	Aston Villa	8	-	4 (1)	-
92-93	Aston Villa	10 (4)	-	1	-
93-94	Aston Villa	8 (1)	-	3	-
94-95	Aston Villa	5	-	-	-
TOTAL		31 (5)	-	8 (1)	-

★ An *England Under-21 international.*

NIGEL SPINK

Born Chelmsford,
8th August 1958
Joined Villa January 1977
from Chelmsford City
Villa debut v Nott'm
Forest, League (a),
26/12/79.

Always ready and waiting when required
to step into the action.

Nigel played in the European games
against Inter Milan and Trabzonspor and
made other spasmodic appearances
when first-choice Bosnich was either
unavailable or off-form.

His high spot was playing in the final
game at Norwich and helping in the 1-1
draw which assured the club of safety.

Career Record:

Season	Club	League Apps	Gls Ag	Cups Apps	Gls Ag
79-80	Aston Villa	1	2	-	-
80-81	Aston Villa	-	-	-	-
81-82	Aston Villa	-	-	-(1)	0
82-83	Aston Villa	22	23	8	9
83-84	Aston Villa	28	43	13	16
84-85	Aston Villa	19	22	1	3
85-86	Aston Villa	31	53	11	15
86-87	Aston Villa	32	55	7	9
87-88	Aston Villa	44	41	7	11
88-89	Aston Villa	34	52	8	10
89-90	Aston Villa	38	38	13	14
90-91	Aston Villa	34	54	11	13
91-92	Aston Villa	23	21	3	2
92-93	Aston Villa	25	29	8	7
93-94	Aston Villa	14 (1)	21	3	1
94-95	Aston Villa	12 (1)	-	5	-
TOTAL		357 (2)	454	98 (1)	110

★ *Full England international (1 cap).*

STEVE STAUNTON

Born Drogheda, Ireland,
19th January 1969.
Joined Villa August 1991
from Liverpool, £1.1m.
Villa debut v Sheff. Wed.
League (a), 17/8/91.
Scored the winner.

Was made club skipper to replace Kevin
Richardson and had yet aother superb
season at Villa Park.

Injury kept him out of the team just
before and just after Brian Little's
appointment but then he came back to
battle away unceasingly for the rest of
the season.

His powerful dashes down the left side
and explosive delivery of centres and
shots were a feature of Villa's game and
one which the opposition knew they
had to counteract.

Career Record:

Season	Club	League Apps	Gls	Cups Apps	Gls
86-87	Liverpool	-	-	-	-
87-88	Liverpool	-	-	-	-
(loan)	Bradford City	7 (1)	-	3	-
88-89	Liverpool	17 (4)	-	8	1
89-90	Liverpool	18 (2)	-	4 (2)	3
90-91	Liverpool	20 (4)	-	9	2
91-92	Aston Villa	37	4	6	-
92-93	Aston Villa	42	2	9	-
93-94	Aston Villa	24	3	9	-
94-95	Aston Villa	34 (1)	5	8	-
Villa record		*137 (1)*	*14*	*32*	*-*
TOTAL		199 (12)	14	56 (2)	6

★ *Full Republic of Ireland international (59 caps,
5 goals – up to and including 11/6/95).*

● NOTE: Career records of goalkeepers Nigel Spink (left) and Mark
Bosnich (p131) list number of goals conceded in the goals columns.

IAN TAYLOR

Born Birmingham,
4th June 1968.
Joined Villa December
1994 from Sheffield
Wednesday.
Villa debut v Arsenal,
League (a), 26/12/94.

Signed by Brian Little from Sheffield Wednesday in exchange for Guy Whittingham because of his industrious capacity to work ceaselessly from one penalty area to the other.

The Birmingham-born midfield player made his debut at Highbury on Boxing day and, on his home debut against Chelsea two days later 'signed in' with a headed goal in front of the Holte End where he used to stand.

After that his goals supply dried up disappointingly but his work-rate persisted and, significantly, Little selected him as an ever-present from the moment he joined the club.

Career Record:

Season	Club	League Apps	Gls	Cups Apps	Gls
92-93	Port Vale	41	15	15	4
93-94	Port Vale	42	13	8	3
94-95	Sheff. Wed.	9 (5)	1	2 (2)	1
	Aston Villa	21	1	2	-
Villa record		*21*	*1*	*2*	*-*
TOTAL		113 (5)	30	27 (2)	8

SHAUN TEALE

Born Southport,
10th March 1964.
Joined Villa July 1991
from Bournemouth,
£300,000.
Villa debut v Sheff Wed,
Lge (a), 17/8/91.

Distinctly a season of two halves for Teale who began the season injured and then gashed his arm in a domestic accident.

As Ugo Ehiogu took over his centre-back role, alongside Paul McGrath, Teale was seeking a move until the managerial change.

Little then recalled him to the side against Leicester City at Filbert Street, where he gave an outstanding, battling display, and he never looked back.

Chosen at either full-back or centre of defence his qualities of strength, defiance and skill were a crucial element in the battle for survival.

Career Record:

Season	Club	League Apps	Gls	Cups Apps	Gls
88-89	Bournemouth	19 (1)	-	-	-
89-90	Bournemouth	34	-	6	-
90-91	Bournemouth	46	4	10	1
91-92	Aston Villa	42	-	9	1
92-93	Aston Villa	39	1	8	1
93-94	Aston Villa	37 (1)	1	13	1
94-95	Aston Villa	28	-	4	-
Villa record		*146 (1)*	*2*	*34*	*3*
TOTAL		245 (2)	6	50	4

ANDY TOWNSEND

Born Maidstone,
27th July 1963.
Joined Villa July 1993
from Chelsea, £2.1m.
Villa debut v Queen's
Park Rangers, Lge (h),
14/8/93.

The Irish Republic World Cup skipper continued to gain an automatic place in midfield when not ruled out by injury or suspension.

Townsend's experienced and powerful presence in midfield was a valuable asset to the team throughout a difficult season when nerve and commitment were essential qualities.

Along with Taylor he formed the regular centre midfield partnership, giving Little both confidence and continuity of selection. Like Taylor, however, it was a slightly disappointing season on the goal-scoring front along with the rest of the team.

Career Record:

Season	Club	League Apps	Gls	Cups Apps	Gls
84-85	Southampton	5	-	-	-
85-86	Southampton	25 (2)	1	5 (5)	-
86-87	Southampton	11 (3)	1	2 (1)	-
87-88	Southampton	36 (1)	3	5	-
88-89	Norwich	31 (5)	5	7 (1)	2
89-90	Norwich	35	3	9	-
90-91	Chelsea	34	2	11	3
91-92	Chelsea	35	6	10	1
92-93	Chelsea	41	4	7	3
93-94	Aston Villa	32	3	15	1
94-95	Aston Villa	32	1	8	1
Villa record		*64*	*4*	*23*	*2*
TOTAL		317 (11)	29	79 (7)	11

★ *Republic of Ireland international (54 caps, 6 goals – up to and including 26/4/95).*

GUY WHITTINGHAM

Born Evesham,
10th June 1964.
Joined Villa August 1993
from Portsmouth,
£1.1m.
Villa debut As sub v Man.
Utd, Lge (h), 23/8/93.

The former soldier, signed after his record-scoring season with Portsmouth, was never quite able to live up to that promise at Villa Park.

He did, however, score three goals in seven full appearances without managing to secure a regular place.

After the change of manager Guy moved to Sheffield Wednesday in exchange for Ian Taylor soon after Brian Little's appointment.

Career Record:

Season	Club	League Apps	Gls	Cups Apps	Gls
89-90	Portsmouth	39 (3)	23	4	1
90-91	Portsmouth	34 (3)	12	5 (1)	8
91-92	Portsmouth	30 (5)	11	4 (4)	2
92-93	Portsmouth	46	42	10	5
93-94	Aston Villa	13 (5)	3	3	-
(loan)	Wolves	13	8	1	-
94-95	Aston Villa	4 (3)	2	3 (2)	1
Villa record		*17 (8)*	*5*	*6 (2)*	*1*
TOTAL		179 (19)	101	30 (7)	17

★ *Scored his 100th league goal against Liverpool at Anfield on October 8th 1994.*

★ *After leaving Villa he scored twice against Everton on his debut for Sheffield Wednesday.*

ALAN WRIGHT

Born Ashton-under-Lyme,
28th September 1971.
Joined Villa March 1995
from Blackburn Rovers,
£900,000.
Villa debut v West Ham
Utd, Lge (h), 18/3/95

Signed by Brian Little from Blackburn
Rovers in early March he instantly
became the regular left back enabling
Steve Staunton to employ his attacking
qualities.

Although lacking the height normally
associated with defenders Wright, who
lost his Ewood Park place through
injury, has all the other essentials.

With his pedigree on the England
international ladder up to and including
the Under-21s he has ambitions to even-
tually continue an international career.

Frustratingly for him, at Blackburn, it
was while he was injured that Kenny
Dalglish bought Graeme Le Saux who
then broke through for full caps.

Career Record:

Season	Club	League Apps	Gls	Cups Apps	Gls
87-88	Blackpool	- (1)	-	-	-
88-90	Blackpool	14 (2)	-	3 (1)	-
89-90	Blackpool	20 (4)	-	9 (3)	-
90-91	Blackpool	45	-	12	-
91-92	Blackpool	12	-	5	-
	Blackburn R.	32 (1)	1	5	-
92-93	Blackburn R.	24	-	9	-
93-94	Blackburn R.	7 (5)	-	2	-
94-95	Blackburn R.	4 (1)	-	- (1)	-
	Aston Villa	8	-	-	-
Villa record		8	-	-	-
TOTAL		166 (14)	1	45 (5)	-

★ *England U21 International.*

DWIGHT YORKE

Born Canaan, Tobago,
3rd November 1971.
Joined Villa December
1989 from Signal Hill in
Tobago, £120,000.
Villa debut v C.Palace,
Lge (a), 24/3/90.

The bubbly West Indian re-established
himself not only as a regular but as an
ever-present from the turn of the year.

His range of skills enabled him to play
either as a wide front man, or as a centre
striker or even as a lone front man.

Yorke can hold the ball up, make good
passes and certainly is capable of scoring
well into double figures, an achievement
which escaped him.

Among Yorke's 1994-95 successes was
his 'action-replay' double strike against
Liverpool at Villa Park in the final home
game of the season.

That 2-0 win, a week before the draw
at Norwich, claimed the three points
which ultimately hauled Villa clear of
Crystal Palace.

Career Record:

Season	Club	League Apps	Gls	Cups Apps	Gls
89-90	Aston Villa	- (2)	-	-	-
90-91	Aston Villa	8 (10)	2	3	-
91-92	Aston Villa	27 (5)	11	8	6
92-93	Aston Villa	22 (5)	6	6 (2)	1
93-94	Aston Villa	2 (10)	2	- (2)	1
94-95	Aston Villa	33 (4)	6	6	2
TOTAL		92 (36)	21	23 (4)	10

★ *Full international with Trinidad & Tobago.*

● *All international records are up to and
including 11th June 1995.*

FIRST TEAM APPEARANCES & GOALSCORERS

	LEAGUE Apps	Gls	FA CUP Apps	Gls	LGE CUP Apps	Gls	UEFA CUP Apps	Gls	TOTAL Apps	Gls
Dalian ATKINSON	11 (5)	3	-	-	2	3	3	1	16 (5)	7
Earl BARRETT	24 (1)	-	2	-	3	-	4	-	33 (1)	-
Chris BODEN	- (1)	-	-	-	-	-	-	-	- (1)	-
Mark BOSNICH	30	-	1	-	3	-	-	-	34	-
Franz CARR	- (2)	-	-	-	-	-	-	-	- (2)	-
Gary CHARLES	14 (2)	-	-		-		-		14 (2)	-
Ugo EHIOGU	38 (1)	3	2	-	3	-	4	1	47 (1)	4
John FASHANU	11 (2)	3	2	-	-	-	1	-	14 (2)	3
Dave FARRELL	-	-	-	-	2	-	-	-	2	-
Graham FENTON	7 (10)	2	-	-	1 (2)	-	-	-	8 (12)	2
Ray HOUGHTON	19 (7)	1	-	-	2	-	3 (1)	1	24 (8)	2
Tommy JOHNSON	11 (3)	4	- (1)	-	-	-	-	-	11 (4)	4
Phil KING	13 (3)	-	-	-	3	-	4	-	20 (3)	-
Nii LAMPTEY	1 (5)	-	-	-	2 (1)	3	-	-	3 (6)	3
Paul McGRATH	36 (4)	-	2	-	3	-	4	-	45 (4)	-
Michael OAKES	-	-	-	-	1	-	-	-	1	-
Garry PARKER	12 (2)	1	-	-	4	-	- (2)	-	16 (4)	1
Kevin RICHARDSON	18 (1)	-	-	-	-	-	4	-	22 (1)	-
Dean SAUNDERS	39	15	2	1	3	1	4	-	48	17
Bryan SMALL	5	-	-	-	-	-	-	-	5	-
Nigel SPINK	12 (1)	-	1	-	-	-	4	-	17 (1)	-
Steve STAUNTON	34 (1)	5	2	-	2	-	4	-	42 (1)	5
Ian TAYLOR	21	1	2	-	-	-	-	-	23	1
Shaun TEALE	28	-	2	-	2	-	-	-	32	-
Andy TOWNSEND	32	1	2	-	2	1	4	-	40	2
Guy WHITTINGHAM	4 (3)	2	-	-	2 (1)	1	1 (1)	-	7 (5)	3
Alan WRIGHT	8	-	-	-	-	-	-	-	8	-
Dwight YORKE	33 (4)	6	2	1	4	1	-	-	39 (4)	8
Own Goal	-	4	-	-	-	-	-	-	-	4

Unused Substitutes:
Nigel Spink 31, Michael Oakes 12, Graham Fenton 9, Mark Bosnich 8, Tommy Johnson 5, Garry Parker 5, Dalian Atkinson 3, Chris Boden 3, Ray Houghton 3, Kevin Richardson 3, Shaun Teale 3, Franz Carr 2, Gary Charles 2, Phil King 2, Earl Barrett 1, Dave Farrell 1, John Fashanu 1, Nii Lamptey 1, Paul McGrath 1, Steve Staunton 1, Andy Townsend 1, Guy Whittingham 1.

Goalscorers in friendly games:
Whittingham 9, Yorke 5, Fenton 4, Saunders 4, Farrell 3, Parker 3, Ehiogu 2, Lamptey 2, Atkinson 1, Cowe 1, Farrelly 1, Houghton 1, Murray 1.

HIGHEST AND LOWEST

Highest home attendance:
40,154 v Liverpool, 6.5.95
Lowest home attendance:
12,433 v Wigan Athletic, 21.9.94
Highest away attendance:
43,795 v Manchester United, 4.2.95
Lowest away attendance:
2,633 v Wigan Athletic, 5.10.94
Biggest victory:
7-1 v Wimbledon (home), 11.2.94
Heaviest defeat:
0-4 v Arsenal (home), 17.4.95
Most goals in a match:
3, Tommy Johnson v Wimbledon (h) 11.2.95
Most goals against:
2, Alan Shearer (Blackburn Rovers) 24.9.94
2, Robbie Fowler (Liverpool) 8.10.94
2, Jürgen Klinsmann (Tottenham) 19.11.94
2, Gareth Southgate (Crystal Palace) 30.11.94
2, Chris Armstrong (Crystal Palace) 30.11.94
2, Uwe Rosler (Manchester City) 31.12.94
2, David Lowe (Leicester City) 22.2.95
2, Peter Beardsley (Newcastle United) 25.2.95
2, John Hartson (Arsenal) 17.4.95
2, Ian Wright (Arsenal) 17.4.95

Clean sheets: 16
Failed to score: 18
Villa scored first: 25
Scored first and won: 19
Scored first and drew: 4
Scored first and lost: 2
Opponents scored first: 25
Lost after opponents scored first: 16
Drew after opponents scored first: 3
Won after opponents scored first: 6
Highest League position: 8th
Lowest League position: 20th

SEQUENCE RECORDS

Most matches undefeated:
8, Dec 26 - Jan 25
Most home matches undefeated:
8, Nov 27 - Feb 22
Most away matches undefeated:
4, Dec 26 - Jan 21
Most wins in succession:
4, Jan 7 - Jan 25

Most home wins in succession:
3, Sep 10 - Sep 29 and Jan 14 - Feb 11
Most away wins in succession:
2, Jan 7 - Jan 21
Longest run without a win:
6, Nov 27 - Dec 26
Longest run without a home win:
6, Feb 22 - May 3
Longest run without an away win:
5, Nov 30 - Dec 31
Most defeats in succession: **3**
Goals for in successive matches:
7 matches, Nov 1 - Dec 3
Goals against in successive matches:
8, Oct 29 - Dec 3
Longest run without scoring:
410 minutes, Feb 25 - Apr 1
Longest run without conceding a goal:
182 minutes, Mar 4 - Apr 15
Most consecutive appearances:
28 - Shaun Teale, 3.12.94 - 14.5.95
Ever-presents: None

DEBUTANTS

Ten players made their Villa first team debuts in 1994/95 – Chis Boden, Franz Carr, Gary Charles, John Fashanu, Tommy Johnson, Phil King, Nii Lamptey, Michael Oakes, Ian Taylor and Alan Wright.

RED CARDS

Andy Townsend was shown the red card twice in league encounters against Wimbledon and Arsenal, with Mark Bosnich being sent off at Leeds United and Ugo Ehiogu in a Coca-Cola Cup tie at Crystal Palace. The only opposition player to receive his marching orders was Tranzonspor's Ogün Termizkanoglu in the UEFA Cup tie at Villa Park.

QUICK OFF THE MARK

Dwight Yorke netted Villa's fastest goal of the season, after just three minutes, in Villa's 1-0 win at Coventry City.

The earliest conceded goal was Stuart Pearce's second minute penalty during Nottingham Forest's 2-0 victory at Villa Park.

FINAL TABLE

		Home					Away					Total					
	Pl	W	D	L	F	A	W	D	L	F	A	W	D	L	F	A	Pts
1 Blackburn Rovers	42	17	2	2	54	21	10	6	5	26	18	27	8	7	80	48	89
2 Manchester United	42	16	4	1	42	4	10	6	5	35	24	26	10	6	77	28	88
3 Nottingham Forest	42	12	6	3	36	18	10	5	6	36	25	22	11	9	72	43	77
4 Liverpool	42	13	5	3	38	13	8	6	7	27	24	21	11	10	65	37	74
5 Leeds United	42	13	5	3	35	15	7	8	6	24	23	20	13	9	59	38	73
6 Newcastle United	42	14	6	1	46	20	6	6	9	21	27	20	12	10	67	47	72
7 Tottenham Hotspur	42	10	5	6	32	25	6	9	6	34	33	16	14	12	66	58	62
8 Queens Park Rangers	42	11	3	7	36	26	6	6	9	25	33	17	9	16	61	59	60
9 Wimbledon	42	9	5	7	26	26	6	6	9	22	39	15	11	16	48	65	56
10 Southampton	42	8	9	4	33	27	4	9	8	28	36	12	18	12	61	63	54
11 Chelsea	42	7	7	7	25	22	6	8	7	25	33	13	15	14	50	55	54
12 Arsenal	42	6	9	6	27	21	7	3	11	25	28	13	12	17	52	49	51
13 Sheffield Wednesday	42	7	7	7	26	26	6	5	10	23	31	13	12	17	49	57	51
14 West Ham United	42	9	6	6	28	19	4	5	12	16	29	13	11	18	44	48	50
15 Everton	42	8	9	4	31	23	3	8	10	13	28	11	17	14	44	51	50
16 Coventry City	42	7	7	7	23	25	5	7	9	21	37	12	14	16	44	62	50
17 Manchester City	42	8	7	6	37	28	4	6	11	16	36	12	13	17	53	64	49
18 Aston Villa	42	6	9	6	27	24	5	6	10	24	32	11	15	16	51	56	48
19 Crystal Palace	42	6	6	9	16	23	5	6	10	18	26	11	12	19	34	49	45
20 Norwich City	42	8	8	5	27	21	2	5	14	10	33	10	13	19	37	54	43
21 Leicester City	42	5	6	10	28	37	1	5	15	17	43	6	11	25	45	80	29
22 Ipswich Town	42	5	3	13	24	34	2	3	16	12	59	7	6	29	36	93	27

ROLL OF HONOUR

Champions: Blackburn Rovers
Runners-up: Manchester United
Relegated: Crystal Palace, Norwich City, Leicester City, Ipswich Town
FA Cup winners: Everton
Coca-Cola Cup winners: Liverpool

FACTS & FIGURES

Of the 462 games played, 205 resulted in home wins, 123 in away wins and 134 in draws. A total of 1,195 goals were scored, (the same number as the previous season) an average of 2.58 per game, 697 by the home clubs and 498 by the away clubs.

Most goals: 80, Blackburn Rovers
Most home goals: 54, Blackburn Rovers
Most away goals: 36, Nottingham Forest
Least goals: 34, Crystal Palace
Least home goals: 16, Crystal Palace

Least away goals: 10, Norwich City
Least goals conceded: 27, Manchester United
Least home goals conceded: 4, Manchester Utd.
Least away goals conceded: 18, Blackburn R.
Most goals conceded: 93, Ipswich Town
Most home goals conceded: 37, Leicester City
Most away goals conceded: 59, Ipswich Town

Highest goals aggregate: 129, Ipswich Town
Lowest goals aggregate: 83, Crystal Palace

Best home record: 53pts, Blackburn Rovers
Best away record: 36pts, Blackburn Rovers and Manchester United
Worst home record: 18pts, Ipswich Town
Worst away record: 8pts, Leicester City

Highest home score:
Manchester United 9 Ipswich Town 0, 4.3.95

Highest away score:
Sheffield Wednesday 1 Nottingham Forest 7, 1.4.95

GOALSCORERS & ATTENDANCES

LEADING SCORERS

(Including Cup & European games)

37 Alan Shearer (Blackburn Rovers)
31 Robbie Fowler (Liverpool)
30 Ian Wright (Arsenal)
29 Jurgen Klinsmann (Tottenham Hotspur)
29 Matthew Le Tissier (Southampton)
27 *Andy Cole (Manchester United)
26 Les Ferdinand (Queens Park Rangers)
25 Stan Collymore (Nottingham Forest)
25 *Ashley Ward (Norwich City)
23 Teddy Sheringham (Tottenham Hotspur)
22 Uwe Rosler (Manchester City)
21 Chris Sutton (Blackburn Rovers)
19 Ian Rush (Liverpool)
18 Chris Armstrong (Crystal Palace)
18 *Paul Kitson (Newcastle United)
17 Dean Saunders (Aston Villa)
16 Dion Dublin (Coventry City)
16 Paul Rideout (Everton)

Includes goals for other clubs

Highest home score:
9-0 Man. Utd v Ipswich 4.3.95

Highest away score:
1-7 Sheff. W. v Nottm F. 1.4.95

Five goals in a match:
Andy Cole (Man. U.) v Ipswich 4.3.95

Three goals in a match:
Chris Sutton (Blackburn) v Coventry 27.8.94
Robbie Fowler (Liverpool) v Arsenal 28.8.94
Andrei Kanchelskis (Man. U.) v Man. C. 10.11.94
Alan Shearer (Blackburn) v QPR 26.11.94
Teddy Sheringham (Spurs) v Newcastle 3.12.94
Tony Cottee (West Ham) v Man. C. 17.12.94
Alan Shearer (Blackburn) v W.Ham 2.1.95
Alan Shearer (Blackburn) v Ipswich 28.1.95
Tommy Johnson (A.Villa) v Wimbledon 11.2.95
Peter Ndlovu (Coventry) v Liverpool 14.3.95
Anthony Yeboah (Leeds) v Ipswich 5.4.95
Ian Wright (Arsenal) v Ipswich 15.4.95

Highest attendance:
43,868 Man. Utd v Sheffield Weds. 7.5.95

Lowest attendance:
5,268 Wimbledon v Manchester City 21.3.95

THE GATE LEAGUE

	Best	Average
Manchester United	43,868	43,681
Arsenal	39,377	35,377
Newcastle United	35,626	34,691
Liverpool	40,014	34,175
Leeds United	39,426	32,964
Everton	40,011	31,367
Aston Villa	40,154	29,756
Tottenham Hotspur	33,040	27,258
Sheffield Wednesday	34,051	26,595
Blackburn Rovers	30,545	25,271
Nottingham Forest	28,882	23,537
Manchester City	27,850	22,747
Chelsea	31,161	21,057
West Ham United	24,783	20,175
Leicester City	21,393	19,531
Norwich City	21,843	18,620
Ipswich Town	22,559	16,907
Coventry City	21,885	15,977
Crystal Palace	18,224	14,801
Southampton	15,210	14,689
Queens Park Rangers	18,948	14,595
Wimbledon	18,224	10,206

PONTIN'S LEAGUE DIVISION ONE TABLE

	P	W	D	L	F	A	Pts
Bolton Wanderers	34	22	5	7	69	46	71
Everton	34	17	10	7	63	32	61
Leeds United	34	19	4	11	53	37	61
Sheffield United	34	17	8	9	49	36	59
Tranmere Rovers	34	16	9	9	65	53	57
Derby County	34	15	7	12	51	52	52
Notts County	34	15	6	13	46	48	51
West Bromwich A.	34	13	8	13	53	54	47
Wolverhampton W.	34	12	11	11	40	52	47
Manchester United	34	12	9	13	45	45	45
Stoke City	34	12	7	15	46	44	43
Blackburn Rovers	34	10	12	12	31	37	42
Liverpool	34	11	9	14	41	48	42
Nottingham Forest	34	9	11	14	45	46	38
Sunderland	34	10	8	16	49	56	38
Aston Villa	34	11	4	19	41	53	37
Coventry City	34	8	7	19	30	45	31
Rotherham United	34	7	5	22	34	67	26

PONTIN'S CENTRAL LEAGUE

Aug	20	H	**Derby County**	2-0	Fenton, Whittingham
Aug	23	A	Manchester United	0-2	
Aug	30	A	Sheffield United	2-4	Whittingham, Fenton
Sep	7	A	Sunderland	2-1	Fenton, Farrell
Sep	12	H	**Notts County**	0-2	
Sep	19	A	Wolverhampton W.	2-1	Scimeca, Whittingham
Sep	26	H	**Liverpool**	1-0	Whittingham
Oct	6	H	**Leeds United**	2-0	Davis, Berry
Oct	12	A	Blackburn Rovers	0-0	
Oct	20	A	Stoke City	3-3	Boden, Fenton (2)
Oct	27	H	**Nottingham Forest**	3-1	Scimeca (2), Farrell
Nov	10	A	Tranmere Rovers	0-2	
Nov	16	H	**Bolton Wanderers**	0-2	
Nov	23	A	West Bromwich Albion	1-2	Scimeca
Dec	1	H	**Stoke City**	0-1	
Dec	6	A	Derby County	3-1	Pearce, Scimeca, Murray
Dec	21	H	**Rotherham United**	2-3	Scimeca, Lamptey
Jan	18	H	**Everton**	2-2	Davis, Berry
Jan	26	A	Nottingham Forest	1-1	Parker
Feb	1	H	**Tranmere Rovers**	0-2	
Feb	8	A	Bolton Wanderers	3-4	Scimeca, Cowe, Farrell
Feb	20	H	**Manchester United**	2-0	Scimeca, Davis
Mar	9	H	**Wolverhampton W.**	1-2	Cowe
Mar	20	A	Liverpool	0-2	
Mar	23	A	Notts County	1-2	Cowe
Mar	27	A	Coventry City	2-1	Cowe, Davis
Mar	29	H	**Sunderland**	1-3	Murray
Apr	4	A	Rotherham United	1-0	Berry
Apr	13	H	**Sheffield United**	2-3	Cowe, Browne
Apr	18	A	Everton	0-1	
Apr	26	H	**Coventry City**	0-1	
May	1	H	**West Bromwich Albion**	1-2	Lamptey
May	3	A	Leeds United	0-2	
May	10	H	**Blackburn Rovers**	1-0	Lamptey

BIRMINGHAM COUNTY FA SENIOR CUP

Nov	21	A	Banbury United (Rd 2)	9-2	Berry (4), Scimeca (2), Farrell (2), Cowe
Dec	13	A	Burton Albion (Rd 3)	3-1	Cowe (2), Evans
Feb	6	A	Hednesford Town (Rd 4)	3-3	Scimeca, Davis, Cowe
Feb	21	A	Hednesford Town (Rd 4R)	2-1	Boden, Scimeca
Mar	14	H	**Paget Rangers** (SF)	5-0	Boden (2), Davis, Berry, Scimeca
Apr	24	H	**Solihull Borough** (Final)	0-2	

League and Cup double for Youths but Reserves are relegated

Although the Reserve team suffered a difficult and disappointing season in losing their Pontins League First Division status, the youths did far better.

New manager Brian Little was quick to emphasise that the importance of the development side is in bringing individuals through to first team status rather than the building of successful reserve and youth teams.

There was a considerable upheaval behind the scenes with the departure of staff including youth coach Colin Clarke who was replaced by Tony McAndrew. Significant signs that this department of the club was moving along the right lines came with the progress of several excellent YTS players.

Their input led to a treble being achieved of Purity League and League Cup plus the winning of a prestigious international youth tournament in Japan. They also reached the semi-final of the FA Youth Cup.

Meanwhile, Villa continued to attract a flow of young players to the club at all age levels with the accent heavily on local talent.

SOUTHERN JUNIOR FLOODLIT CUP

Aug 22	A	Oxford United (Rd 1)	4-0	Byfield (3), Burgess
Nov 2	H	**Northampton T.** (Rd 2)	6-3	Byfield (2), Moore, Collins, Walker, Hendrie
Nov 29	A	Wimbledon (Rd 3)	2-5	Byfield, Moore

FA YOUTH CUP

Oct 22	H	**Derby County** (Rd 1)	1-1	Senior
Nov 21	A	Derby County (Rd 1R)	3-0	Moore, Burchell, Hendrie
Dec 7	H	**Leeds United** (Rd 2)	1-0	Burgess
Jan 11	H	**Leyton Orient** (Rd 3)	1-0	Impey
Jan 30	H	**Colchester Utd** (Rd 4)	4-0	Hendrie, Burchell, Byfield, Burgess
Feb 28	H	**Manchester Utd** (Rd 5)	2-3	Burgess, Walker

MIDLAND YOUTH CUP

Oct 19	H	**Derby County** (Rd 1)	2-3	Moore, Burgess

MIDLAND PURITY YOUTH LEAGUE CUP

Nov 26	H	**Northampton T.** (Rd 2)	8-0	Walker (2), Burgess (2), Burchell (2), Hendrie, Byfield
Mar 8	A	Wolverhampton W. (Rd 3)	3-2	Jaczeszun, Walker, Hendrie
Apr 22	H	**Derby County** (SF)	2-0	Hendrie, Burgess
May 15	H	**Birmingham City** (F)	2-1	Hendrie, Burchell

MIDLAND PURITY YOUTH LEAGUE

Aug	14	H	**Birmingham City**	4-1	Walker (2), Moore, Byfield
Aug	20	A	Coventry City	4-2	Byfield (2), Collins, Walker
Aug	27	H	**Derby County**	3-2	Byfield (2), Senior
Sep	3	A	Grimsby Town	5-0	Moore, Senior, Walker, Byfield, Hendrie
Sep	10	H	**Leicester City**	4-1	Byfield (2), Walker, Burgess
Sep	16	A	Lincoln City	2-0	Hendrie (2)
Sep	24	H	**West Bromwich Albion**	5-0	Burgess (3), Petty, Hendrie
Oct	1	A	Northampton Town	3-1	Hines, Walker, Byfield
Oct	8	H	**Notts County**	4-1	Hendrie (2), Byfield (2)
Oct	15	A	Nottingham Forest	3-0	Byfield (2), Walker
Oct	29	A	Port Vale	3-0	Burchell, Walker, Byfield
Nov	12	H	**Shrewsbury Town**	6-0	Burchell (3), Walker (2), Byfield
Nov	19	A	Stoke City	3-1	Hines, Byfield, Hendrie
Dec	3	A	West Bromwich Albion	4-2	Impey, Burchell, Byfield, Hendrie
Dec	10	H	**Peterborough United**	4-1	Burgess (2), Walker, Hendrie
Dec	17	H	**Wolverhampton W.**	3-1	Hines, Walker, Byfield
Jan	14	A	Birmingham City	2-0	Walker, Burgess
Jan	21	H	**Coventry City**	3-2	Walker (2), Burchell
Feb	4	A	Derby County	1-0	Burchell
Feb	11	H	**Walsall**	1-0	Hendrie, Walker
Feb	18	H	**Lincoln City**	6-3	Byfield (2), Moore, Lescott, Walker, Hendrie
Feb	24	A	Mansfield Town	4-2	Walker (2), Burchell, Byfield
Mar	11	A	Notts County	1-2	Burchell
Mar	15	H	**Northampton Town**	8-0	Kirby (3), Walker (3), Burgess, Burchell
Mar	18	A	Walsall	4-3	Hines, Burgess, Walker, Byfield
Mar	22	A	Leicester City	2-3	Mitchell, Burchell
Mar	25	H	**Nottingham Forest**	4-1	Impey, Kirby, Burchell, Byfield
Apr	1	A	Peterborough United	3-0	Kirby, Walker, Burgess
Apr	8	H	**Port Vale**	4-0	Byfield, Lee, Kirby, Burchell
Apr	12	A	Wolverhampton W.	2-0	
Apr	15	A	Shrewsbury Town	3-0	Lee, Kirby, Burchell
Apr	19	H	**Grimsby Town**	1-1	Mitchell
Apr	26	H	**Stoke City**	3-4	Lee (2), Hendrie
May	13	H	**Mansfield Town**	2-1	Hines, Byfield

RESERVE & YOUTH TEAM APPEARANCES

	CENTRAL LGE		SENIOR CUP		YOUTH LGE		YOUTH CUPS	
	Apps	Gls	Apps	Gls	Apps	Gls	Apps	Gls
Nasser Abdellah	3	-	-	-	-	-	-	-
Dalian Atkinson	2	-	-	-	-	-	-	-
Earl Barrett	1	-	-	-	-	-	-	-
Trevor Berry	17 (3)	3	3 (1)	5	-	-	-	-
Chris Boden	21 (1)	1	5	3	-	-	-	-
Stuart Brock	2	-	1	-	14	-	7	-
Ian Brown	14 (1)	-	2 (1)	-	-	-	-	-
Paul Browne	32 (2)	1	6	-	-	-	-	-
Lee Burchell	1	-	-	-	24 (4)	14	14	5
Richard Burgess	-	-	-	-	12 (13)	10	5 (5)	8
Darren Byfield	- (2)	-	-	-	27 (2)	25	13 (1)	8
Franz Carr	4	-	-	-	-	-	-	-
Lee Collins	-	-	-	-	19 (2)	1	9 (1)	1
Steven Cowe	18 (1)	4	6	4	-	-	-	-
Neil Davis	11 (9)	5	4	2	-	-	-	-
Darren Evans	27 (1)	1	5 (1)	1	-	-	-	-
Dave Farrell	27 (1)	3	2 (2)	2	-	-	-	-
Gareth Farrelly	15 (4)	-	4 (1)	-	-	-	-	-
Graham Fenton	18	5	-	-	-	-	-	-
Lee Hendrie	- (1)	1	- (1)	-	21 (1)	11	14	7
Leslie Hines	-	-	-	-	27 (3)	6	13 (1)	-
Ray Houghton	1	-	-	-	-	-	-	-
David Hughes	-	-	-	-	17 (1)	-	2	-
Jamie Impey	-	-	-	-	12 (1)	2	2	1
Tommy Jaczeszun	-	-	-	-	9 (5)	-	2 (2)	1
Tommy Johnson	2	-	-	-	-	-	-	-
Phil King	6	-	-	-	-	-	-	-
Alan Kirby	-	-	-	-	23	7	2 (2)	-
Nii Lamptey	12	3	-	-	-	-	-	-
Alan Lee	-	-	-	-	7 (3)	4	- (1)	-
Jonathan Miley	-	-	-	-	20 (2)	-	11 (1)	-
Andrew Mitchell	-	-	-	-	19 (5)	2	9 (2)	-
Darrell Mooney	2	-	1	-	-	-	-	-
David Moore	-	-	-	-	26 (2)	4	13	4
John Murphy	1 (3)	-	2 (1)	-	-	-	-	-
Scott Murray	11 (4)	2	5 (1)	-	-	-	-	-
Michael Oakes	22	-	3	-	-	-	-	-
Garry Parker	8	1	-	-	-	-	-	-
Dennis Pearce	20 (4)	-	5	-	-	-	-	-
Ben Petty	-	-	-	-	27 (1)	1	10 (1)	-
Adam Rachel	2	-	2	-	18	-	7	-
Kevin Richardson	3	-	-	-	-	-	-	-
Riccardo Scimeca	25 (4)	8	6	5	-	-	-	-
Marc Senior	-	-	-	-	7 (2)	2	5 (1)	1
Bryan Small	19	-	1	-	-	-	-	-
Nigel Spink	8	-	-	-	-	-	-	-
Shaun Teale	8	-	1	-	-	-	-	-
Andy Townsend	1	-	-	-	-	-	-	-
Richard Walker	-	-	-	-	30	24	13	5
Danny West	3 (2)	-	2	-	-	-	-	-
Guy Whittingham	7	4	-	-	-	-	-	-

Also played for the youth team: Freestone 1 app (Lge); George 1 app (Lge); Hadland 1(2) apps (Lge); Hazell 2(1) apps (Lge); Hickman 1(1) app (Lge); Hutchings -(1) app (Lge); Lescott 4(1) apps 1gl (Lge); Michael 1app (Lge); Tallentire 1 app (Lge)

VILLA'S ALL-TIME LEAGUE RECORD – CLUB BY CLUB

	Home						Away				
	P	W	D	L	F	A	W	D	L	F	A
Accrington	10	4	0	1	26	12	1	2	2	9	10
Arsenal	132	36	13	17	133	93	20	13	33	78	109
Barnsley	10	3	2	0	9	2	4	1	0	13	2
Birmingham City	96	23	13	12	82	60	16	12	20	68	74
Blackburn Rovers	126	33	17	13	135	83	17	11	35	86	136
Blackpool	62	16	9	6	65	39	10	7	14	44	51
Bolton Wanderers	126	34	15	14	137	81	15	13	35	64	126
Bournemouth	4	1	1	0	3	2	1	0	1	2	4
Bradford Park Avenue	10	4	0	1	12	4	1	2	2	8	16
Bradford City	28	9	2	3	32	12	4	4	6	17	23
Brentford	6	2	1	0	12	4	3	0	0	8	3
Brighton & Hove Albion	16	6	2	0	16	4	3	2	3	8	7
Bristol City	32	10	3	3	27	19	5	6	5	18	14
Bristol Rovers	8	3	1	0	8	3	2	1	1	4	4
Burnley	94	28	12	7	109	47	11	8	28	71	113
Bury	52	17	6	3	59	31	10	6	10	39	39
Cardiff City	44	14	3	5	39	20	8	2	12	23	30
Carlisle United	10	4	1	0	5	1	2	2	1	6	6
Charlton Athletic	38	10	6	3	41	18	5	6	8	22	33
Chelsea	96	27	12	9	104	67	15	9	24	59	73
Chesterfield	8	2	1	1	7	4	3	0	1	8	3
Coventry City	42	11	10	0	30	10	9	6	6	28	26
Crystal Palace	22	7	2	2	19	8	2	5	4	5	9
Darwen	4	2	0	0	16	0	1	1	0	6	2
Derby County	104	33	10	9	130	58	17	11	24	71	90
Doncaster Rovers	4	1	1	0	4	3	0	0	2	1	3
Everton	160	37	19	24	149	112	20	20	40	98	149
Fulham	34	8	5	4	30	22	2	5	10	20	34
Gillingham	2	1	0	0	2	1	0	1	0	0	0
Glossop	2	1	0	0	9	0	0	0	1	0	1
Grimsby Town	20	5	3	2	29	19	5	1	4	16	20
Halifax Town	4	1	1	0	2	1	1	0	1	2	2
Huddersfield Town	64	20	9	3	74	31	7	10	15	32	51
Hull City	16	4	3	1	21	8	2	2	4	7	12
Ipswich Town	40	11	6	3	40	17	5	4	11	20	30
Leeds United	62	14	10	7	52	40	6	10	15	31	54
Leicester City	68	17	6	11	73	52	6	9	19	48	87
Leyton Orient	10	4	1	0	8	3	1	2	2	3	6
Lincoln City	2	0	1	0	1	1	0	1	0	0	0
Liverpool	140	35	16	19	147	90	12	14	44	78	160
Luton Town	32	10	1	5	29	15	1	3	12	8	24
Manchester City	122	32	19	10	114	66	14	15	32	79	117

	Home					Away				
	P	W	D	L	F	A	W	D	L	F	A
Manchester United	124	31	15	16	131	92	10	13	39	61	132
Mansfield Town	4	0	0	2	0	2	0	1	1	1	3
Middlesbrough	102	29	9	13	120	59	17	14	20	66	78
Millwall	18	4	4	1	14	8	3	2	4	9	12
Newcastle United	114	31	12	14	114	62	12	9	36	75	128
Northampton Town	2	0	0	1	1	2	0	0	1	1	2
Norwich City	46	14	6	3	42	25	4	7	12	28	41
Nottingham Forest	102	32	9	10	105	52	16	14	21	73	96
Notts County	66	23	7	3	83	29	12	8	13	49	52
Oldham Athletic	30	9	3	3	34	8	7	6	2	29	17
Oxford United	14	4	2	1	9	3	1	3	3	8	11
Plymouth Argyle	14	5	1	1	19	9	2	2	3	12	12
Portsmouth	60	19	7	4	73	39	8	7	15	42	65
Port Vale	4	2	0	0	3	0	0	1	1	4	6
Preston North End	98	37	3	9	108	44	13	11	25	64	90
Queen's Park Rangers	36	7	4	7	28	24	3	3	12	14	28
Reading	4	2	0	0	4	2	2	0	0	7	3
Rochdale	4	2	0	0	3	0	0	1	1	1	2
Rotherham United	8	3	0	1	8	3	2	1	1	6	3
Scunthorpe United	2	1	0	0	5	0	1	0	0	2	1
Sheffield United	120	40	12	8	145	55	17	16	27	85	111
Sheffield Wednesday	118	42	8	9	150	60	15	8	36	83	127
Shrewsbury Town	6	3	0	0	6	0	1	1	1	4	4
Southampton	40	10	7	3	33	16	2	7	11	17	38
Stockport County	2	1	0	0	7	1	1	0	0	3	1
Stoke City	88	31	7	6	108	36	13	13	18	54	66
Sunderland	138	45	11	13	143	88	14	21	34	88	134
Swansea City	14	7	0	0	19	0	4	0	3	12	10
Swindon Town	10	3	1	1	10	5	2	2	1	6	4
Torquay United	4	1	0	1	5	2	0	1	1	2	3
Tottenham Hotspur	104	22	13	17	80	73	17	9	26	85	107
Tranmere Rovers	4	2	0	0	3	0	1	1	0	2	1
Walsall	4	0	2	0	0	0	0	1	1	1	4
Watford	12	3	2	1	11	6	0	2	4	9	16
West Bromwich Albion	124	39	8	15	118	74	19	15	28	86	99
West Ham United	64	18	4	10	68	44	4	10	18	38	76
Wimbledon	16	3	1	4	11	9	2	2	4	12	14
Wolverhampton Wan.	96	26	10	12	109	64	15	12	21	67	86
Wrexham	4	1	0	1	5	4	2	0	0	5	2
York City	4	2	0	0	5	0	1	1	0	2	1
TOTALS	3786	1094	411	388	3980	2163	510	452	931	2421	3439

VILLA'S ALL-TIME LEAGUE RECORD

Season	Div	Teams	Pos	P	W	D	L	F	A	W	D	L	F	A	Pts	Cup Honours
1888-89	1	12	2nd	22	10	0	1	44	16	2	5	4	17	27	29	*(FAC Winners in 1886-87)*
1889-90	1	12	8th	22	6	2	3	30	15	1	3	7	13	36	19	
1890-91	1	12	9th	22	5	4	2	29	18	2	0	9	16	40	18	
1891-92	1	14	4th	26	10	0	3	63	23	5	0	8	26	33	30	*FAC Runners-up*
1892-93	1	16	4th	30	12	1	2	50	24	4	2	9	23	38	35	
1893-94	**1**	**16**	**1st**	**30**	**12**	**2**	**1**	**49**	**13**	**7**	**4**	**4**	**35**	**29**	**44**	
1894-95	1	16	3rd	30	12	2	1	51	12	5	3	7	31	31	39	***FAC Winners***
1895-96	**1**	**16**	**1st**	**30**	**14**	**1**	**0**	**47**	**17**	**6**	**4**	**5**	**31**	**28**	**45**	
1896-97	**1**	**16**	**1st**	**30**	**10**	**3**	**2**	**36**	**16**	**11**	**2**	**2**	**37**	**22**	**47**	***FAC Winners***
1897-98	1	16	6th	30	12	1	2	47	21	2	4	9	14	30	33	
1898-99	**1**	**18**	**1st**	**34**	**15**	**2**	**0**	**58**	**13**	**4**	**5**	**8**	**18**	**27**	**45**	
1899-00	**1**	**18**	**1st**	**34**	**12**	**4**	**1**	**45**	**18**	**10**	**2**	**5**	**32**	**17**	**50**	
1900-01	1	18	15th	34	8	5	4	32	18	2	5	10	13	33	30	*FAC Semi-finalists*
1901-02	1	18	8th	34	9	5	3	27	13	4	3	10	15	27	34	
1902-03	1	18	2nd	34	11	3	3	43	18	8	0	9	18	22	41	*FAC Semi-finalists*
1903-04	1	18	5th	34	13	1	3	41	16	4	6	7	29	32	41	
1904-05	1	18	4th	34	11	2	4	32	15	8	2	7	31	28	42	***FAC Winners***
1905-06	1	20	8th	38	13	2	4	51	19	4	4	11	21	37	40	
1906-07	1	20	5th	38	13	4	2	51	19	6	2	11	27	33	44	
1907-08	1	20	8th	38	9	6	4	47	24	8	3	8	30	35	43	
1908-09	1	20	7th	38	8	7	4	31	22	6	3	10	27	34	38	
1909-10	**1**	**20**	**1st**	**38**	**17**	**2**	**0**	**62**	**19**	**6**	**5**	**8**	**22**	**23**	**53**	
1910-11	1	20	2nd	38	15	3	1	50	18	7	4	8	19	23	51	
1911-12	1	20	6th	38	12	2	5	48	22	5	5	9	28	41	41	
1912-13	1	20	2nd	38	13	4	2	57	21	6	8	5	29	31	50	***FAC Winners***
1913-14	1	20	2nd	38	11	3	5	36	21	8	3	8	29	29	44	*FAC Semi-finalists*
1914-15	1	20	13th	38	10	5	4	39	32	3	6	10	23	40	37	
First World War																
1919-20	1	22	9th	42	11	3	7	49	36	7	3	11	26	37	42	***FAC Winners***
1920-21	1	22	10th	42	11	4	6	39	21	7	3	11	24	49	43	
1921-22	1	22	5th	42	16	3	2	50	19	6	0	15	24	36	47	
1922-23	1	22	6th	42	15	3	3	42	11	3	7	11	22	40	46	
1923-24	1	22	6th	42	10	10	1	33	11	8	3	10	19	26	49	*FAC Runners-up*
1924-25	1	22	15th	42	10	7	4	34	25	3	6	12	24	46	39	
1925-26	1	22	6th	42	12	7	2	56	25	4	5	12	30	51	44	
1926-27	1	22	10th	42	11	4	6	51	34	7	3	10	30	49	43	
1927-28	1	22	8th	42	13	3	5	52	30	4	6	11	26	43	43	
1928-29	1	22	3rd	42	16	2	3	62	30	7	2	12	36	51	50	*FAC Semi-finalists*
1929-30	1	22	4th	42	13	1	7	54	33	8	4	9	38	50	47	
1930-31	1	22	2nd	42	17	3	1	86	34	8	6	7	42	44	59	
1931-32	1	22	5th	42	15	1	5	64	28	4	7	10	40	44	46	
1932-33	1	22	2nd	42	16	2	3	60	29	7	6	8	32	38	54	
1933-34	1	22	13th	42	10	5	6	45	34	4	7	10	33	41	40	*FAC Semi-finalists*
1934-35	1	22	13th	42	11	6	4	50	36	3	7	11	24	52	41	
1935-36	*1*	*22*	*21st*	*42*	*7*	*6*	*8*	*47*	*56*	*6*	*3*	*12*	*34*	*54*	*35*	
1936-37	2	22	9th	42	10	6	5	47	30	6	6	9	35	40	44	
1937-38	**2**	**22**	**1st**	**42**	**17**	**2**	**2**	**50**	**12**	**8**	**5**	**8**	**23**	**23**	**57**	*FAC Semi-finalists*
1938-39	1	22	12th	42	11	3	7	44	25	5	6	10	27	35	41	
Second World War																
1946-47	1	22	8th	42	9	6	6	39	24	9	3	9	28	29	45	
1947-48	1	22	6th	42	13	5	3	42	22	6	4	11	23	35	47	
1948-49	1	22	10th	42	10	6	5	40	36	6	4	11	20	40	42	
1949-50	1	22	12th	42	10	7	4	31	19	5	5	11	30	42	42	

Season	Div	Teams	Pos	P	W	D	L	F	A	W	D	L	F	A	Pts	Cup Honours
1950-51	1	22	15th	42	9	6	6	39	29	3	7	11	27	39	37	
1951-52	1	22	6th	42	13	3	5	49	28	6	6	9	30	42	47	
1952-53	1	22	11th	42	9	7	5	36	23	5	6	10	27	38	41	
1953-54	1	22	13th	42	12	5	4	50	28	4	4	13	20	40	41	
1954-55	1	22	6th	42	11	3	7	38	31	9	4	8	34	42	47	
1955-56	1	22	20th	42	9	6	6	32	29	2	7	12	20	40	35	
1956-57	1	22	10th	42	10	8	3	45	25	4	7	10	20	30	43	*FAC Winners*
1957-58	1	22	14th	42	12	4	5	46	26	4	3	14	27	60	39	
1958-59	1	22	21st	42	8	5	8	31	33	3	3	15	27	54	30	*FAC Semi-finalists*
1959-60	2	22	1st	42	17	3	1	62	19	8	6	7	27	24	59	*FAC Semi-finalists*
1960-61	1	22	9th	42	13	3	5	48	28	4	6	11	30	49	43	*LC Winners*
1961-62	1	22	7th	42	13	5	3	45	20	5	3	13	20	36	44	
1962-63	1	22	15th	42	12	2	7	38	23	3	6	12	24	45	38	*LC Runners-up*
1963-64	1	22	19th	42	8	6	7	35	29	3	6	12	27	42	34	
1964-65	1	22	16th	42	14	1	6	36	24	2	4	15	21	58	37	*LC Semi-finalists*
1965-66	1	22	16th	42	10	3	8	39	34	5	3	13	30	46	36	
1966-67	1	22	21st	42	7	5	9	30	33	4	2	15	24	52	29	
1967-68	2	22	16th	42	10	3	8	35	30	5	4	12	19	34	37	
1968-69	2	22	18th	42	10	8	3	22	11	2	6	13	15	37	38	
1969-70	*2*	*22*	*21st*	*42*	*7*	*8*	*6*	*23*	*21*	*1*	*5*	*15*	*13*	*41*	*29*	
1970-71	3	24	4th	46	13	7	3	27	13	6	8	9	27	33	53	*LC Runners-up*
1971-72	**3**	**24**	**1st**	**46**	**20**	**1**	**2**	**45**	**10**	**12**	**5**	**6**	**40**	**22**	**70**	
1972-73	2	22	3rd	42	12	5	4	27	17	6	9	6	24	30	50	
1973-74	2	22	14th	42	8	9	4	33	21	5	6	10	15	24	41	
1974-75	2	22	2nd	42	16	4	1	47	6	9	4	8	32	26	58	*LC Winners*
1975-76	1	22	16th	42	11	8	2	32	17	0	9	12	19	42	39	
1976-77	1	22	4th	42	17	3	1	55	17	5	4	12	21	33	51	*LC Winners*
1977-78	1	22	8th	42	11	4	6	33	18	7	6	8	24	24	46	
1978-79	1	22	8th	42	8	9	4	37	26	7	7	7	22	23	46	
1979-80	1	22	7th	42	11	5	5	29	22	5	9	7	22	28	46	
1980-81	**1**	**22**	**1st**	**42**	**16**	**3**	**2**	**40**	**13**	**10**	**5**	**6**	**32**	**27**	**60**	
1981-82	1	22	11th	42	9	6	6	28	24	6	6	9	27	29	57	*EC Winners*
1982-83	1	22	6th	42	17	2	2	47	15	4	3	14	15	35	68	*ESC Winners*
1983-84	1	22	10th	42	14	3	4	34	22	3	6	12	25	39	60	*LC Semi-finalists*
1984-85	1	22	10th	42	10	7	4	34	20	5	4	12	26	40	56	
1985-86	1	22	16th	42	7	6	8	27	28	3	8	10	24	39	44	*LC Semi-finalists*
1986-87	*1*	*22*	*22nd*	*42*	*7*	*7*	*7*	*25*	*25*	*1*	*5*	*15*	*20*	*54*	*36*	
1987-88	2	23	2nd	44	9	7	6	31	21	13	5	4	37	20	78	
1988-89	*1*	*20*	*17th*	*38*	*7*	*6*	*6*	*25*	*22*	*2*	*7*	*10*	*20*	*34*	*40*	
1989-90	1	20	2nd	38	13	3	3	36	20	8	4	7	21	18	70	*FMC Area Finalists*
1990-91	1	20	17th	38	7	9	3	29	25	2	5	12	17	33	41	
1991-92	1	22	7th	42	13	3	5	31	16	4	6	11	17	28	60	
1992-93	P	22	2nd	42	13	5	3	36	16	8	6	7	21	24	74	
1993-94	P	22	10th	42	8	5	8	23	18	7	7	7	23	32	57	*LC Winners*
1994-95	P	22	18th	42	6	9	6	27	24	5	6	10	24	32	48	

	P	W	D	L	F	A	Pts
Home	1893	1094	411	388	3980	2163	2739
Away	1893	510	452	931	2421	3439	1543
Total	3786	1604	863	1319	6401	5602	4282

Other honours: World Club Championship runners-up 1982-83
FA Charity Shield joint winners 1981-82
FA Charity Shield runners-up 1910-11, 1957-58, 1972-73

2pts for a win up to season 1980-81
3pts for a win from season 1981-82

FAC = FA Cup; LC = League Cup; FMC = Full Members' Cup;
EC = European Champions' Cup; ESC = European Super Cup.
Championship seasons in **bold** type, relegation seasons in *italics*.

SUBSCRIBERS ROLL CALL

0001 Neil Gallagher
0002 Colin Askey
0003 Neil Byrne
0004 Jason Wardle
0005 Brian C. Seadon
0006 Frank McNally
0007 Oliver Eagle
0008 Susan Eagle
0009 David Eagle
0010 Gary Wood
0011 Debbie Wood
0012 Dave Nicholson
0013 Lisa Newman
0014 Shaun Lee Kett
0015 Lee Mark Cashman
0016 Martin Primmer
0017 Elizabeth Dunbar
0018 Lyndsey Dunbar
0019 Yusuf Patel
0020 David Hitchman
0021 Peter Hitchman
0022 Richard Betteridge
0023 Philip Gray
0024 Lisa J. Statham
0025 James Merriman
0026 Martin A. Bird
0027 Miss J.E. Elson
0028 James Bayliss
0029 Hannah Darlington
0030 Miss L.J. Bowdler
0031 Sheena B. Meredith
0032 Mark Stoneman
0033 Kevin Cole
0034 G. Walden
0035 Alan Smith
0036 Richard Ian Stait
0037 Wendy S. Jordan
0038 Ted Timmins
0039 Colin James Walker
0040 Anthony Woolley
0041 Julia Smith
0042 Andrew Fieldhouse
0043 Alison Smith
0044 Nigel Asher
0045 Craig Asher
0046 Loyd Asher
0047 Luke Horsfall
0048 Michelle Banks
0049 Louise Grace
0050 Mark Attwood
0051 Mary J. Sutton
0052 Edward McNeill
0053 Stuart T. Swann

0054 J.R. Onyon
0055 Ralf Schulz
0056 Lisa Robinson
0057 Harry W. McDivitt
0058 Warren H. McDivitt
0059 Guy D.A. Cooke
0060 Laura Anne Jordon
0061 Paul Palmer
0062 Trevor Statham
0063 S. James Dyke
0064 Barry Geddis
0065 Cyril Hood
0066 Norman Hood
0067 Doe Hood
0068 Ellena Burchell
0069 Alan Mark Scrivens
0070 Melissa Newman
0071 Andrew Webster
0072 Mrs Jan Bolton
0073 Scott Dunn
0074 Rob Rodway
0075 Martin Lockley
0076 Simon 'Wilf' Wheeler
0077 Kieran Sheridan
0078 Wally Baylis
0079 Clive Jordan
0080 Helen Jordan
0081 Ann Jordan
0082 Ross Clifford
0083 Neal King
0084 Phil Cotter
0085 Tim Cotter
0086 Martin K. James
0087 Richard Crowley
0088 Matthew John Collinge
0089 Carl Murphy
0090 Carl Dickens
0091 Lee Dickens
0092 Mark Dickens
0093 Pamela Harris
0094 Chris Dennis
0095 Mark T. Lowndes
0096 Kevin Knight
0097 Lisa Ansell
0098 Julie Ansell
0099 A. Hotton
0100 Andrew Harris
0101 Matthew Ansell
0102 Chris Harris
0103 Daniel J.C. Appleby
0104 David J. Appleby
0105 Tracey J. Appleby
0106 Sarah L. Appleby

0107 Mark Oliver
0108 Debbie Bennett
0109 Sarah Clives
0110 Richard Hodgkins
0111 Emma Mackay
0112 Eric Mackay
0113 Jamie Taylor
0114 Bob Peach
0115 Christine Rossiter
0116 Ian Rossiter
0117 Emma Ray
0118 Frances Ray
0119 Terence Ray
0120 Mark Ray
0121 Nigel Mills
0122 Ignace Van de Sype
0123 Lorenzo Van de Sype
0124 Daniel Kirby
0125 Malcolm Kirby
0126 Anthony John Beaman
0127 Master Lewis Dickens
0128 Neil Jones
0129 Jane Benton
0130 Bob Morton (AP Rovers Old Boy)
0131 Scott Fisher
0132 Geraldine Coffey
0133 Alan Chambers
0134 Claire Jones
0135 David Ward
0136 Gavin Roberts
0137 Craig Roberts
0138 Anthony McKay
0139 Keith Stokes
0140 Gareth Stokes
0141 Kirsty Stokes
0142 Michele Platman
0143 Clive Platman
0144 Sonia Greaves
0145 Adrian Spray
0146 Pedro Badlan
0147 Caroline Badlan
0148 Carol Badlan
0149 Andrew James Harper
0150 Mark Greenway
0151 Philip Greenway
0152 Stephen Greenway
0153 Bob Daniels
0154 Edward McGuinness Snr.
0155 Robert Hughes
0156 Ian Checkley
0157 Anthony Wright
0158 Robbie Wright
0159 Neale Wright

0160 Gary Tranter	0212 Leigh A. Robinson	0264 Andrew Ralphson
0161 Mick Tranter	0213 Kevin Fowler	0265 Marc Wesson
0162 Paul McCairn	0214 Sundeep P. Nischal	0266 Alison O'Regan
0163 Mark Barratt	0215 Simon Targett	0267 Joy Harris
0164 Robin D. Elshout	0216 Claude Cripps	0268 P.J. Hadoulis
0165 Karen F. McDivitt	0217 Judi Neal	0269 Sharon Morris
0166 Ellena S. McDivitt	0218 Sylvia Neal	0270 Dean Morris
0167 Natalie Clarke	0219 Neal James	0271 Brian Etheridge
0168 Matthew Stubbs	0220 Craig Brooks	0272 S.C. Tovey
0169 D.L.T. Butler	0221 Wesley Brooks	0273 Michael Lawrence Lawlor
0170 Mrs Carole Stevens	0222 Craig Vigurs	0274 Adam Kelcey
0171 Michael Aberley	0223 Ray Matts	0275 Andrew Gullick
0172 Simon Timerick	0224 Phillip O'Reilly	0276 Fred Gray
0173 Paul Calvey	0225 Amanda Tustin	0277 Dr Mark Wilson
0174 Aaron Davie	0226 Sarah Kinsman	0278 Linda Davies
0175 Terri Donnello	0227 Robert Patterson	0279 Michael Jinks
0176 Michael Bishop	0228 Jennifer Beale	0280 Cara Lauren O'Keeffe
0177 Alex Jalland	0229 Debbie Wilcox	0281 M. Jones
0178 Nigel Smith	0230 Nathan Doyle	0282 Master M. Jones
0179 Miss Siobhan McElkearney	0231 Cliff Paget	0283 R. Bird
0180 Laura Carruthers	0232 Peter Birch	0284 Anita D. Harris
0181 Miss Annette Jones	0233 Tracey Haigh	0285 Joseph Gerard Martin
0182 Barbara Coll	0234 David Woodley	0286 John O'Brien
0183 Gavin Morris	0235 Mrs Anne Kathleen Horrocks	0287 David Ball
0184 Miss Lauren Bolton	0236 Andy Munn	0288 Steve Maddocks
0185 David Ian Jones	0237 Scott Read	0289 Kieran Scanlon
0186 Mark Glyn Jones	0238 Michael Maskill	0290 John Howard
0187 Glyn Jones	0239 Tony C. Dacey	0291 Miss Maggie Eades
0188 Shirley Ann Jones	0240 Robert Barlett	0292 Emma Bennett
0189 Raymond Warr	0241 Ian Parkes	0293 Mark S. Waldron
0190 Tracey and Roy H.	0242 Micky Fishwick	0294 Jennifer Lowe
0191 Dean Strange	0243 Jamie Thomas	0295 James Kieran Murray
0192 Adam Organ	0244 Paul Wood	0296 Kevin Murray
0193 Mark Zeidan	0245 Mark Mortimer	0297 Gavin Watton
0194 Andrew James Short	0246 Thomas Mortimer	0298 Blaine Watton
0195 Sean Escritt	0247 Martha Osborne	0299 Robert Nolan
0196 Simon Peter Rawlins	0248 Danielle McKain	0300 Michael Louis Wilde
0197 Andy Congrave	0249 Kelly McKain	0301 Alan Whitecross
0198 Helen Bale	0250 Linda McKain	0302 Paul Drumm
0199 Peter Bale	0251 Ricardo Leith	0303 Daniel Flynn
0200 Ramon Halford	0252 Tony Friel	0304 Ashley Victoria Francis
0201 Andy Perry	0253 Andrew Krasnik	Charlotte Grimes
0202 H.C.W. Perry	0254 Katherine Krasnik	0305 Aaron Vincent Frederick
0203 W. Fielder	0255 Darren Paul Hunt	Christopher Grimes
0204 John William Nend	0256 Paul Kenna	0306 Claire Wheeler
0205 Louise Crowley	0257 Philip J. Santos	0307 Rob Till
0206 Anthony Read	0258 Dewi Jones	0308 John Seale
0207 Ben Halford	0259 G.S. Clarke	0309 Sean G.M.J. Adkins
0208 Spencer Hawkesford	0260 Thomas Morris	0310 Mitchell Mole
0209 Shane Byse	0261 Tony Fenlon	0311 Benjamin Eaton
0210 John R. Ward	0262 Arron Malpass	0312 Pamela Gormley
0211 Leni D. Ward	0263 Frank MacDonald	0313 Louise Gormley

0314 Sid Jeewa
0315 Paul Perry
0316 Ian Mellen
0317 Reine Bladh
0318 James Cooke
0319 Ken Noon
0320 Paul Noon
0321 Peter Noon
0322 Keith Hall
0323 Pamela Wood
0324 Richard Hinton
0325 Adrian Goddard
0326 Charlene Townsend
0327 Roy Farmer
0328 Michael Shrimplin
0329 Darren Johnston
0330 Michelle Prosser
0331 Trevor McGarrigle
0332 Jenny Bailey
0333 Paul Bailey
0334 N.F. Ingram
0335 Nathan David Stevens
0336 Richard Ford
0337 Sue Ford
0338 Dan Ford
0339 Robert Gough
0340 Vicki Hodgson
0341 Gill Evans
0342 Phil Lees
0343 Doug James
0344 Val James
0345 Michael Trevor Tilley
0346 Kev Buttery
0347 Judith Griffiths
0348 Craig 'Frog' Barnsley
0349 Richard Benham
0350 Michael Benham
0351 Richard Lakin
0352 G. Furness
0353 Craig Lee
0354 Claire Hall
0355 Terry Wright
0356 Christopher Jones
0357 John Joseph Hanna
0358 Serena Bailey
0359 Dapinder Bhara
0360 M. Murphy
0361 Paul Loveridge
0362 Peter Davies-Findell
0363 Kevin Smith
0364 Benjamin Neil Smith
0365 M.F.C. Graham
0366 Mark Ford

0367 Nigel Iwanski
0368 D.H. Perry
0369 David Robert John Barlett
0370 Andrew Robert Taylor
0371 John Andrew Clover
0372 Jonathan Adams
0373 Peter N. Appleby
0374 Stephen Taylor
0375 Paul Robert Taylor
0376 Thomas Blomberg (Sweden)
0377 Dean Davies
0378 Keith Viney
0379 Martin Greenslade
0380 Darren Bedford
0381 Charlotte Bird
0382 Joe Ridout
0383 Emily Ridout
0384 M. Talbot
0385 James Allsop
0386 Steven Hudson
0387 Mark Cobb
0388 Wayne Perrins
0389 Des Bourne
0390 Caroline Bayliss
0391 James A. Flynn
0392 R. Pearson
0393 David John Peachey
0394 Michael Garry Fallaize
0395 Dean Tindall
0396 Michael Thomas Tindall
0397 Donna Hanna
0398 Paul Hawkins
0399 B.W. Hughes
0400 R. Townsend
0401 Nigel Steven Parker
0402 Keith Potter
0403 Sue Tilt
0404 Mick Tilt
0405 James Isham
0406 Adam Hamlet
0407 Morten Esbjerg
0408 Sharon Hudson
0409 David Hudson
0410 Adam K. West
0411 Matthew Slater
0412 David Yeomans
0413 Sarah Payne
0414 Erica Farmer
0415 George Purser
0416 Paul Ford
0417 Karen J. Cooper
0418 Lucy Mulligan
0419 Lee Gough

0420 Rob Wardle
0421 Karen Wardle
0422 Samantha Wardle
0423 Robbie Wardle
0424 Alex Wardle
0425 Andrew Elston (HE 1725)
0426 Roger Rowlands
0427 Russell Turvey
0428 Derek Day
0429 Kerry Day
0430 Carly Day
0431 Jean Day
0432 Emma Spink
0433 Damien Francis Richard Lee
0434 Sarah Louise Nicholls
0435 Gordon Cull
0436 Mark Phillips
0437 Jeremy Fallowfield
0438 Adam Parker
0439 James Potter
0440 Claire Cooper
0441 Peter Downes
0442 Paul Cummins
0443 Damian Barrow
0444 Mark Barrow
0445 Paul Nicholas Randle
0446 Scott MacIver
0447 Gavin MacIver
0448 Roger Nicklin (Tamworth)
0449 Matthew Stephen Allen
0450 Douglas A. Rooker
0451 May Rooker
0452 Paul D. Rooker
0453 Kelly L. Rooker
0454 Oliver A. Rooker
0455 Richard R. Carter
0456 Simon Kerr-Edwards
0457 Jason Kennedy
0458 Geoff Underhill
0459 Gemma Goodhead
0460 Paul J. Edwards
0461 Carol Maguire
0462 Jennifer A. Birch
0463 Jennine Starkey
0464 Paul Starkey
0465 Helena Cerfontyne
0466 Richard Money
0467 Alex Money
0468 Stephen Mullins
0469 Stephen Hicks
0470 Alex Swinfen
0471 Robin Peck
0472 Teresa Meredith

0467 Alex Money	0520 James W. Johnstone	0573 Natalie T. D'Abreu
0468 Stephen Mullins	0521 Rod Snelson	0574 Mike D'Abreu
0469 Stephen Hicks	0522 Mark Thornley	0575 Paul Anderton
0470 Alex Swinfen	0523 Danny Porter	0576 Liam Foley
0471 Robin Peck	0524 John Christopher Parsons	0577 Andrew Collins
0472 Teresa Meredith	0525 Keith Rickett	0578 Hilary Jennings
0473 Amanda Louise Pollard	0526 Graham Rickett	0579 Michael Halaj
0474 Ian Walsh	0527 Gary J. Webber	0580 Alice Pursglove
0475 J.A. Walsh	0528 Stanley Frank Randle	0581 Doreen Pursglove
0476 Paul Steven Felton	0529 Mark Thomas Randle	0582 Stephen Wilkinson
0477 Danny Behan	0530 Daniel Appleby	0583 Daniel Coleman
0478 Alan Jasper	0531 Keith Powell	0584 Nick Bowles
0479 David Jasper	0532 Trevor John Baker	0585 Kelly Fitzsimmons
0480 Belinda Smith	0533 Alexander Berwick	0586 James Richard Hipkiss
0481 Andrew Williams	0534 Connor Emms	0587 Darren Felsenstein
0482 William Stevens	0535 Ashley Goodwin	0588 Isaac Hunt
0483 Gordon Parton	0536 Dawn McCarrick	0589 Mike Hunt
0484 Andrew Neale	0537 Ted Elwell	0590 Iain Pickup
0485 George Clamp	0538 Roger L. Elwell	0591 Stephen Lammas
0486 Philip Kirwon	0539 Mrs Edith Jones	0592 Steven J. Giles
0487 Stuart Palmer	0540 Stephen Merriman	0593 Rebecca Small
0488 David Jones	0541 Alan Chilton	0594 Ken Wootton
0489 Tony R. Wright	0542 David Alan Turner	0595 Natalie Pearce
0490 Dexter Lawlor	0543 Paul Durber	0596 Peter J. Davies
0491 Anthony Beese	0544 Martin E. Woodcock	0597 Stephen Sturman
0492 E. Collins	0545 Mark Pym	0598 J.A. Kibble
0493 Ricky Smith	0546 Thomas Johansson	0599 Paul Aros
0494 Stephen Spittle	0547 Emily McPake	0600 G.C. Tipper
0495 Christian Fletcher	0548 Alice McPake	0601 Matt Palmer
0496 Miss Janeve Fletcher	0549 Stewart Marsh	0602 Danny Palmer
0497 Adam Livesey	0550 Andrew Cole	0603 Frank Allen
0498 Claire Cooper	0551 Frank Beach	0604 Becky Tompkins
0499 Colin A. Forknall	0552 Lee Keith Chapman	0605 Rob Thompson
0500 Claire Bates	0553 Rob Harvey	0606 Jamie Robert Casley
0501 Gido Kirfel	0554 Deanne Groucutt	0607 Paul Casley
0502 Alison K. Francis	0555 Gary J. Fletcher	0608 Graham Watkiss
0503 Sebastian Power	0556 Adrian Garraty	0609 D. Cowan
0504 Frank McNally	0557 Brian Johnson	0610 W.A. Harvey
0505 I.D. Beech	0558 Portland Johnson	0611 Michael P. McTiernan
0506 Robin D. Wilkes	0559 Miss Jennifer Waring	0612 Helen Hollywell
0507 Alan Cole	0560 Miss Leigh Waring	0613 Peter Brett
0508 Bob Nicholls	0561 Jill Waring	0614 H.B.L. Flanagan
0509 Clive Nicholls	0562 Tim Hale	0615 Scott Faulkner
0510 Richard Guy Linley	0563 Paul Jarvis	0616 Edward Mills
0511 Timothy Michael Linley	0564 Robert Dutton	0617 Kevin A. Williams
0512 Gary Beresford	0565 Rev Leo Osborn	0618 Peter Harrold
0513 Alison Halfpenny	0566 Mark Pearce	0619 K.G. Farley
0514 Ross P. Lippitt	0567 Andrew Mitchell	0620 Adrian Rogers
0515 Gemma Jones	0568 Craig Haines	0621 Nick Walker
0516 Peter James	0569 Malcolm Morley	0622 Antony Richard Joyner
0517 Gary James	0570 Adrian M. D'Abreu	0623 D. Poole
0518 Margaret James	0571 Christine D'Abreu	0624 Susan Pudge
0519 Lisa Collins	0572 Nathan J.M.P. D'Abreu	0625 Michael Kirk

0626 Iain Sheppard	0679 Warrick Vowler	0732 Barbara McKain
0627 Richard Shutt	0680 C.P. Screech	0733 Dean Shepherd
0628 The Foden Boys	0681 Kerry-Anne Screech	0734 Joseph Shepherd
0629 Cheryl Bolton	0682 Nigel Sadler	0735 Karen Ellis
0630 Graham N. Willetts	0683 Jonathan Bent	0736 Shelley Parker
0631 Mark Alexander Smith	0684 A.A. Bent	0737 Jason Davin
0632 Matthew Gregory	0685 David Southall	0738 Keith Stubbs
0633 Jack Pinnock	0686 Philip Forletta	0739 Martin Attwood
0634 Leo Pinnock	0687 Mark Forletta	0740 Kieran Collins
0635 Steven Seatherton	0688 Vera Ellen Ragsdale	0741 Robert Collins
0636 Nathan Collins	0689 Jason Russell Perry	0742 Michael English
0637 Lindsey Roberts	0690 Colin Brown	0743 Nicholas English
0638 James Marcantonio	0691 David John Edward Clayton	0744 Richard Henman
0639 Chris Marcantonio	0692 Martin Hodson	0745 Jordan Adams
0640 Kenneth J. Marriott	0693 Karen Green	0746 B.M. Dain
0641 David Foster	0694 Matthew Graham	0747 Paul Middleton
0642 Dave Barker	0695 Vincent Mullooly	0748 Dave Skinner
0643 Phil Barker	0696 Sean Mullooly	0749 Tom Crowe Junior
0644 Miss J. Bowyer	0697 Miss Clare Mullooly	0750 Mike Chew
0645 Adrian Hill	0698 Mark Lench	0751 Claire Griffin
0646 Lisa Hill	0699 Mary D'Abreu	0752 Emma Brooking
0647 Antony Morris	0700 Lewis D'Abreu	0753 Graham Jinks
0648 Cathryn Evans	0701 S.J. Lavery	0754 Neil Jinks
0649 Miss Stephanie Julie Jones	0702 D.S. Tansey	0755 Helen North
0650 Martyn Jones	0703 M.A. Cooper	0756 Sean Christopher Starrs
0651 Mark Ferriday	0704 Michele Carbutt	0757 Mark Hamblett
0652 Nicola Ferriday	0705 Terry Carbutt	0758 Joseph James Moore
0653 Albert Knowles	0706 Lauren Carbutt	0759 Chris Newton
0654 Anthony Baker	0707 Rebecca Carbutt	0760 Matthew Pond
0655 Zosia Mace	0708 Ian Fakes	0761 Michael Morgan
0656 Kevin Marshall	0709 James H.W.T. Soden	0762 Philip Goldie
0657 Paul Rostance	0710 H.W.T. Soden	0763 Antonio Durante, Italy
0658 Geoff Elkington	0711 Phil Jones	0764 Steve Matthews
0659 Saul C. Gray	0712 Alison Royles	0765 Nigel Snowden
0660 Stephen Wall	0713 Nicola Royles	0766 Nick Timothy
0661 Pete Abrahams	0714 Mrs Gwenfyl Royles	0767 John Timothy
0662 Pam Bridgewater	0715 Gary Arthurs	0768 Albert Crowton
0663 Dave Bridgewater	0716 Michael Alan Coldrick	0769 Kevin Stratford
0664 John Duffy	0717 Christopher Mansfield	0770 Thomas Kirby
0665 G.W. Padmore	0718 Edward Knott	0771 Matthew Bond
0666 Simon Padmore	0719 Dave Smith	0772 Patrick F.J. O'Reilly
0667 Ken Phipp	0720 Anthony J. Roberts	0773 Roy Stringer
0668 Robert Mark Feasey	0721 Roger Levicki	0774 George Stringer
0669 Mark John Feasey	0722 Andrew Levicki	0775 Howard Stringer
0670 Matthew Cannings	0723 Tim Levicki	0776 Nicholas Jones
0671 Bryan Harte	0724 David Cox	0777 Paul Virgo
0672 Mark Fairbrother	0725 John Kimberley	0778 Andrew R. Blythe
0673 Andrea Warren	0726 Neal Kimberley	0779 Phillip Bagnall
0674 Ryan Cox	0727 Darren Bray	0780 B.R. Veal
0675 Kelvin Cox	0728 Kevin Tinsley	0781 B. Bindoff
0676 Tracy Piper	0729 Jamie Skinner	0782 N.J. Bindoff
0677 Kevin Piper	0730 Gregory McKain	0783 Master G.A. Bindoff
0678 Philip Piper	0731 Ricky McKain	0784 Dave Silver

0785 Alison Silver	0838 Albert 'Jim' Walton	0891 John Stammers
0786 Steven Silver	0839 Chris McCormack	0892 R.E. Garratt
0787 Tony Kenny	0840 Dawn H. Mann	0893 Simon Burchell
0788 Kevin Gledhill	0841 John Simmonds	0894 Mark Rowland (Skully)
0789 Peter Gledhill	0842 Ben Stephenson	0895 Maurice Carter
0790 Philip J. Etheridge	0843 Matthew Tector	0896 Barrie Bailey, Plymouth
0791 Bernard Flynn	0844 Steven Hood	0897 Gordon Telfer
0792 Donna Scarle	0845 Anthony Williams	0898 Jonathan Handley
0793 Daniel Baldwin	0846 Julian Smith	0899 John Alan Dunn
0794 Sally Beadsmore	0847 R.A. Jones	0900 Steve A. Heath
0795 Philip Williams	0848 Dean Beresford	0901 Andrew R. Owen
0796 David Daniel	0849 Jim Foat	0902 Graham L. Garvey
0797 Mark Whorton	0850 James Daly	0903 Ben Ashford
0798 Dawn Banks	0851 Colin Daly	0904 Esther Rawlings
0799 Charles Southby	0852 Matthew Idoine	0905 Ray Rawlings
0800 Philip John Shakespeare	0853 Chris Deakin	0906 Bill Willcox
0801 Thomas Shakespeare	0854 Brett Rotheroe	0907 Adrian Chamberlain
0802 Lee Petch	0855 Colin Mann	0908 David Smart
0803 John Lacey	0856 Cheryl Harris	0909 P.L. Day (Tenby)
0804 Gary Lacey	0857 Alyn Harris	0910 Mick Turner
0805 Mervyn Aston Arscott	0858 Keith Taylor	0911 Leonard Rawlings Layton
0806 Paul Mervyn Arscott	0859 Malcolm Taylor	0912 David Fortnam
0807 Kevin Lowbridge	0860 C. Duncan	0913 Luke Farrington
0808 Martin Colin Roberts	0861 T. Brown	0914 Peter Lee Maddocks
0809 Charlotte Louise Briggs	0862 C.R. Walster	0915 Neil P. Gaskell
0810 Neal Sawyer	0863 John Peter Reidy	0916 Dave Buet
0811 Adam Peter O'Connor	0864 Richard Wilson	0917 Marg Buet
0812 Alexander George O'Connor	0865 Mark H. Whitehouse	0918 Paul Buet
0813 Angie O'Connor	0866 Alan Green	0919 Vincent R. Green
0814 Christopher Henman	0867 Thomas Green	0920 Graham E. Anderson
0815 Barry Curtis	0868 Keith Andrew Birch	0921 Naomi Collett
0816 Lynn Curtis	0869 M.E.C. Wilson	0922 Daniel Collett
0817 Jonothan Curtis	0870 Andrew K. Clark	0923 Hayley Collett
0818 Martell Beckford	0871 Nigel Thompson	0924 Aaron Collett
0819 G.P. Upton	0872 Mark Rogers, Codsall	0925 Andrew Dawes
0820 Richard Winter	0873 Asten Perry	0926 J.A. Tooth
0821 Paul Dyde	0874 Vic Millward	0927 Mark Napier
0822 Selina Travers	0875 Graham Perry	0928 Neil Stuart Brailsford
0823 Aidan Travers	0876 Liam Kiernan	0929 Desmond Brennan
0824 Alice Rebecca George	0877 Michael Kiernan	0930 David Ostojitsch
0825 Katie Makepeace	0878 Natalie Langford	0931 Matthew Seymour
0826 Sarah Davies	0879 Jonathan Muir	0932 Jackson Hunt
0827 David Hodges	0880 Brendan Shields	0933 Russ Brown
0828 Claire Allsop	0881 B.H.L. Flannagan	0934 Stuart Sherrard
0829 Kevin O'Toole	0882 Kevin Whittick	0935 Rachael - Wales
0830 Robert J. Smith	0883 Paul Cox	0936 James Michael Deeley
0831 Tracie Peagram	0884 John Gillingham	0937 Tony Morris
0832 Sarah Reynolds	0885 Andrew Gillingham	0938 D. Higgins
0833 Robin Nicholas Pleaden	0886 Mark David Goodwin	0939 Robert J.L. Allison
0834 Alyx Sara Pleaden	0887 Scott Ratcliffe - Germany	0940 Stephen J. Allison
0835 Karen Spencer	0888 David Smith	0941 Jeff Corfield
0836 Laura Pollard	0889 James Powell	0942 G. Bateman
0837 Bill Pollard	0890 Terence Stone	0943 Neal Strange

0944 Darren Hudson-Wood	0997 Jon G. Jones	1050 Adrian J. Mullis
0945 Matthew Buck	0998 John Arthur Westwood	1051 Sue Ramsay
0946 Mark Wheeler	0999 John Brealey	1052 Matthew Smith
0947 Ian David Parkes	1000 Andrew Morgan	1053 Daniel Smith
0948 C. Stephens	1001 Adam Morgan	1054 Carol Grove
0949 Malcolm Corfield	1002 Neil Hansen	1055 Tony D. Wilkes
0950 Julia Greenfield	1003 Gavin William Handley	1056 Michelle Angela McDonough
0951 Ted Geary	1004 A. Rogers	1057 Dean Kevin Spooner
0952 John Holmes	1005 Nicholas Cox	1058 Mrs M.O. Downey
0953 G.C. Jones (Bristol)	1006 Dominic Moore - Pongo	1059 Scott Bradley (Evesham)
0954 Duncan K.S. Laws	1007 D.S. Willetts	1060 Christopher Swann
0955 Debbie & Kevin Joynes	1008 Philip Chandler	1061 Adrian Batsford
0956 Peter Caunt	1009 John Simmonds	1062 Scott Hemmens
0957 Jim Stelfox	1010 Pauline A. Holloway	1063 Luke John Clarke
0958 Bruce Veitch	1011 Paul Geraghty	1064 C.J. Whitaker
0959 Neil & Toni Alcock	1012 Alison O'Brien	1065 Gerald H. Lodwick
0960 Jackie Rawlings	1013 P. Pilkington	1066 Tony Starbuck
0961 Iain Rawlings	1014 Nigel Ainge	1067 Aaron Hickman
0962 John Fairfield	1015 Mark Dodd	1068 Andrew John Francis
0963 Carl John Roberts	1016 John Richard Hollywell	1069 A.F. Jalland
0964 Keith Puttick	1017 Roger Bailey (Nottingham)	1070 Susan Higginbotham
0965 Mark Jenkins	1018 Carly Nichols	1071 Adam France
0966 Michael J. Reidy	1019 Craig Nichols	1072 Jonathan Betts
0967 Alex Wier	1020 Robert Michael Milne	1073 Robert Meadows
0968 Karen Jeffery	1021 Maria Ganner	1074 Ian Taylor
0969 Bob Tomkins	1022 Emma Ganner	1075 Carl Wayne Davies
0970 K.G. Wilkinson	1023 Clare Ganner	1076 Kelly-Ann Feely
0971 Derek T. Hough	1024 Simon Blake	1077 Aidan Jeffery
0972 Martin Weaver	1025 Stephen C. Tovey	1078 Caroline James
0973 Mark Harrell	1026 Jennifer Blake	1079 Ian J. Walker
0974 Gerald Leek	1027 Robert Taylor	1080 Michael J. Taylor
0975 Jens Martin	1028 Gordon Reynolds	1081 Derek Anthony Price
0976 Darren Wilkins	1029 Paul Aldhouse	1082 Gihan Ibrahim
0977 Mick Wilkins	1030 John A. Gould (1934)	1083 Davey Jones
0978 Darren Woodfield	1031 Daniel Stefan O'Gorman	1084 Julie Anne Harrison
0979 Lee Symonds	1032 Andrew Steward	1085 Vass & E.U. Lions
0980 Adam Glaudot	1033 David Bray 'The Raver'	1086 Ross Griffith
0981 Doyle Family	1034 Clare Beswick	1087 Jason Ashley
0982 Karl Linder	1035 Richard Bennett	1088 Terence Anthony Barker
0983 Jon Linder	1036 Paddy Fenlon	1089 David Barron
0984 James C. Flood	1037 Gwyn David Brewer	1090 Vincent J. McKenna
0985 John Henry Lane	1038 Owen Suter	1091 David Clarkson
0986 John Adkins	1039 Steven McCabe	1092 Stephen Knott
0987 Tony Broadhurst	1040 Vicky Lee	1093 Andrew Mateer
0988 Lee Day	1041 Nick Becerra	1094 Raymond John Paul Feely
0989 Simon Booker	1042 David Knight	1095 Ralph & Wendy, M'bro
0990 Christopher C. Fleming	1043 Craig Holman	1096 D.P. Shipley
0991 Anthony William	1044 H.E. Holman	1097 Scott Marsden
0992 Jim McDonald	1045 Matthew Plant	1098 Andy Hooper
0993 Darren Seaton	1046 Stephen Williams	1099 Richard Allen
0994 Aden Cole	1047 James Williams	1100 Keith Gleadall
0995 Daren Reynolds	1048 Alan Adrian West	1101 Ian Campbell
0996 Mrs S.M. Scott	1049 Sid Walton	1102 David Hockenhull

SUBSCRIBERS ROLL CALL

1103 Elizabeth Medcraft	1156 Joanna Tarabilda	1209 Phillip Jemmison
1104 Stephen Donnelly	1157 Anton Tarabilda	1210 Mark Clews
1105 Nick Blewer	1158 Ruth Simmons	1211 Joanne DaCosta
1106 Howard Benbow	1159 Matthew Pond	1212 K.J. Williams
1107 Michael David Bromwich	1160 Kevin Portley	1213 Craig Harris
1108 Michelle Walters	1161 Trevor Hartley	1214 Shaun Harris
1109 Philip Walters	1162 Ian Pestridge	1215 John Harris
1110 Peter Goakes	1163 Philip Pestridge	1216 Richard Pike
1111 Ian Smith	1164 Michael O'Brien	1217 Dennis Rebbeck
1112 Paul Gray-Davis	1165 Anthony McAllister	1218 Andy Downes
1113 Nigel Renshaw	1166 Tony Lennon	1219 Andy Knight
1114 Stephen Renshaw	1167 Louise Lennon	1220 Andrew Clayton
1115 Rob Hale	1168 Ian Levell	1221 Ross McCarthy
1116 Adam Thomas Barrett	1169 Emma Hurcombe	1222 Jonathan Giffin
1117 Stewart Ray	1170 Christopher Homewood	1223 Robert Cooley
1118 Peter Houghton	1171 Derek Hollis	1224 Jonathan Morgan
1119 Richard & Steven Baker	1172 Christina M. Clay	1225 Geoff Morgan
1120 Theresa Donner	1173 G.C. Carlin	1226 Matthew Robert Oakes
1121 Joanne Barber	1174 Daniel Richard Evans	1227 Karyn Hasson
1122 Robert Lerner	1175 Brig Flounders	1228 J.K. Winters
1123 Jonathan Grossman	1176 Craig Winstone	1229 Shirley & Geoff Blizard
1124 Mrs. T. Roberts	1177 Michelle Diggins	1230 Craig Marriott
1125 John Treadwell	1178 Kevin Cox	1231 Andrew Hart
1126 M. Weller	1179 Ian Edward Beesley	1232 Amanda Grove
1127 Nigel Groves	1180 John Donohoe	1233 Gordon Grove
1128 Nick Yates	1181 Richard A. Hales	1234 Jonathan Tebbutt
1129 Simon Lawrie Turner	1182 Brent Aston	1235 Stephen A. Underhill
1130 T.J. Hall (South Africa)	1183 Marc Troth	1236 Simon Phillips
1131 J.E. Jones	1184 Andy (Telford) Seal	1237 P.J. Byrne
1132 Paul Hughes	1185 Geoff Baker	1238 Dek Bird Shaw
1133 Peter Aldridge	1186 Neil Harris	1239 Mandy Shaw
1134 Ian R. Wilson	1187 Christopher James Hearn	1240 Andrew Rollason
1135 Eddie Gajny	1188 Emma Rock	1241 R.W.C. Kitley
1136 Ron Vincent	1189 Gavin Harris	1242 Scott Davidson
1137 Rob Vincent	1190 "Bully, Lisa & Leanne"	1243 Zoe E. Gough
1138 Richard Vincent	1191 Robert Head	1244 Warren Enon
1139 Carl Thornton	1192 Martin John Watson	1245 Chris Russell
1140 Martyn R. Smith	1193 Mick Brown	1246 Barry Wall
1141 Nick Salter	1194 Hayden Wakeling	1247 Steven John Green
1142 Andrew Wibberley	1195 Frank A. Francies	1248 Chris Michell
1143 Shaun & Jack Welch	1196 Allen Souch	1249 Tony Hall
1144 Paul Taylor	1197 Adam Coles	1250 Liam Hall
1145 Sheila Bourke	1198 Leslie John Stoddart	1251 John A. Williams
1146 Tony A. Bill	1199 Nicholas Watts	1252 Iris Ann Ball
1147 Amanda Ann Evans	1200 David Pinner	1253 Harjinder Dosanjh
1148 David Cleminson	1201 Adam Rooke	1254 David England
1149 Robert Cleminson	1202 Robert Abbotts	1255 Chris Rigby
1150 Simon Giles	1203 Emma Abbotts	1256 John W. Daw
1151 Stuart Middleton	1204 Lisa Abbotts	1257 Mark Freer
1152 Anna Mendonca	1205 Kieran James Gennoy	1258 Ross Underhill, Co. Cork
1153 Roisin Mendonca	1206 Thomas Philip Gennoy	1259 Malcolm Everall
1154 Julie Nerney	1207 Paul Dann	1260 Francesca Duff
1155 Robert York	1208 H. John Desaulles	1261 William Duff

1262 Nicola Bullivant	1315 P. Tilbury	1368 Christopher Newman
1263 Leighton Bullivant	1316 Gerard Hayrabian	1369 Darren Sheffield
1264 Frank Antram	1317 Carlos Apezteguia Bosch	1370 Adrian Thorne
1265 Matthew Woodhouse	1318 J.H. Van de Pol	1371 Paul Tierney
1266 Darren Fisher	1319 Nakano Tomio	1372 Mary J. Sutton
1267 Talia Homer	1320 Didier Mestre	1373 Julie 'AVFC' Richardson
1268 David Goodyear	1321 Jason 'Nobby' Crowley	1374 Jack Barrington Stewart
1269 Simon Goodyear	1322 Jim French	1375 Paul Biddlestone
1270 Robert Brooke	1323 Suzanne French	1376 Alan Bowdler
1271 Peter Askey	1324 Martyn Bacchus	1377 Fran Bowdler
1272 Alexander Thomas Berry	1325 Brigham Flounders	1378 P.J. Stocker
1273 Brian Cowling	1326 Miss Angela Weir	1379 Ian Stringer
1274 Nigel Rose	1327 Stephen James Murphy	1380 Ruth Edwards
1275 Mark Pugh	1328 Lee Pendry	1381 Pete Edwards
1276 Alex Ashford	1329 W.J. Mottram	1382 Alison Jones
1277 Jack David Roberts	1330 T.D. Measey	1383 C.J. Lally
1278 Rob Davis	1331 L.N.E. Barlow	1384 Alan Gee
1279 John Hadgkiss	1332 Lloyd Hutchings	1385 Rhys Howard Dawson
1280 M.E. Shelton	1333 Stewart J. Draper	1386 Darran Boulter
1281 Sioned Enlli	1334 Katharine Jackson	1387 Robert Cooper
1282 Sion Ynyr	1335 Claire Hill	1388 Clive Foster
1283 Frank Croft	1336 Mark Howes	1389 David Foster
1284 Simon Croft	1337 R.O. Evans	1390 Gary Foster
1285 Paul Anthony Webb	1338 Mark Deeley	1391 Benito Elsker Rikke
1286 Andrew Haigh	1339 Steven Chapman	1392 Matthew Dale
1287 Gareth Powell	1340 Susan Myatt	1393 Nathan Rose
1288 Sam Jones	1341 D. Byrne	1394 Charles R.J. Clarke
1289 Julian M. Turner	1342 Ron Gumbley	1395 Julie Ann Dodman
1290 J.E.S. Cook	1343 Mark Green	1396 Philip R. Haynes
1291 Richard Prvulovich	1344 Louise Barnsley	1397 Gordon W. Price
1292 Iain Fenwick	1345 Simon Bull	1398 Ryan Spybey
1293 Tracey Louise Hatfield	1346 Paul Groves	1399 Kris Hinde
1294 Robert Kench	1347 V.A.P. Kiely	1400 Louise Hinde
1295 J.E. Reeves	1348 Roger W. Linney	1401 I.R. Hoskison
1296 Trond Hagenes	1349 Stanley T.T. Jones	1402 Colin Cameron
1297 Stephen Morris (France)	1350 Richard Wiseman	1403 Rebecca Lowe
1298 Jürgen Hohmann	1351 Lisa Whitmore	1404 Paul Fogarty
1299 Derek Wisdom	1352 Terry Whitmore	1405 Michelle Thickett
1300 Jørgen Esbjerg	1353 Mark A.J. Ward	1406 Anthony Thickett
1301 S. Lewis	1354 Robert Andrew Taylor	1407 Melvin James Thickett
1302 Kevin Abraham	1355 Robert Leonard Taylor	1408 Miss Sharon Thickett
1303 Reza Bodiat	1356 Daniel Tonka Taylor	
1304 David B. Sims	1357 Tony Spraggon	
1305 M.A. Gajny	1358 G. Padmore	
1306 Stefan Wally	1359 Robert F. Rea	
1307 Juan Ma Alfaro Lozano	1360 John Smith	
1308 Taisuke Kotani	1361 Mary Smith	
1309 Joachim H. Quade	1362 Shaun Smith	
1310 L.B.A. Dumay	1363 Chris Riordan	
1311 D. Dekker	1364 C.G. Millard	
1312 A.C. Legall	1365 J.C. Noden	
1313 John Gondo	1366 Barbara Warman	
1314 Louis Nicollin	1367 David Warman